4450/D

MISSION IN TORMENT

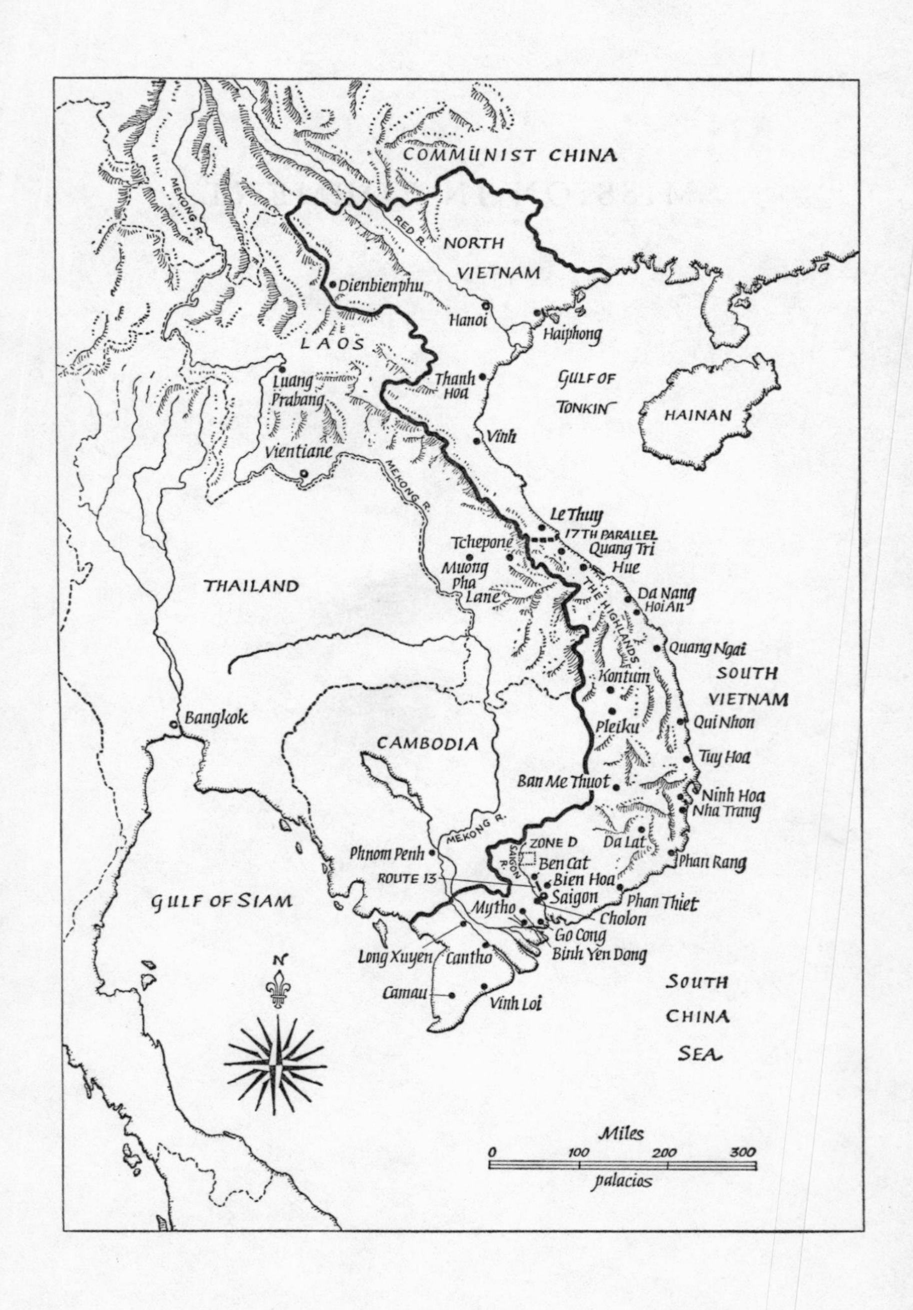
COMMUNIST CHINA
MEKONG R.
RED R.
NORTH
VIETNAM
Dienbienphu
Hanoi
Haiphong
LAOS
Luang
Prabang
Thanh
Hoa
GULF OF
TONKIN
HAINAN
Vinh
Vientiane
MEKONG R.
Le Thuy
17TH PARALLEL
Tchepone
Quang Tri
Hue
Muong
Pha
Lane
THAILAND
THE HIGHLANDS
Da Nang
Hoi An
Quang Ngai
SOUTH
VIETNAM
Kontum
Pleiku
Qui Nhon
Bangkok
CAMBODIA
Tuy Hoa
Ban Me Thuot
Ninh Hoa
Nha Trang
MEKONG R.
ZONE D
SAIGON R.
Da Lat
Phnom Penh
Ben Cat
Phan Rang
ROUTE 13
Bien Hoa
Saigon
GULF OF SIAM
Mytho
Phan Thiet
Cholon
Go Cong
Binh Yen Dong
N
Long Xuyen
Cantho
Camau
Vinh Loi
SOUTH
CHINA
SEA
Miles
0
100
200
300
palacios

MISSION IN TORMENT

An Intimate Account of the U.S. Role in Vietnam

by

John Mecklin

1965

DOUBLEDAY & COMPANY, INC.

GARDEN CITY, NEW YORK

Library of Congress Catalog Card Number 65–10632
Copyright © 1965 by JOHN MECKLIN
All Rights Reserved
Printed in the United States of America
First Edition

327.73
M487m

To my mother,
and the memory
of my father.

41954

CONTENTS

Introduction

Over a drink one evening in Saigon, when things looked even more hopeless than usual, a friend suggested that at least I could write a book about it. We talked about calling it "Two Years in a Squirrel Cage." This was the way I often felt about my job, but that kind of approach would nevertheless be out of order. Indeed perhaps it is a symptom of U.S. frustration that our effort in Vietnam has failed uniquely to generate an anthology of humor.

Vietnam is an intensely tragic land. It might be called the Poland of Asia. The Vietnamese, like the Poles, are racially and culturally related to a mighty, predatory neighbor, and this has produced a proud, intelligent, hardy breed. Like the Poles the Vietnamese have been victims of aggression for centuries, occupied and reoccupied by foreign armies, yet they have never lost their courage, nor their determination to be free. Like the Poles the Vietnamese deserve better than history, to date, has granted. It is a country that often gets under an American's skin.

This was the case with me when I worked there as a newsman in 1953–55. It was there that I first began thinking seriously of government service, after more than a decade as a foreign correspondent. I wanted to try to do something myself about such problems, rather than simply writing about them from the outside looking in. My chance came in 1961, midst the bright promise of the New Frontier, when I was invited to become a foreign service reserve officer of the U. S. Information Agency. A British friend in Germany, where I was working at the time, neatly pinpointed the troubles to come with my former colleagues of the press by remarking with a huge guffaw that I was "a poacher turned gamekeeper."

On leave of absence from my employers, Time Inc., I was first assigned to Paris as public affairs advisor to the U. S. Mission to the Organization for Economic Cooperation and Development (OECD). After a few months, by a remarkable quirk of fate, the Agency asked me to transfer to Saigon.

I was aware of the truth later articulated by the New York *Times* (June 28, 1963) that Vietnam is "a graveyard for the reputations of American diplomats and soldiers." The pull of that tortured country nevertheless was still there, and I was eager to go. Twenty-one months later, the assignment ended in despair—and no doubt another headstone in the graveyard. In March 1964 I resigned from USIA to write this book and then return to Time Inc.

Why the book?

Partly to have my own say on that astonishing and controversial period in Saigon. Partly perhaps as a catharsis, to try to get Vietnam out of my system. (My wife has suggested correctly that it would have been less trouble to go to an analyst.) Partly it reflects a reporter's instinct that somehow the job is not finished until it has been put down on paper, a form of atavism in my case perhaps.

My main objective, however, is to try to stir more sympathetic interest in Vietnam by telling the story in a personalized and hopefully dramatic fashion, to try to communicate something of the human side of this remote struggle. I hope that an account of my own education in the complexities of the problem, in the nature of American involvement, and in the errors we made, may help at least to stimulate new thinking about Vietnam. Of course I have a high regard for the opinions expressed (they are one hundred percent personal), but even if they are badly wrong, they may be useful in provoking new thinking, and perhaps in countering some of the weary boredom of many Americans with this endless, sickening crisis.

I particularly hope that my book may contribute toward better understanding and appreciation of the hardships, courage and personal sacrifices of the Vietnamese people, and of the men and women of the U. S. Government with whom I was privileged to associate in Vietnam.

The writing has been difficult because the book was an afterthought—certainly the last thing from my mind while I was in Vietnam. I kept no personal records, except for an incomplete collection of newspaper and magazine clippings, and there were many gaps in my memory of those hectic months. Such research as was possible in the time available had to be limited to unclassified sources which were often skimpy. There is no information in the book which has not been published elsewhere, or would not have been available to a determined reporter. And of course I was harassed by the knowledge that Vietnam might be gone by the time the book was published, or even before I could finish writing it.

It was my original intention to write mainly about the so-called "press problem" in Vietnam—the feud between the newsmen who said 2 + 2 = 3 and the officials who said 2 + 2 = 5—since this was my primary responsibility. I soon found, however, that this could not be reported understandably without including extensive material on the overall dilemma of Vietnam itself. As I got into that, I gradually realized that the press problem was less earth-shaking than we had thought at the time. The book evolved into a narrative of the history of the period, as seen from my own relatively limited viewpoint.

An authoritative, specialized book on the role of the newsmen in the fall of the Diem regime nevertheless remains to be written, and should be written. American reporters in Vietnam achieved an influence in the making of U.S. foreign policy that had been equaled in modern times only by the role of the New York newspapers in precipitating the Spanish-American War more than a half century earlier. There was a significant difference. In the earlier case it was deliberate, as suggested by William Randolph Hearst's famous message to the artist Frederic Remington in Cuba: "You furnish the pictures; I'll furnish the war." In Vietnam, a major American policy was wrecked, in part, by unadorned reporting of what was going on.

My story touches only occasionally on the work of the U. S. Information Service in Vietnam in the field of psychological operations to try to turn the Vietnamese people against the Viet Cong. This was a large part of my responsibility, but it was also a specialized activity which does not fit into the framework of this undertaking. It is a story that should be written. It was an important part of our education, e.g. in the reminder that effective advertising requires a good product.

I had hoped to omit names of individuals as much as possible, especially in a derogatory context. My idea was to stimulate thinking about Vietnam, not to stir up new bitterness. This was possible to some extent, but there were repeated occasions when names had to be named for the discussion to make sense. By the nature of things this meant mainly the senior American and Vietnamese officials in Saigon who were running the show, and often the point could not be made with a pulled punch.

I hope, however, that this will not obscure my central thought: that we were all Americans in an uncommonly difficult spot, that the errors and successes were American errors and successes, and that specific individuals were incidental to this uncomfortably basic reality.

Finally, for the patience and encouragement of my wife and two sons, and for the invaluable help of a friend who must remain anonymous, a heartfelt word of thanks from this short-time gamekeeper.

JM

San Francisco
March 1965

MISSION IN TORMENT

CHAPTER ONE

"Be Nice to the Goddam People"

(1)

Deep in the night over Pakistan and India, Burma and Thailand, moonlight glinted on the tapered wing outside, and flickered occasionally on the water of a paddy far below. I talked with a friend about the work ahead. He was returning to his post in the American Embassy in Saigon. I was reporting for duty as Public Affairs Officer in Saigon, returning to Vietnam after seven years' absence.

He was a big, gentle man, slouched in his seat, his fingers nervously tightening and then relaxing around a drink in which the ice had long melted. "I think we are making progress," he said, "but it is slow, very, very slow."

As he talked on, dwelling on a score of problems and frustrations with which he had learned to live, I tried to think how it would be this time. It had been my fortune as a news correspondent to witness the agonized collapse of French colonialism in Vietnam in 1954, and the subsequent intervention of U.S. power to shore up the beleaguered, newly independent government of Ngo Dinh Diem. Now this commitment was being put to arduous trial by renewed Communist guerrilla warfare against the Diem regime, the same stealthy, ugly warfare in the jungles and hip-deep slime of the paddies that I recalled so well. Could we succeed, where the French had failed?

It was midday, May 1, 1962, when the pilot cut the engines of the weary DC-3 of Air Vietnam that had brought us from Bangkok, the last leg of the journey, and I stepped out into the searing glare of the Saigon airport. In an instant the confident, bureaucratically tidy briefings I had received in Washington were forgotten. It took only a glance around the airport to sense something of what it meant for my own country now to be so inextricably involved in this foul and bitter struggle.

It was like a time machine. The airport was cluttered with military aircraft. An armed policeman stood at the foot of the landing gangway, still more at various points around the terminal. There was a heavy leavening of men in uniform in the airport crowds. Nothing had changed. Except the markings on the aircraft. Instead of the French tricolors, there were the black and white symbols of the United States Air Force and the United States Army. And the men in uniform. Instead of crew-cut Frenchmen, or black Moroccans, or lean German Foreign Legionnaires, there were lean, crew-cut, and sometimes black Americans.

Memories flooded back . . .

The futile, murderous battles I had witnessed between the French and the swarming, elusive Vietminh (Communist guerrillas), an enemy of "termites" as Jean Lartéguy was later to call them in his superb novel *The Centurions*. A column of two thousand men in tanks, armored cars and armored halftracks, stalled on a road along a dike between the paddies in the Red River Delta by Vietminh mines, and hidden snipers. The reply of the sweating, sun-tanned French colonel when I asked how the operation was going: "*Comme toujours, Viets partout*" (As always, Vietminh everywhere) . . .

The night I circled for hours in a command plane high over the doomed garrison of Dienbienphu, the lonely pinpoint of a shielded navigation light in the inky depths below, and the intermittent slow-motion blossoms of garish red flames from Vietminh mortars falling among the paratroopers we were dropping into the pitifully small French perimeter. The steady young voice on the garrison's radio link to our plane, advising that the paratroopers had landed, and concluding "*rien à signaler*" (nothing to report) . . .

The arrogant French motorcycle courier I watched one day near Hanoi as he playfully crowded a trudging column of heavily laden peasants into the ditch—an eloquent glimpse of why the French were hated, and why they lost . . .

The French forces evacuating Hanoi in 1955 in their throbbing tanks and halftracks and six-by-six trucks, towing their useless artillery (all American aid), to be replaced by silent, expressionless Vietminh troops on foot, wearing sneakers. Western technological genius, Western industrial might, outflanked and routed by Asian peasants . . .

General René Cogny, the defeated French commander in North Vietnam, standing on the beach at Haiphong one day in 1955 for the departure of his last rearguard troops on a waiting LST. His towering frame guidon-straight, his voice loud and steady, but a telltale glistening in his eye. "France is proud of you," he cried. "You have fought well. *Vive la France!*" He saluted as the Tricolor was lowered for the last time. Quickly he then boarded a helicopter. A storm of swirling dust and he was gone, ending French power north of the 17th Parallel . . .

In Saigon, later that year, cynical French plotting with a Vietnamese gangster mob called the Binh Xuyen to destroy Ngo Dinh Diem because he had refused to take orders. Diem's lonely courage. Some twenty blocks of Cholon, the Chinese quarter of Saigon, swathed in black smoke and flames from Binh Xuyen mortars. The French journalist watching, sipping his Pernod at a sidewalk café, sneering that Diem's troops were "cowards" as they filed stolidly into the inferno to wipe out the Binh Xuyen in less than forty-eight hours. The frail American hope that Diem might be the leader so desperately needed . . .

French despair, mixed with petulant, insensate arrogance as the reality of defeat settled upon them. Their vindictive resentment of American support for Diem. "Children leading children" sneered a French businessman who had made a fortune selling French textiles to Vietnamese peasants at exorbitant prices fixed by colonial authorities. Threats against American newsmen for reporting the sordid spectacle of French maneuvering against Diem. My hurt dismay when my friend M. Boyer, proprietor of l'Amiral, my favorite restaurant, refused to serve me.

It was no homecoming to return to Vietnam. But few Americans have ever worked there without finding themselves emotionally involved, as I had been, with the land and with its sturdy, tormented people. As we drove into the city, along the broad, tree-lined boulevards left by the French, I was pleased to be back, yet also fearful, for I knew something of the elusive dangers of this contested nation. In Vietnam I had known France at her finest, and her shabbiest. In many ways Vietnam was now to provide a similar glimpse of the United States.

(2)

Remote and unknown though Vietnam was to most Americans, there was nothing exceptional about U.S. involvement there. It developed as part of the worldwide U.S. effort after World War II to contain Communist imperialism. The problem was, however, considerably more difficult and complex than such similar commitments as Greece, Turkey, West Germany, the Philippines and even Korea, because Vietnam emerged from the war as one of the untidiest corners of an untidy world.

The very name Vietnam was suppressed for nearly a century before 1950 by its French colonial rulers. It is pronounced Vee-Yet-Nahm. To call it "Veet-naam," as many Americans do, is not only wrong, but insulting. In the Vietnamese language this pronunciation translates as "sick duck."

Vietnam is one of the world's oldest nations. Its recorded history reaches back nearly three thousand years. Its people are believed to be a mixture of Indonesians and Mongols from Central Asia who migrated southward to escape marauding Chinese warlords. Vietnamese culture is basically Chinese and the language is a monosyllabic Chinese dialect. It was originally written in Chinese characters, until a French missionary priest, Alexandre de Rhodes, devised a Latin script in the seventeenth century.

Like the Chinese the Vietnamese have always been primarily an agricultural people. They settled in the fertile lowlands of the Red River Delta in the north, the Mekong River Delta in the south, and along the thin strips of coastal plain in between. This created a freakish sickle-shaped country fifteen hundred miles long and only twenty-five to three hundred miles wide. Its spinal rain-forest highlands are populated by a half million aborigines of uncertain origin who dress in loincloths and hunt with crossbows. They are called *montagnards* (mountaineers) by the French, *moi* (savages) by the Vietnamese.

Vietnam was occupied by the Chinese for a millennium, from 111 B.C. until A.D. 939 when the Vietnamese united to win their independence. For centuries thereafter the Vietnamese were alternately invaders and invaded. They fought off repeated Chinese assaults, hurling back even the hordes—reputedly a half million strong—of Kublai Khan, whose defeat stirred a Vietnamese leader to say: "This ancient land shall live forever." The Chinese then, as today, hungered for the rich ricelands of Vietnam. A vastly more energetic people than their neighbors, the Vietnamese in turn repeatedly fought the Lao, Cambodians and even the Thai, extending their hegemony on occasion well beyond the present Cambodian capital of Phnom Penh. This created a fear and hatred among their neighbors that lingers pathetically today in the hysterical pro-Chinese policy of Cambodia's Prince Norodom Sihanouk.

For the latter centuries of this era, the emperors who made their imperial capital at Hue, in the central coastal area, were the dominating power in Vietnam. Saigon in those days was a mere outpost of empire. Even the name Saigon derives from ancient words meaning "Western Tribute" because it was there that the western colonies paid their taxes. The last of the Vietnamese emperors was the playboy Bao Dai, who collaborated successively with the Japanese, Chinese Nationalists, Communists, French and the Binh Xuyen gangsters in Saigon. He capped this unlovely record by retreating, with his mistresses, to the French Riviera while his countrymen died by the thousands at Dienbienphu in 1954.

The French won control of Vietnam in the mid-nineteenth century, consolidating European commercial and missionary penetration that began three hundred years earlier. They quickly extended their sway as well over Cambodia and Laos, attempting to obliterate national identities by naming the whole peninsula French Indo-China. The French brought highways and a railroad, lovely colonial homes, Parisian-style avenues, and some industry, but most of all French culture, which remains strong in all three countries today. One of their main economic efforts was the development of rubber plantations which made Vietnam the world's fifth biggest producer. Throughout most of World War II the area was controlled by the Vichy regime, which permitted the Japanese to operate freely from Vietnamese soil. The airfield at Saigon was the base of the planes that sank the British battle cruiser *Repulse* and the dreadnaught *Prince of Wales* in December 1941.

In the months during and after the Japanese collapse in 1945, parts of Vietnam were occupied variously by British, Chinese Nationalist and French forces—while hundreds of thousands of Vietnamese died of famine in the resulting chaos.

The situation was ripe for the Vietnamese again to assert their historic determination to be free, and indeed they did. But this time the leader who stimulated the rebellion was a lean, goateed, Communist pro-consul named Nguyen Ai Quoc who broke into the world's headlines under the alias of Ho Chi Minh (The Enlightened One). He was a veteran Moscow agent whose revolutionary activities in Southeast Asia have been traced back to the Twenties when he was the principal Comintern agent for the region. Using standard Communist camouflage as a nationalist, Ho was able to rally enough military and political strength to occupy Hanoi and proclaim an independent government in August 1945.

This provoked a period of complicated international maneuvering—much of it sordid—among the French, British, Chinese Nationalists and Ho's Vietminh (an abbreviation of the Vietnamese term *Viet-Nam Doc-Lap Dong Minh Hoi* which translates as the Revolutionary League for the Independence of Vietnam). The French initially went through the motions of negotiating with Ho, even inviting him to Paris. At the same time, however, they rapidly built up their military forces in Vietnam. In the fall of 1946 they broke off negotiations and resorted to force. On November 23, 1946, the French cruiser *Suffren* bombarded the northern port city of Haiphong, slaughtering thousands of Vietnamese. Ho fled to the jungle and launched a guerrilla rebellion, exploiting the hatred stirred by French brutality. It culminated in victory eight years later at a remote village called Dienbienphu in the hills of northwest Vietnam.

Despite its overwhelming military dominance at the end of World War II, the United States initially stayed out of the Southeast Asian shambles. American inclinations, reflecting President Roosevelt's idealism, favored an end to European colonialism in the area. But political realities—notably the exposed nerve ends of our British, Dutch and French allies—made it impractical to do much about it. By the late forties the option in Vietnam was virtually ended, in any case, because Ho Chi Minh was rapidly creating a situation where the only visible alternative to French colonialism was Asian Communism.

Then in 1949 came a cataclysmic event that ended U.S. detachment decisively and permanently. This, of course, was the fall of China, bringing Mao Tse-tung's forces to the Vietnamese frontier, and abruptly stiffening U.S. policy in Asia. In 1950 the U. S. recognized the puppet French regime headed by Bao Dai. (It was during this period that the French belatedly revived the name Vietnam in an effort to rally Vietnamese nationalism against the Vietminh.) Also in 1950 the United States contributed $25 million to help the French effort against the Vietminh. By 1954 this had mushroomed to more than $1 billion.

American policy during that period was little more than blank-check support for the French. This dismayed a good many liberal-minded Americans, including the then Senator John F. Kennedy, who visited Saigon in 1953. In a speech in the Senate in 1954 Kennedy said: "I am frankly of the belief that no amount of American military assistance in Indo-China can conquer an enemy which is everywhere, and at the same time nowhere, 'an enemy of the people' which has the sympathy and covert support of the people." By then, however, events had forced the U. S. into such a box that a better policy was hard to come by.

On one hand it would have been disastrous to abandon the French. On the other the French were in such an emotional state that they were unwilling to listen to American advice on anything. (Diem was a paragon of sweet reasonableness by comparison.) As late as 1953, furthermore, there was reason to hope that the French could defeat the Vietminh, just as Ramón Magsaysay had destroyed the Communist Huks in the Philippines and the British were then crushing the Communist guerrillas in Malaya. Even today there are competent authorities who believe that the French could have prevailed if they had made a greater effort.

Instead, the French blundered in a hundred ways—to a degree, in retrospect, that seems unbelievable. They behaved as though they had never heard of Mao Tse-tung and the elusive guerrilla techniques that had toppled Chiang Kai-shek—which Ho and his military commander Vo Nguyen Giap had adopted and elaborated. The French forces holed up in fortified watch towers and isolated themselves from the Vietnamese people, in effect ceding control of the countryside to the Vietminh by default. They tried to use tanks and planes and artillery against an invisible enemy—like attacking mosquitoes with a sledgehammer. In frustrated fury they repeatedly wiped out whole villages with shells and napalm on mere suspicion of concealed Vietminh troops, adding to the people's hatred.

Even by classic principles of warfare, they were persistently wrong. The French commander, General Henri Navarre, for example, committed thirty-odd battalions of infantry to a futile operation on the Annamese coast just before Dienbienphu, thus denying himself reinforcements that might have averted disaster. Perhaps most seriously of all, the French treated even friendly Vietnamese with arrogant contempt—e.g. addressing them mostly with the intimate pronoun *tu* (you) as though they were servants. A man with any sort of personal integrity was sorely tempted to join the Vietminh—and thousands of non-Communist Vietnamese did just that.

Inevitably the French failed militarily, but in French fashion they did so gloriously—in their gallant stand in the mud and filth and gangrene of Dienbienphu, suffering four thousand useless dead to stir the world's admiration.

Equally inevitably the sequel to military disaster was political collapse. This too was done in French fashion—ingloriously.

At the Geneva Conference of 1954 the French gave up the northern half of Vietnam, accepting partition at the 17th Parallel and neutralization of Cambodia and Laos. Ho Chi Minh became President of the "Democratic Republic of Vietnam." But instead of accepting the evidence that they were finished in Vietnam, the French tried one last series of maneuvers in the South. They persuaded Ngo Dinh Diem, who was just about the last true nationalist of any weight who had not joined the Vietminh, to return from self-imposed exile to become premier by promising real independence at long last. Then they tried to manage Diem, as they had his predecessors. When he refused to be managed the French tried to oust him by such trickery as their secret support for the Binh Xuyen gangster rebellion, as noted earlier—and failed.

Once he had consolidated his position Diem quickly eliminated what remained of French political influence in Saigon. France's last days in Vietnam were deeply humiliating. The French never forgot. Officially, of course, they supported U.S. efforts to save the South, but many Americans in Saigon had a visceral feeling that emotionally the French wanted us also to fail. There was surely a suspicion of this in President de Gaulle's 1963 proposal to "neutralize" Southeast Asia, which probably would mean its eventual loss to the Communists.

In any case Diem's surprising success in frustrating French conniving in 1955 by no means settled the crisis. The French departure had created a power vacuum. The South was demoralized. And no sensible observer thought for an instant that Ho Chi Minh would settle for only half the country. There was equally little doubt that still another Communist triumph would be disastrous to Western interests in the whole region. For a second time the United States thus was forced into a larger commitment in Vietnam by circumstances beyond its control.

This inescapably meant coming to the support of the man in power, Ngo Dinh Diem. The cost was high in frustration, frazzled nerves and disillusion among the long procession of American officials who had to try to deal with this stubborn, unimaginative, distant man in the years that followed.

American performance during the late fifties has become a matter of controversy. Apart from the basic question of our wisdom in supporting a man like Diem at all, competent critics charge that the U. S. failed to foresee that Ho Chi Minh would again resort to the guerrilla techniques that had worked so spectacularly against the French. The critics charge that the U. S. inexplicably built up South Vietnam, instead, to beat off a conventional attack across the 17th Parallel—despite floods of intelligence indicating that the Communists had concluded after Korea that it was an error to challenge Western industrial power in conventional warfare. The evidence suggests that there was truth to such charges.

American economic aid between 1955 and 1959 accented long-term infra-structure projects, such as highways, airports, dams and harbor improvements, in effect treating Vietnam like any other underdeveloped country. The program led to impressive economic progress. The gross national product jumped a healthy average of three percent annually during this period, despite the massive problems of resettling 900,000 anti-Communist refugees from the North. But there were relatively few "impact" programs of immediate benefit to the peasants which would help persuade them to resist Communist subversion. Such efforts as the U. S. did make in that direction, moreover, were often sabotaged by the Vietnamese Government. American experts helped prepare a sweeping land reform program, for example, but only about fifteen percent of it was ever implemented.

Similarly U.S. military aid was programmed in more or less the same fashion as for countries like Turkey and Korea, where guerrillas were not a threat. The Vietnamese armed forces not only were equipped with tanks, planes, artillery and similar hardware that has relatively little value against guerrillas—as the French had discovered so painfully, and the Pentagon apparently had not noticed. They were also trained to depend on that kind of big bang support in battle, reducing both their capability and their psychological willingness to get out and fight the guerrillas the only way that works: with rifles, close in.

The U. S. persisted in these policies, furthermore, with little apparent regard for multiplying reports on Communist activities during this period. For the first year or two after Geneva, the stay-behind Communist apparatus in the South was relatively quiescent, presumably because Ho Chi Minh needed time to consolidate his position in Hanoi and also perhaps because he hoped to invest the South by political maneuvers. Around 1957, however, he began preparing actively for renewed guerrilla war.

On one hand Ho's agents set about systematic organization of the South Vietnamese countryside. Clandestine organizers concentrated on exploiting peasant grievances to turn them against the Diem government—and no doubt were delighted with the failure of the land reform effort. Where persuasion failed they resorted to terror, creating both an underground political system and guerrilla military units. Between 1957 and 1959 the Vietnamese Government reported the murders of no fewer than sixty-five village officials who had tried to resist.

On the other hand the Communists proceeded with a remarkable clandestine buildup of arms and ammunition. During the same two years, the Vietnamese Government discovered some three thousand secret dumps and, of course, the number it did not discover must have been vastly greater. Some of this materiel, protectively greased and packaged, was hidden at the time of Geneva, when the Vietminh supposedly evacuated the South. More was infiltrated on jungle trails from the North across the 17th Parallel, often through Laos, where a coordinated guerrilla rebellion had already made a mockery of the solemn Communist promises at Geneva.

In mid-1959 Ho Chi Minh was ready and the signal was flashed to his commanders in their deep jungle command posts. Once again Vietnam was engulfed in war. Hanoi Radio proclaimed that the objective was destruction of the Diem regime and achievement of "national unity," meaning reunification of Vietnam under Communist control. Something called the "National Liberation Front"—composed of faceless unknowns who remain unknown today—was proclaimed as a cover for Hanoi's political control. The Viet Cong (literally Vietnamese Communists), as the guerrillas were now called to distinguish them from the Vietminh in the North, mounted attacks on government troops and installations in every corner of the country.

In a matter of months it was clear that the Diem regime was desperately unequal to the challenge. In November 1960 it was nearly toppled by a coup d'état attempted by some of its own paratroopers. It failed mainly because they lost their nerve at the last moment. By mid-1961 the regime was perilously close to total collapse.

For a third time, the U. S. faced a no-choice challenge in Vietnam. Despite his disapproval of President Eisenhower's policy in Vietnam five years earlier, President Kennedy found himself doing the same thing, but more so. Following a special mission headed by General Maxwell Taylor in October 1961, Kennedy ordered a massive increase in American support that was to boost U.S. military personnel in Vietnam from about six hundred in 1961 to twenty-three thousand by the beginning of 1965. Their task was to train, supply and advise the Vietnamese forces, but not to engage in combat themselves. It was an unprecedented undertaking: U.S. prestige laid squarely on the line, in a struggle of critical importance to Free World security, yet with no command authority except for such advice as we could persuade the remote and intractable Ngo Dinh Diem to accept.

(3)

What happened next was a wonderfully typical bureaucratic performance, in which I had now become a supporting player. Overnight in Washington, Vietnam became fashionable, a priority country, and everyone above the rank of Pfc scrambled to share in the resulting top level attention. Since there was no precedent, there were no rules, no inter-agency jurisdictional limitations, and just about everyone made it. It was like a contest among a dozen teams of carpenters to see who could build the same house fastest, simultaneously, on the same lot.

A special, emergency, inter-agency group called the Vietnam Task Force was created (to be replaced later by the Vietnam Working Group, which later became part of the Southeast Asia Task Force, which was replaced by the Vietnam Coordinating Committee) to organize the effort. In Saigon new American outfits and command posts began appearing like crabgrass; some were understandable, like a Navy Hospital, others utterly mysterious either because of their alphabetical names, like HEDSUPPACT (a supply organization), or their semicovert missions. The Embassy telephone book was regularly out of date before it could be printed.

Traffic of U.S. military personnel in and out of Vietnam was so confused that the Saigon PX soon found itself stuck with several thousand dollars in bad checks that could not be traced. A story circulated that the Pentagon itself lost track and eventually had to resort to a computer to sort out its personnel situation in Vietnam. Housing in Saigon became such a problem that U.S. agencies began bidding against each other until houses for senior officials were bringing rents as high as one thousand dollars a month, to the delight of local businessmen. The French, of course, had never permitted any such windfalls as that.

Two big officers' clubs, complete with slot machines, thirty-five-cent martinis and Sunday-night barbecued steaks, blossomed on the rooftops of a hotel and apartment building in the heart of Saigon. Back-alley bars mushroomed with B-girls and names like "The Florida Club," "21," "Honeymoon Lane" and "Uncle Sam's" to attract U.S. servicemen. An Armed Forces Radio network went on the air in Saigon and several other locations. The American Women's Association of Saigon went into the cocktail glass rental business in a brave effort to meet the community's burgeoning social requirements.

Visiting senior officers from Washington cluttered Saigon to the point where American general officers in the country often outnumbered the Vietnamese generals. More than a dozen American generals and admirals were permanently stationed in Saigon, though the total number of men for them to command was equal to only one infantry division. Briefings, meetings with Diem and other top Vietnamese officials, and other arrangements became so time-consuming that Admiral Harry Donald Felt, the able U.S. commander-in-chief for the Pacific (CINCPAC), eventually ordered that no more senior officers could junket to Vietnam without CINCPAC permission.

Washington adopted something close to a wartime psychology vis-à-vis Vietnam—and rightly so—with the result that almost anything Saigon requested was forthcoming as quickly as possible, including money. Indeed I once heard a VIP visitor from the Pentagon brush aside a question about additional funds by remarking: "We have a fifty billion dollar budget and this is our only war. Don't worry about money."

Bureaucratically, the result of the crash, unprecedented buildup in Vietnam to perform an unprecedented function was a Rube Goldberg contraption that no man could wholly understand. At the top of the military pyramid, for example, there emerged something called the Military Assistance Command, Vietnam (commonly known as MACV, pronounced Mack-Vee), headed by a four-star general, Paul D. Harkins. Even the name was a contradiction, since the U. S. had no true "command" function in Vietnam, except, of course, over its own people. It was all nicely compounded, moreover, by retention (until mid-1964) of the existing Military Assistance Advisory Group (MAAG) under a two-star general, Charles J. Timmes—who fortunately was one of the ablest and most personable Americans in Vietnam.

Timmes was broadly under Harkins' command, of course, but he retained considerable independent authority and primary responsibility for supply and training. MACV assumed primary responsibility for advice to the Vietnamese Government on operational matters and command authority over the limited American units in combat roles, mainly Air Force and helicopter outfits. It worked out that American officers in the field reported to MAAG on some of their activities, to MACV on others.

On the civilian side the Saigon station of the Central Intelligence Agency, headed by John H. Richardson, was deeply involved in advisory assistance to the Vietnamese Government on such matters as creation of a modern intelligence system and training of para-military organizations, in addition to its own normal functions. The U. S. Operations Mission (the local name for the AID office), headed by Joseph L. Brent, was engaged in economic assistance ranging from radio transmitters to fertilizer, often in direct support of military operations. The U. S. Information Service, of which I was director, worked closely with the Vietnamese Government in developing propaganda programs. Almost everything any of us did related to some degree to parallel activities by other American agencies, creating a labyrinth of fast-changing requirements for co-operation.

There was a Saigon joke that the U. S. Mission was "like a log floating down a stream, covered with ants, each one of whom thinks he is steering."

Despite the seeming absurdities, however, the system worked. This was mainly to the credit of the two top American officials in Saigon: Ambassador Frederick E. ("Fritz") Nolting, Jr., and General Harkins.

Nolting, who held a doctor's degree in Philosophy, was forty-nine when he arrived in Vietnam in May 1961. He was a career foreign service officer, most recently in Paris in the U. S. Mission to NATO, and had never before served in Asia. He was a hulking, big-boned man with inexhaustible energy, gentle in voice and manner in keeping with his Virginia background, yet a sensitive, emotional man who chain-smoked cigarettes as he wrestled with impossible problems in his lonely sixth floor office. He liked to relax with tennis and a swim with his lovely wife and three daughters at Saigon's Cercle Sportif.

Before he went to Vietnam, Nolting was told in Washington that it would be a miracle if South Vietnam lasted three months longer. Nolting merits much credit for the fact that the miracle happened. He was dedicated to his job and to the conviction that U.S. support for Diem was what he frequently called "a winning program." He was savagely criticized for his seemingly unbending defensiveness about Diem—which he maintained even with his intimates—but there were occasional hints that he had no illusions about this. Diem was notorious for his compulsive monologues which would often keep his visitors fighting drowsiness for hours. At a dinner one evening the conversation touched on the bombing of Diem's palace by two renegade Vietnamese pilots in early 1962, and the story about a carpenter working on the floor above who is supposed to have fallen into Diem's bedroom.

Nolting quipped gently: "And how many hours did the President keep him?"

Harkins, who was then fifty-seven, arrived in Vietnam in February 1962. A Bostonian whose father had been a newspaperman, he served on General George Patton's staff in World War II. Before the Vietnam assignment, he was Felt's deputy at Honolulu. He lived a spartan military life in Saigon, traveling almost daily around the country in small planes to keep in touch with the war.

Harkins shared Nolting's determination to keep Diem in power. The two men also got along well personally. This was particularly fortunate because of the complex balance of authority between them. U.S. tradition is that the Ambassador is the supreme U.S. authority in a foreign country in peacetime, while the theater commander is supreme in wartime. Technically Vietnam qualified as "peace" with the Ambassador thus the head man. Harkins, however, had four stars and responsibility for thousands of men, and he was also commander of MAC-Thai (Military Assistance Command, Thailand), making him a "theater" commander in a sense. American bureaucracy being what it is, this kind of two-headed system was loaded with the ingredients for damaging disputes. Nolting and Harkins were big enough men to put aside jealousies and make it work.

As the contraption eventually evolved, the U. S. Mission, meaning all the Americans in Vietnam, was run by the Country Team. This was an official institution, which exists in other U.S. missions, composed of the Ambassador as chairman, the chiefs of the other U.S. agencies represented at the post, plus the service attachés and several other key officers. In Vietnam there was a smaller group called the Country Task Force composed of the Ambassador and agency chiefs only, supposedly functioning as an extension of the Vietnam Task Force in Washington. We also had a number of specialized inter-agency committees to coordinate such activities as intelligence, economic development and psychological operations.

The Country Team met regularly at nine-thirty Tuesday mornings in the Ambassador's office. A list of the problems we discussed would be a catalog of frustrations such as few, if any, American missions had ever had to live with.

(4)

So what—as so many Americans asked—were we doing with all those people and all that money over there if we were not fighting the Viet Cong ourselves? And in any case why should we invest such a big effort in support of a regime that was so weak, inefficient and unpopular that it could not by itself control a rebellion by a few thousand poorly armed peasants?

The answer lay in the inconvenient reality that this was exactly the kind of regime that is always most vulnerable to Communist subversion. It had happened repeatedly elsewhere, e.g. Iran, Greece, the Congo, and it would surely happen again. Apart from the compelling strategic reasons for denying the Communists another victory in Southeast

Asia (or anywhere else for that matter), it was undeniably more in the American interest to try to find ways to help such a regime win its own war than to commit U.S. combat forces. Such a policy would soon find us fighting in brush-fire rebellions all over the world.

Vietnam was special only in the sense that we had never before come to the aid of a country so badly demoralized, and in such desperate trouble, short of overt enemy attack across its frontier.

In effect, what the U. S. did in Vietnam was to set up a shadow government—though it would have been heresy to describe it that way publicly because of Vietnamese sensitivities. The shadow's function was to try to figure out what needed to be done and then to try to persuade the government of Vietnam to do it. Thus the justification for so many generals and other senior Americans; senior Vietnamese, being Orientals and therefore "face" conscious, would have been reluctant to take advice from Americans of lesser rank. The advisory relationship was the nub of U.S. frustrations in Vietnam.

Unlike the British who crushed a similar Communist insurgency in Malaya, the U. S. had no authority in Vietnam. It was true that General Taylor exacted a long list of promises from Diem in 1961, mostly relating to urgently needed reforms. It was also true that the U. S. theoretically could use its aid as leverage to have its way with Diem. In fact, Diem accepted only such advice as was least painful and ignored many of his promises. He was so consummately stubborn, and proud, that he eventually committed what amounted to suicide rather than bend to U.S. pressures. He regarded them as an unacceptable violation of Vietnamese sovereignty.

Paradoxically, moreover, it was desirable for the U. S. to preserve and honor Vietnamese sovereignty, even though it was the main block to effective American influence on the war effort. In a nation so recently liberated from colonialism, open foreign domination would be a block to true popular support for the regime. This was particularly true in view of the Viet Cong propaganda line that Diem was an American "puppet." The U. S., in short, faced three indigestible alternatives: to support Diem with all his faults, or to use our power to unseat him with the risk of resulting chaos, or to go home in defeat. We were in exactly the same box with the regimes that followed Diem.

In characteristic American fashion the U. S. Mission reacted to these maddeningly frustrating circumstances by rationalizing the word "advice" into something close to a form of warfare. It came to have a meaning similar to words like combat, operations, or objective—often, unfortunately, becoming psychologically an end in itself. For example, I recall a sign over the entrance to the offices of a divisional advisory team in the Mekong Delta that read something like: "Through These Portals Pass the Best Darned Advisors in the United States Army."

Similarly the word "counterpart" acquired unique meaning and importance. A counterpart was the Vietnamese official whom any given American was supposed to be advising. Inevitably this led to slogans like: "If you do not first-name your counterpart, you are not doing your job." The counterpart system was soon developed to an extraordinary degree, reaching deep into the fabric of the whole Vietnamese Government and military establishment. The U.S. armed forces, USOM and CIA all maintained full-time advisors inside the Vietnamese Government and a good many Embassy and USIS officers spent much of their time in the advisory business.

In practice this meant that Americans were intimately involved in literally hundreds of Vietnamese Government activities: police, intelligence, harbor maintenance, airport control towers, radio broadcasting, motion picture production, printing, traffic engineering, highway construction, railroad maintenance, education, health and medical training, industrial development, banking, taxation, rural development, pig raising, monetary controls, and, of course, at every level down to company or equivalent of the Vietnamese Army, Navy and Air Force. By mid-1963, at least one American—and usually several—participated in nearly every military operation of any significance initiated by the government, whether a simple patrol or an assault with several thousand men.

More than any other accomplishment, Nolting and Harkins merit the highest kind of praise for establishment of the counterpart system which was at once massively complex and politically explosive because it amounted to foreign infiltration of every arm of a sovereign government with hair-trigger pride.

My own counterpart was a likable former newspaperman named Phan Van Tao, the director-general of information, who first won attention among his countrymen with a book called *The Bladder of the Pig*—a personalized story about his childhood in a northern village and the big, periodic event of the slaughter of a pig when the kids would scramble for the bladder to blow up and use as a ball. Tao often approved of my ideas, or so he said anyway, but he was almost always overruled, usually by the President's brother Ngo Dinh Nhu. Tao was arrested and jailed after the November 1 coup, for reasons that were not made public.

Like "advice" and "counterpart," there was a third expression that Washington, reacting to the Vietnam crisis, clasped to its breast. This was "counter-insurgency," also known as "CI" and "COIN." Nobody knew who invented it. There was a movement to abolish it on the grounds it was too negative. (One proposed substitute was "nation building" which thankfully had not caught on.) It was the official tag for what we were trying to do in Vietnam. Insurgency, in Pentagon usage, meant the type of conflict that comes between subversion, when there is enemy activity against the legal government but no shooting, and limited war, when there is conventional warfare in a limited theater without recourse to nuclear weapons, e.g. Korea. Insurgency, in short, essentially meant warfare conducted by irregulars who generally avoided toe-to-toe combat between military formations, striking instead by surprise, from ambush, at points where the enemy was weak, dispersing rapidly when reinforcements arrived. The Communist term was "revolutionary wars of liberation."

This kind of fighting, of course, was as old as mankind. Caesar complained of guerrilla harassment in Gaul. The American Indians used guerrilla tactics against the white settlers of the New World. The word guerrilla itself originated among the Spanish patriots who harassed Napoleon and means "little war." The French *maquisards* confounded the Germans in World War II with much the same techniques used by the Viet Cong. It was my fortune for a few days in France in 1944 to be a prisoner of the Germans. I vividly recall a German soldier lying horribly wounded on a stretcher in a hospital. My German guard said he had been hit by a "criminal," meaning a guerrilla. Why criminal? I asked. "Because they don't wear uniforms," said the guard. "They don't fight fair."

It remained, however, for the Asian Communists to hone the guerrilla weapon to a new effectiveness. It was the starting point of the monumental revolution that led to the capture of China. Perhaps even more significantly, the Chinese Communists then exported their techniques for use against foreign regimes. Besides the Vietminh success in Indo-China, Communist guerrilla rebellions almost worked in Malaya and the Philippines. The Communists developed guerrilla warfare into an extraordinarily dangerous device to bypass Western industrial power, for destroying pro-

Western regimes without offering a target by posing as indigenous, nationalist uprisings.

Characteristically the Communists also developed guerrilla warfare as a sort of politico-military doctrine. Mao Tse-tung's writings became a textbook, must reading in the Pentagon. They are full of pronouncements like the famous line that "The people are the water and the army is the fish," meaning that guerrillas cannot survive without help from the population and therefore must win the population's support by propaganda, good deeds and, if necessary, force. It is rigid Maoist law, for example, that a guerrilla soldier must treat the people courteously, help the people when he can, pay for such food as he takes and otherwise be kind and lovable. Mao was adapted for Vietnam's special conditions by Ho Chi Minh's military commander, Vo Nguyen Giap, in a book called *People's War, People's Army*.

As reported earlier, the United States erred in failing to prepare the Vietnamese for this kind of fighting in its military assistance program during the fifties. There was still a disturbing lack of coherent Pentagon doctrine and organization for effective counter-insurgency programs in the early sixties. Vietnam in fact had become a laboratory. The United States, unlike the French in their war, tried to learn from the challenge.

On President Kennedy's personal direction, a high-level course in counter-insurgency was required of senior officials of all agencies who were heading overseas. A super-elite "Special Group, Counter-Insurgency" (commonly known as the C. I. Group) was set up in Washington with Attorney General Robert Kennedy as chairman. An Office on Counter-Insurgency and Special Activities, commanded by a two-star general, was set up in the Pentagon directly under the joint chiefs. It became an asset for young officers to attend the U. S. Army Special Warfare School at Fort Bragg, and vastly more of an asset to do a tour in Vietnam.

All this apparently was sinking in, too. Shortly after I arrived in Saigon, I overheard a hard-bitten colonel, who had spent most of his career in tanks, explaining to a friend that counter-insurgency was not hard to understand. "The way I figure it," he said, "it's mostly being nice to the goddam people."

In a speech in Chicago in September 1962, Roger Hilsman, then director of intelligence and research in the State Department, who had himself fought the Japanese as a guerrilla in World War II, articulated official American doctrine somewhat more sedately. "To fight guerrillas," he said, "you must adopt the tactics of the guerrilla himself."

This was one of the basic objectives of the whole, massive U.S. advisory effort in Vietnam—to drain the water away from the Viet Cong fish. On the political level, we pressed the government toward such reforms as punishment of dishonest village officials. In the economic field, we developed a far-reaching program ($20 million in Fiscal 1963 alone) of direct help to the peasants, e.g. fertilizer and thousands of pigs. In the propaganda field, USIS produced innumerable pamphlets, magazines, radio programs, films, and leaflets covering everything from how to cultivate turnips to a code of behavior urging Vietnamese troops not to steal chickens nor otherwise molest the villagers. There was similar accent in a wide area of U.S.-engineered covert actions.

Most of all, it was the young American officers attached to field military units—mostly captains and majors—who carried the weight of the U.S. advisory effort. They were men of whom Americans could be justly proud. They lived with the Vietnamese, ate their food and suffered their hardships. I was at an advisors' mess at Hue one time, for example, when an officer returned after forty-odd days in the jungle on patrol with a Vietnamese unit. He had lost thirty-five pounds but planned to return to the bush a few days later. Our field advisors were repeatedly involved in combat with the Viet Cong, and captured V.C. documents revealed orders to shoot first at Americans, as was confirmed all too much by mounting U.S. casualty figures. It was rough, dangerous, but rewarding duty.

There were no rulebooks. Probably the most valuable asset these men had was their American background of general knowledge, ingenuity and common sense. On one occasion, for example, a Vietnamese patrol trapped a Viet Cong in a canal. He was standing up to his knees in water, hands raised, trying to surrender, but the troops continued firing at him. An American advisor tried to stop them by shouting, then in desperation jumped down into the canal himself and ran toward the Communist, gesturing to the troops to cease firing, at obvious great risk. It worked. The man was taken prisoner with superficial wounds. The American then directed a medic to take care of him. The prisoner was so surprised and grateful that he pointed out three more Viet Cong among the crowd of curious villagers who were watching.

Yankee ingenuity blossomed all over Vietnam, to the point where Harkins' headquarters began collecting new ideas in a periodic bulletin entitled "Lessons Learned." I knew a paratrooper captain, for example, who observed that when the Viet Cong ambushed a government column they always tried first to knock out vehicles with radio masts, figuring that these were command vehicles. The captain forthwith installed fake radio masts on all his unit's vehicles. Also to frustrate ambushes, the captain persuaded the unit commander never to use the same spacing between vehicles in convoy that he had on the previous sortie, thus making it impossible for the Viet Cong to observe the unit's habits and spot their men accordingly along the road. It was American influence in promoting a British practice in Malaya that gradually led Vietnamese outfits to remodel their trucks so that infantry could ride on benches facing outward, adding a few seconds to their response to ambushes.

In Saigon and back in the U. S., American technical skill was applied to development of new weapons and equipment for guerrilla fighting. Results ranged all the way from the "Huey" (HU-1A) helicopters loaded with rockets and machine guns to protect troop-carrying helicopters, to "instant *nuoc mam*," a dehydrated form of the fish sauce that is a staple of the Vietnamese diet.

Most of all, however, the problem was to persuade the government forces to get out into the muck and filth of the jungle, to seek out the Viet Cong in their safe havens, to patrol constantly, night and day, and to be just as tough and ready for hardship as the Communists—in short, to forget about their American tanks and artillery and similar tempting psychological crutches.

The point was dramatically made in a notice posted on a bulletin board outside the war room at Admiral Felt's headquarters in Honolulu. It purported to be the standing orders of Rogers' Rangers in the French and Indian Wars more than two hundred years ago, and somebody had headlined it: "Injun Fightin' 1759. Counter-Insurgency 1962." The orders:

1. Don't forget nothing.
2. Have your musket clean as a whistle, hatchet scoured, sixty rounds powder and ball, and be ready to march at a minute's warning.
3. When you're on the march, act the way you would if you was sneaking up on a deer. See the enemy first.
4. Tell the truth about what you see and what you do. There is an army depending on us for correct information. You can lie all you please when you tell other folks about the Rangers, but don't never lie to a Ranger or officer.
5. Don't never take a chance you don't have to.

6. When we're on the march we march single file, far enough apart so one shot can't go through two men.
7. If we strike swamps, or soft ground, we spread out abreast, so it's hard to track us.
8. When we march, we keep moving till dark, so as to give the enemy the least possible chance at us.
9. When we camp, half the party stays awake while the other half sleeps.
10. If we take prisoners, we keep 'em separate till we have had time to examine them, so they can't cook up a story between 'em.
11. Don't ever march home the same way. Take a different route so you won't be ambushed.
12. No matter whether we travel in big parties or little ones, each party has to keep a scout 20 yards ahead, twenty yards on each flank, and twenty yards in the rear, so the main body can't be surprised and wiped out.
13. Every night you'll be told where to meet if surrounded by a superior force.
14. Don't sit down to eat without posting sentries.
15. Don't sleep beyond dawn. Dawn's when the French and Indians attack.
16. Don't cross a river by a regular ford.
17. If somebody's trailing you, make a circle, come back onto your own tracks, and ambush the folks that aim to ambush you.
18. Don't stand up when the enemy's coming against you. Kneel down, lie down, hide behind a tree.
19. Let the enemy come till he's almost close enough to touch. Then let him have it and jump out and finish him up with your hatchet.

Major Robert Rogers, 1759

CHAPTER TWO

Tragic Legacy

(1)

For all its enthusiasm, ingenuity, and high price tag, the American effort to save South Vietnam by shoring up the Diem regime was a spectacular, heartbreaking failure. Two years after the Taylor mission, the regime collapsed, Diem and his brother Ngo Dinh Nhu were dead, and the Viet Cong were on a rampage, gaining everywhere.

The failure resulted from a combination of unique and complex factors, and who was wrong about what probably will be argued for years to come. There can be no debate, however, that the single most important cause of the failure was the regime itself.

The Ngo Dinh family (Diem is a given name, the usual designation in Vietnamese usage) claims its origin in the tenth century when an ancestor, Ngo Quyen, led the army that finally expelled the Chinese. Under the Hue emperors, the Ngo Dinh belonged for centuries to the Mandarinate, the aristocracy of privileged officials. The family was converted to Roman Catholicism some three hundred years ago, and almost wiped out in 1870 when an anti-Christian mob herded about one hundred of its members into a church and burned them alive.

Diem (pronounced Zee-Yem), who was born in 1901, was something of an eccentric from his earliest youth, given to uncontrolled tantrums, for example, when his studies were interrupted. He set out to become a priest, but then abandoned the idea on the surprising grounds, according to one of his brothers, that the church was "too worldly." Instead Diem took a vow of chastity and spent hours daily throughout his life in deep meditation. He became a Mandarin (official) in the French colonial system, eventually rising to provincial governor (1929) and then interior minister (1933) for a French puppet emperor; he quit after a few months in protest against French interference.

For the next eleven years Diem lived in virtual solitude. Then in 1944 the Japanese invited him to become a puppet prime minister; Diem refused. In 1946 Ho Chi Minh invited him to join his provisional government in Hanoi; Diem refused. In 1949 Bao Dai asked him to be prime minister; Diem refused. Whatever his faults Diem was a genuine patriot, and he wanted public office again only in a free Vietnam. In 1950 he left the country, living in monasteries in Japan, New York, and Belgium until the French persuaded him to return to become premier in 1954.

As a journalist I became acquainted with Diem in those early frenetic days, when he was struggling among the French, Communists, Binh Xuyen gangsters and the Americans to survive. One of my last dispatches from Saigon, in March 1955, was a lengthy report about him. He had then been in office for nine months. Except for minor details, what I wrote in 1955 was equally applicable to the man I found when I went back to Saigon in 1962, which is a glimpse in itself of the immutability that made Diem so difficult.

Excerpts from my 1955 report:

"'Diem is a fine choice for President,' said a French officer sipping his Cinzano the other day at one of Saigon's sidewalk cafés. 'He is an honest man. This is surely no time for a realistic man.' Brutal but true. . . .

"Seldom has a man undertaken such a tough job with such a curious set of credentials. When Diem stepped off the plane in Saigon last June 26, he had not worked for a living in 21 years. His whole lifetime had been an unbroken series of negative decisions: not to be a priest, not to study in France, not to remain in the Annamese cabinet, not to work for the Japanese or Ho Chi Minh or the French, and finally not to remain in his country during the period of its greatest peril.

"Of his own choice he had denied himself a normal family life, seeking emotional satisfaction instead in an extreme form of religious contemplation which, however worthy, had inevitably affected his personality, isolated him from the world. He had never fired a rifle in anger, never fought with his hands for anything, however strong his principles, yet he came to a country torn by war. He had no organized popular support. A vast majority of his countrymen had never heard of him. . . .

"At the same time, so many people so many times had asked him to take the job he had now accepted that he came to Saigon with a grade-A Messiah complex, superimposed on almost total ignorance of the problems he faced. . . .

"Seldom has a leader stood more sublimely alone than Ngo Dinh Diem during those first weeks. However considerable his faults, a man with that kind of guts is a rare asset.

"During his first few months in office, unfortunately, that was about the only good thing to be said for Diem. He revealed himself quickly as a humorless, egotistical, incredibly stubborn perfectionist, who refused to act on any question, however trivial, without exhaustive meditation and ideal conditions. He was neurotically suspicious of everyone except his family, refused advice, refused to delegate power. He was a Messiah with a persecution complex. . . .

"Said a prominent American journalist after his first interview: 'Sort of a screwball, isn't he? His eyes don't even focus.' A senior American official calls him 'a stubborn little gink.' Another American who has dealt with Diem frequently says 'he's a dead loss. We should drop him as soon as we can.'

"Only a minority group is ready to condemn him that strongly, but nobody is enthusiastic about Diem. . . . For lack of any alternative, we are stuck with a marginal man, at least so far, and to rate him as anything else would be a great disservice. . . .

"Despite his enormous reading he flounders in almost any subject. He says he believes in popular democracy, but he cannot define it. He cannot take criticism, much less organized political opposition. He says he believes in social 'reforms' but he is so ignorant of his country's social conditions that he does not know what reforms are needed, and resists being told. He is at ease with peasants but knows nothing about their thinking. . . .

"A disturbing, if inevitable, tendency is developing among Americans here, and I think Washington, to freeze our policy too tightly to Diem. . . . The freeze is having the effect of making Diem overconfident. It is blacking out Vietnamese public opinion, however little of it there is. Yet the hard fact is that Diem is not doing well enough for any kind of confidence."

This was the opinion of a large segment of the American community in Saigon in 1955. The operative word for Diem always was "marginal."

Support for Diem, moreover, really meant support for the Ngo Dinh family. By 1962 its control of all decisions of any significance was total: Diem as President and minister of national defense; Brother Nhu as his political counselor and alter ego; Brother Can as pro-consul in Central Vietnam (i.e. the northern part of the South); Brother Thuc, an archbishop, leader of the nation's two million Roman Catholics; Brother Luyen, Ambassador to London; Tran Van Chuong, Nhu's father-in-law, Ambassador to Washington; Mme. Chuong, Vietnamese observer at the United Nations; and of course Diem's spectacular sister-in-law, Mme. Nhu, as "First Lady" and leader of the Women's Solidarity Movement. Other than the family, only one man possessed any real authority at all, and he was little better than a respected special assistant. This was Nguyen Dinh Thuan, secretary to the presidency and assistant minister of national defense.

Altogether there probably had never before in American foreign affairs been a phenomenon comparable to our relations with the Ngo Dinh family. It was like dealing with a whole platoon of de Gaulles.

Almost none of the standard clichés about Oriental dictatorships applied to the Ngo Dinh. There was an element of corruption. The Nhus had an elegant house in Dalat, and they were supposed to have secreted a fortune in Swiss banks, though this was never proved. Brother Can (executed by the Khanh regime), who lived like a recluse at Hue, controlled a virtual monopoly of Central Vietnam's economy. Petty corruption among minor officials, like kickbacks on wages, was commonplace. But the degree of corruption was tolerable by Asian standards, and it would have been irrelevant if the regime had been otherwise effective.

Similarly it was not a power-mad regime. Diem was motivated by honorable, patriotic principles, and the same probably could be said of Nhu, though this was more debatable.

The regime's greatest errors were subjective rather than aggressive, self-protective rather than despotic, and thus the more difficult to correct. One of its main weaknesses was its refusal to delegate authority. This was partly a reflection of the family's aristocratic background and its distrust of the masses. It also reflected a profound, increasingly irrational suspicion of almost everyone outside the family as a result of repeated attempts to overthrow the regime. In 1955 this was already developed to the point where Diem spent hours of his time reviewing personally such details as applications for entry visas. After the attempted coup d'état in 1960, no troop movements of any significance were permitted without Diem's personal approval. After two renegade pilots bombed the palace in 1962, Diem took away his Air Force's five-hundred-pound bombs—like dangerous toys denied to a child.

The more the regime drew inward upon itself, the less it knew of the massive problems plaguing the nation, and the more it was possessed by the conviction that only the family really understood what was right for Vietnam. With the Ngo Dinh, power was initially an obligation to duty, later an essential to survival, never an end in itself.

It was a posturing regime in some ways. Diem loved to command the diplomatic corps to attend trivial ceremonies, like the opening of a school. They usually began at seven-thirty in the morning. We were always invited for a half hour in advance, and directed to wear white suits, which became a sort of uniform. We would rise respectfully as the cabinet arrived, then the chief of the Supreme Court, then the president of the assembly, then the vice president, and finally Diem—at five-minute intervals, each with a flourish of martial music, while we sweated under a blazing sun. Then came endless speeches in Vietnamese which few of the foreigners could understand. We were never sure whether Diem thought he was honoring or humiliating us, but there was one memorable occasion when Mme. Nhu delivered a harangue wherein she repeatedly insulted the U. S. The senior American present, not understanding a word, politely applauded when she finished. Thereafter we demanded English texts in advance, or simultaneous translation.

If the regime had learned to run the war as well as it could stage a ceremony, the Viet Cong would have been annihilated years ago.

Despite his relish for this kind of posturing, Diem scorned mass demonstrations of the sort in which most dictators—like his neighbor, Prince Sihanouk in Cambodia—love to revel. He even barred the general public from the annual military parade on the October 26 National Day.

The U. S. spent some $7 million on a radio network in the hope that Diem would use it to bring his government closer to the people and thus perhaps generate a nationalistic spirit to the detriment of the Viet Cong. But it was almost impossible to persuade him to use it, despite the spectacular successes with radio of contemporary leaders like Nasser and Castro. Once I asked him why. His inexplicable reply: "Bao Dai made a lot of speeches. Look what happened to him."

He was equally unwilling to be filmed speaking to his people for the weekly U.S.-subsidized national newsreel. He made frequent trips into the countryside, and he talked easily to the peasants. I was with him on one occasion in 1962, for example, when he asked about some kind of turnip bug. Told that the region was infected, Diem straightaway squatted in the mud and poked around the base of a plant, turned up some of the bugs and then discussed the problem at length with a woman carrying a squalling, naked baby. It would have made a fine newsreel item, but cameramen, as usual, had been forbidden to come along. I suspect he thought that sort of publicity was undignified.

Diem seemed to feel that popular support, and even affection, could be taken for granted. Where the Viet Cong cynically propagandized the peasants with promises of good things they would do for the people, Diem and Nhu talked repeatedly about the people's "duty" to the government. Their line was that the government should give only what the people had earned. They were disdainful of the practice among American advisors in the field of passing out candy to the kids in the villages, often the first candy any of them had tasted. The regime was possessed by the idea that its policies should be morally correct, in a straight-laced puritanical sense, and it refused repeatedly to bow to American suggestions that good works were what counted in the villages, where the literacy rate was fifty percent at best, and the living standards close to the survival level.

It was characteristic, for example, that Diem and Nhu came up with the term "strategic hamlets" for the program of fortified communities that became a key part of the effort against the Viet Cong, rejecting terms like "new villages" which the British had used for a similar program in Malaya. There is no single word meaning "strategic" in the Vietnamese language. The concept is formed by two words meaning "fight" and "plan." The peasants thus were invited to support the "fight-plan hamlets," which was just as meaningless to them as it sounds to an American. Once I negotiated for several weeks with Nhu to decide on a slogan to be printed on U.S. aid materials for the hamlets. I wanted to say "Build strategic hamlets for a better life." Nhu initially wanted a "slogan" of fifteen or twenty words about the philosophical virtues of the hamlets. We finally compromised on "Build strategic hamlets for a new society." He was adamant in refusing any language that might imply material improvements for the peasants.

The regime, in effect, asked its people to oppose the Communists because Communism was wrong. The Vietnamese peasant was no less responsive to right and wrong than anyone else, but not as applied to intellectual abstractions like Communism. The wrongs that counted in a Vietnamese hamlet were those committed by corrupt local officials, or a greedy landlord. All too often the regime condoned this kind of wrong, while the Viet Cong promised to put it right. The Diem regime could not be faulted on principle, but it was a sorry match for the Viet Cong in a struggle where the decision would go to the side that could win the people.

If the foregoing suggests that the Diem regime was essentially negative (as I think it was), this was not its purpose. Diem and particularly Nhu rationalized their policies under a doctrine called *Nhan Vi* which was usually translated by the word "Personalism." A number of orientalists have written lengthy treatises about Personalism, and there is no doubt that it was a legitimate philosophy.

Diem has been quoted as calling it "intellectual loyalty and noble morality, an acute consciousness and clear vision of the compass of one's duties toward the Creator, the country, and toward one's self, as well as toward one's fellow man." Nhu was generally recognized as its high priest. I once heard him say that one of the original Personalists was Walt Whitman.

At a meeting with Diem, Ambassador Nolting once remarked: "You may be surprised to know that most Americans who have ever heard of Personalism think it means the glorification of your own person as chief of state." Such Vietnamese as had ever heard about Personalism apparently had a similar attitude. It died a sudden, unlamented death with the end of the Diem regime.

The foregoing presents a chaotic picture of the Diem regime, but this was essentially how we saw it from inside the American Mission in Saigon. Even among its most dedicated American supporters, there were endless debates, endless despair on what it was all about. The regime was not malicious, not evil, not concerned particularly about material gain or glory. It was vigorously anti-Communist and genuinely wanted to cooperate, in its own peculiar way, with the U. S. But instead of grappling with its problems, it behaved as though they did not exist.

There were those who thought the whole family was mad. It was at least conceivable that this could have been confirmed clinically, particularly during its final months when it seemed to be consumed by a death wish. There could be no doubt at all, however, that the regime was an anachronism in the twentieth century, a tragic legacy of Vietnam's tragic past.

(2)

During the nine years that the U. S. tried to live with Diem, a majority of the foreign affairs experts in the press and elsewhere back home regularly complained that the incumbent Ambassador in Saigon, whoever he was and whatever his policy, was doing the job the wrong way. Over the years the critics variously proclaimed that what the Ambassador should be doing was:

1. Be tough. Diem is an American property and he therefore must do what we say or we will cut off the aid.
2. Be soft. Diem is an inscrutable Oriental but a true patriot. The U. S. therefore must "understand" him and let him do things his way.
3. Dump him. He's hopeless.

The first four Ambassadors who tried to deal with Diem dutifully rotated the "tough" and "soft" approaches. General J. Lawton ("Lightning Joe") Collins (1954–55) tried futilely to run Diem the way he ran the VII Corps in World War II. G. Frederick Reinhardt (1955–57), who had it relatively easy because the Communists were quiescent, was soft and repaired relations. Elbridge Durbrow (1957–61) was so tough that Diem virtually boycotted him. Nolting (1961–63) was soft and wound up in despair. In the U.S. relationship with Diem, the only constant was Diem—until the fifth Ambassador, Henry Cabot Lodge (1963–64), applied the "dump him" policy.

Saigon became a post where a foreign service officer could consider that a tour of duty was successful if he simply stayed even, with neither damage nor profit to his career. Nobody had ever been able to use Saigon as a stepping stone to high position.

It was debatable whether any policy would have worked with Diem, but the burden of evidence favored the soft approach. He could occasionally be persuaded, but he could never be intimidated. The hitch was that the U.S. public ultimately would not tolerate a soft line. In any case, sweetness and light was the rule during most of my tour in Saigon. We treated Diem and his family like a Latin lover seeking the favor of a crotchety, middle-aged heiress.

Unfortunately the regime maintained all the superficial paraphernalia of a modern government, ministries, directorates-general, an extensive civil service. Its official *Liste des Personnalités* ran to one hundred and fifty pages. Except for Diem and Nhu, nobody in the whole book could make decisions of any significance, but everyone's dignity had to be respected. This was because even the lowliest official did have the power to sabotage almost any kind of project with lightning efficiency. (On the rare occasion when I discovered a secondary official who was helpful, I made it a practice not to tell anyone for fear he would be suppressed.) So we wasted incalculable time pretending to process everything through the correct channels.

Inevitably, if the project were at all important, there would then be weeks of silence. On inquiry, we would be told that it was still being "studied." That almost always meant it was stalled in the palace, most likely in the middle of a two-foot stack of papers on Nhu's or Diem's desk. How to get action presented some labyrinthian problems in protocol.

Nhu and his wife had great power, but neither had an official position in the Vietnamese Government, and we did not want to do anything that would boost either their egos or their influence. That meant that the official channel was Diem, even when we knew that Nhu was the man stalling a project. Diem was chief of state so protocol required that the Ambassador or General Harkins should go to see him. This in turn meant that Nolting and Harkins had to involve themselves repeatedly in matters that could have been settled by desk officers in Washington. Yet that was the only way to get action—that is, to try to get action, since nothing happened anyway a good part of the time. Nolting took an average of perhaps a dozen problems with him every time he saw Diem, and seldom if ever got past the first one or two items because he was unable to get Diem to stop talking.

Diplomats in Saigon developed a number of basic principles about meetings with Diem. One was to try for an appointment late in the morning or early evening, making it possible to use a lunch or dinner date as an excuse to escape, though there always remained the hazard of being commanded to stay for the meal with Diem. Another, most important, principle was to raise the main subject immediately upon entering Diem's presence, avoiding any kind of small talk, since a remark that it was a nice day could easily evoke a twenty-minute discourse on Vietnamese meteorology. Once Diem started talking, it was impossible to change the subject, or even to attract his attention.

There must be a psychiatric term for Diem's compulsive talking. His behavior surely was not normal, apart from his apparent indifference to the fact that there was a war on, that he was chief of state, and that hundreds of decisions were always awaiting his attention because of his refusal to delegate authority. A mere two-hour session with Diem was considered a "quickie." An ashen-faced American newsman came directly to my office from the palace one day to report that Diem had kept him for six and one-half hours, from 10 A.M. to 4:30 P.M. with no lunch, and that the last ninety minutes had been spent standing in the doorway after the newsman had gotten up to try to leave.

In the spring of 1963 Diem heard that I was going to the U. S. for medical treatment and called me in to say goodbye. I was there for two and a half hours, and I shall never forget my struggle to stay awake as he droned on and on about agricultural practices in Quang Tri province. It was a hot, humid day and his voice was hypnotic. Desperately I decided the only hope for reviving my senses was somehow to break in and talk for a minute or two myself. After several futile tries to attract his attention, I began talking anyway and continued for perhaps thirty seconds. Diem kept right on going, too. I don't think he even noticed that I had spoken, though he was looking right at me. The shock of this realization at least was enough to wake me up.

Diem was not a man one could dislike. Unlike Nhu and Mme. Nhu, he seldom lost his temper, seldom in fact emerged from the cocoon in which he lived. He was a short, stocky man and walked with a funny, open-toed gait that inevitably tagged him as "The Penguin" among Americans in Saigon. He chain-smoked strong Vietnamese cigarettes, one of those habitual smokers who repeatedly lights up a new one while his last cigarette is still burning in the ashtray. He preferred French to Vietnamese and talked in a monotone, interspersed incessantly with the expression "*n'est-ce pas?*", like a tic; I once counted thirty-three times that he used it in five minutes, which works out at an average of once every ten seconds.

Unlike the cruelty of much Asian humor, Diem's was gentle and forgiving, even as applied to his enemies. At a luncheon one time, for example, I heard him relate the misadventure that made a Viet Cong of Nguyen Huu Tho. Tho, a lawyer by profession, was chairman of the Hanoi-directed "National Liberation Front," supposedly the Viet Cong political executive. Diem said that Tho, whom he had known personally, some years ago became involved in an illicit love affair with a girl in a neighboring town whom he used to visit secretly. The Communists heard about this, according to Diem, intercepted Tho on one of his clandestine trips and threatened to tell all to his wife unless he joined the Viet Cong. I suspect Diem also considered the story worth telling because of its lesson in the hazards of involvement with women.

In some ways Diem was a pathetic man. His marathon dissertations, delivered in a tone that was almost plaintive, gave a superficial impression of vast knowledge of his people and country. He knew the names and something of the personal history of an astonishing number of officials, often down to such lowly levels as battalion commanders and district chiefs. But his information was filtered through such a morass of selfishly motivated bureaucrats that it was often inaccurate, sometimes seriously so. Events were to prove, for example, that neither he nor Nhu was aware of the degree to which the Viet Cong had infiltrated the strategic hamlets, which was the main reason the U. S. Mission was also fooled.

On the rare occasion when Diem could be brought to consider a problem, there was still no assurance of action. Like so many Orientals, Diem had the maddening habit of seldom saying no, and of saying yes when he did not really mean it. The way we usually found out what he thought was to wait a few weeks to see if anything happened, and what did happen often had little relationship to what he had said. The effect of all this on the war effort should not be difficult to imagine. It was remarkable that anything got done at all.

Nhu was nine years younger than Diem and a totally different man, except that he too was a compulsive talker. He and his wife were widely resented, or worse. The two Air Force pilots who bombed the palace in February 1962 aimed only at the wing housing the Nhus, wiping it out with such precision that it looked as though it had been done with a cake knife—a reflection of the excellent training they had gotten from the Americans. The Nhus miraculously survived. In the American community the line was that the pilots evidently felt that "no Nhus is good news." The U. S.

repeatedly tried to persuade Diem over a period of several years to separate the Nhus from the government, which mainly had the effect of outraging Diem and drawing the two brothers closer together.

Like so much else around Saigon, the Diem-Nhu relationship was a psychiatric curiosity. It was best explained by the "Siamese twin" theory, that Diem could not survive without Nhu, whom he trusted absolutely. By 1963 there was evidence that Nhu was undermining the President's authority, taking independent actions that embarrassed him, particularly in permitting Mme. Nhu to become an international notoriety, yet Diem merely became more defensive about Nhu. Nhu, contrarily, frequently criticized his brother to visitors, implying that Diem was something of an unimaginative oaf.

The Nhus were the poison that ultimately destroyed the regime. There is a minority argument that Diem alone could have defeated the Viet Cong. On the contrary, I think, Diem's very unwillingness to separate himself from Nhu was the final measure of his inadequacy.

Nhu was a highly intelligent man. Whether he was evil is debatable. My personal belief is that he was not, that he was misled and irrational, but no less a genuine patriot than Diem. He was fascinated with Communist techniques, which he tried to imitate. Nhu adopted Communist language, for example, like "cadres" for field organizers. He even initiated "self criticism" sessions among government employees. He ran a clandestine, inner-circle political organization called *Can Lao Nhan Vi Dang* (Personalist Labor Party), commonly known as the *Can Lao,* which closely followed Communist methods, such as secret cells inside public and private organizations. This was one of several apparatuses in Nhu's intelligence network.

The evolution of Nhu's power was as elusive as the man himself. He was educated in France, and spent the years before and during the war as custodian of the imperial archives in Hanoi, where he met his wife, the daughter of a Hanoi lawyer. During this period the two brothers seldom saw each other. Almost immediately after Diem's return to Vietnam in 1954, however, Nhu emerged at his side. By 1955 it was clear that he had become a major influence. Soon thereafter he moved into the palace with his family and assumed the title of political counselor, and "Monsieur Le Conseiller" became the correct way to address him.

Nhu concerned himself primarily with internal political matters. He organized the Republican Youth, a uniformed, highly political outfit which eventually grew to some five million members, and was sometimes compared with the Hitler Youth because of its bully-boy behavior. In 1962 Nhu had himself elected "Supreme Leader" and began appearing in public in the blue coverall Republican Youth uniform. There were indications that Nhu regarded the Republican Youth, which he was gradually arming, as insurance against a military coup, though it failed miserably when the test came.

It was the strategic hamlet program, however, that brought Nhu into the heart of the regime's policy making. The main force in getting the program started was probably the British Advisory Mission, which arrived in September 1961 and consisted of a group of old Malaya hands headed brilliantly by Robert G. K. ("Bob") Thompson, who had served in a capacity comparable to minister of defense in Kuala Lumpur. The U. S. Mission was an early convert to the strategic hamlet idea and gave it all-out support. But it was Nhu who got it off the ground, and who eventually claimed full credit for the idea itself. Chauvinistically Nhu insisted that an ancient Vietnamese emperor originally devised fortified hamlets as a defense against Chinese marauders, thus making the program ideologically sanitary.

Nhu became chairman of a special inter-ministerial committee on strategic hamlets. The Nhu Committee, as it came to be called, became the most effective instrumentality inside the government, ultimately achieving a role comparable with the National Security Council in Washington. Ambassador Nolting reacted realistically, creating a parallel inter-agency committee on the American side that was ably headed by the Deputy Chief of Mission, William C. Trueheart. It was revealed after the coup that the program was recklessly overextended, but the program nevertheless did more good than harm.

During a talk with me in November 1962, Nhu volunteered candidly that the strategic hamlets had become a personal *raison d'être*. "Until this task," he said, "I had been drifting, never sure how best to use my energies." He also said with no evident embarrassment that the program required support from all parts of the government, that he had found deplorable inefficiency, and that therefore "I was forced to take charge of many new areas of the government myself." This meant that U.S. agencies in Saigon had to deal increasingly with Nhu to get things done.

Main responsibility for dealing with Nhu was given to the CIA chief in Saigon, John H. Richardson, thus establishing effective U.S. communication without bolstering Nhu's ego and/or influence through open official recognition. Richardson was eminently successful in cultivating Nhu's confidence and respect. The subsequent press attacks upon Richardson, accusing him of being "too close" to Nhu, were unfair and unwarranted. That was his job.

It also became the practice for lesser American officials, including myself, to deal with Nhu on occasion. During the last year of the regime, Nhu and his wife took over direction of the two areas in which USIS was most interested: the regime's stormy feud with the U.S. press, and psychological operations against the Viet Cong. I had a half dozen frustrating sessions with him midst the mountains of books, official documents tied up in ribbons, and tasteless art objects that littered his corner office in Gia Long Palace.

Nhu was a small man, slight of build even for a Vietnamese. He spoke softly with a permanently fixed smile (earning him the nickname "Smiley" in the American community). It was a professorial smile, implying generous tolerance for the listener's stupidity. Nhu was easier to keep on the subject than Diem. He could be eloquent: "In Asia, philosophies are born of the weather, and the seasons, and the crop of rice." But where Diem rambled endlessly on relatively prosaic subjects like farming, Nhu's tangents often made no sense. One of his apologists once tried to explain this by saying that Nhu liked to talk to people on two "planes," one philosophic, the other practical. If he sometimes did not make sense, it was only because he was on his Asian plane, which few Westerners could understand.

I was never sure what Nhu really thought of the United States. He was widely assumed to be strongly anti-American, but I think it was also possible that what bothered him was his country's total, humiliating dependence upon American aid. One of his pet theories, significantly, was that a formula should be worked out for the aid to continue but American advice and political influence to be cut off—"the same way you help Tito without interfering in his affairs," he once said to me. He was particularly bothered by the relatively small number of Americans in politically influential positions, whom he suspected, correctly, of short-circuiting his personal control. These were mainly the sector advisors, the Americans attached to each of the forty-two province chiefs, whose functions included civil administration as well as military operations.

Nhu was an extremist. During one talk with me, for example, he said that if Americans really understood Asians and Communism, we would drop an atomic bomb forthwith on Peking. Paradoxically, however, I think Nhu was also a neutralist, who wanted to escape dependence upon either East or West, which was understandable in view of his profound resentment of the overwhelming American presence in Vietnam. Some of this surfaced near the end when there was evidence that he had begun secret negotiations with the French, and reportedly even with Hanoi, toward some kind of a "neutral" solution, as de Gaulle had suggested. Nhu was bitterly contemptuous of Sihanouk and Soekarno, whom he described as "fools," but ironically I think he was more in tune with their political thinking than anyone else in the Vietnamese Government.

Finally, there was Nhu's catastrophic wife Tran Le Xuan (Beautiful Spring), who was best known as Mme. Nhu. Fate could hardly have chosen a more unfortunate harassment to impose on the chaste, remote Diem and the emotionally chaotic Nhu at a time of their country's agony than this hair-triggered spitfire.

There were a dozen theories, all speculative, on Mme. Nhu's true role in the family. The most persuasive version was that she had few if any original ideas of her own and merely reflected Nhu's tortured thinking. There was no question, however, that she repeatedly forced the initiative, and almost always in the most damaging directions. She boasted to a top American official after the savage government attack on the pagodas on August 21, 1963, for example, that the operation was her idea, and she was fiercely proud of it, despite the fact that it led to final American disengagement from the regime and thus to its fall.

Her motivation? Nobody knew for sure, including her immediate family. Vindictiveness no doubt, born of frustration. But she was not necessarily evil, though she abused her power more than the others. She was certainly stirred by the crisis of her country, however much her antics worsened it. It seemed likely that she was influenced by the crusade that Mme. Chiang Kai-shek undertook in 1942–43 when she visited the United States to plead for greater aid for China. There was certainly a parallel in Mme. Nhu's visit in 1963, with the critical difference that Mme. Chiang had been educated in the United States and understood Americans, while Mme. Nhu did not.

Mme. Nhu, who was about thirty-nine at the time of the regime's fall in 1963, was not a beautiful woman. She had classical delicate Vietnamese features, but she depended excessively on cosmetics, and somehow lacked the depth and charm and softness of true beauty. She was, however, a striking woman, bubbling with energy and flashing, searching (but unrevealing) eyes. Her dress was slightly, but distinctly, overdone, particularly her liking for flashy, expensive jewelry. There were plentiful tales, none confirmed, about her extravagance, like the two-thousand-dollar gold desk set that supposedly was made for her by a Paris jeweler.

Mme. Nhu was a captivating conversationalist, modern, outgoing, quick-witted, often humorous—though the latter was sometimes grotesque, as in her description of the Buddhist protest suicides by burning as "barbecues." She talked like a machine gun in either French or English, and unlike Diem or Nhu, she permitted a dialogue. One soon sensed, however, that she could not be persuaded. This was partly the femininity that she exploited so spectacularly. She often resorted to a trace of a pout that calculating women have used since time immemorial, but there was also an element of the blank-wall irrationality that characterized her husband and brother-in-law. Mme. Nhu intellectually was distinctly shallower than Diem or Nhu, with the result that frustrations angered her more, and complexity infuriated her. As the crisis of the regime deepened, she slipped into what might be called a permanent tantrum.

I first met Mme. Nhu in 1955 when she impressed me as a sparkling, aggressive woman who probably was essentially good for Diem in stirring him to action. Once in 1962, I called on her to try to persuade her to cease insulting the American press, which she had recently accused of being "intoxicated" by Communists. My line—the same one I used, with equal lack of success, on members of the U. S. Mission —was that the American press was one of those things one must learn to live with, that perhaps it should be reformed, but that Saigon was not the place in which to try to do it. To my delight, she indicated a certain amount of acceptance of this.

Three days later, at 8 A.M. on a Sunday, she telephoned me at home, rousing me from sleep, cigarettes out of reach, and harangued in fast French for forty-five minutes. "I have thought about what you said, Monsieur Mecklin," she began, "and last night I could not sleep. I have decided I was wrong to agree with you." It was a tirade, not particularly against me, but against American correspondents, American editors, and by implication almost everything else American. I attempted once or twice to give battle, but she overrode me so decisively that I reverted to "*oui, madame*" and "*très intéressant.*" When she finished I said it was kind of her to go to the trouble of calling me so early on a Sunday morning.

In a sense Mme. Nhu's position was a symptom of what was going wrong in Saigon. She irritated Diem. He told me himself in July 1962 that she had a "*mauvaise caractère*" (bad character) because she harbored grudges. He said he was trying to get her to cease making so much trouble. The hitch was that every time there was an American complaint about her, the family closed ranks—and there were plentiful complaints. The impression in the American community was that Nhu worshiped her, and this seemed to be confirmed by witnesses of the few occasions when they were seen together with their children. This made it the more difficult for Diem to do anything about her.

One of the dominating characteristics of this immensely complicated woman was what appeared to be a fixation against other people having a good time. She was the main force behind a series of puritanical morality laws which wrecked Saigon's reputation as "the Paris of the East."

One of these was the widely publicized ban on dancing, on the grounds that the troops in combat resented that kind of frivolity. The same law also banned cockfights, contraceptives and gambling. Queried about the dancing ban, Mme. Nhu explained that the Vietnamese people were "dancing with death" and that should suffice. As for Americans, she suggested they go elsewhere to dance. The result instead was a proliferation of "black" dancehalls all over Saigon. Mme. Nhu was credited with a decree banning thirty-odd popular Vietnamese songs from the radio on the grounds that they were dangerously sentimental and not sufficiently anti-Communist. She also initiated a revision of the marriage laws making divorce more difficult to obtain. A story circulated that she promoted the latter in order to prevent her sister from divorcing her husband to marry a Frenchman.

Like her husband, Mme. Nhu found her power in devious ways. She was a member of the rubber-stamp national assembly. The press called her the "first lady." She organized and ran the Women's Solidarity Movement, which was supposed to have two or three million members. The movement's ostensible mission was welfare work among the needy, but its main purpose—like Nhu's Republican Youth—was political, as an instrument to generate support for the regime, and to collect intelligence in its defense.

In 1962 Mme. Nhu also created the Women's Paramilitary Corps which undertook to organize and train thousands of young women in armed combat. The newspapers were full of photographs of lovely, wraithlike Vietnamese girls in trim blue coveralls, charging over parapets, squeezing off rounds on a rifle range and assembling machine guns. Mme. Nhu's daughter, Le Thuy, seventeen at the time, turned up as the honor student in one of the first graduating classes.

At the National Day military parade, October 26, 1962, perhaps a thousand smartly trained and uniformed women marched proudly past the reviewing stand, armed with the latest American carbines and submachine guns—which had somehow been quietly diverted from the Vietnamese armed forces without American knowledge, much less permission. Few, if any, of Mme. Nhu's women ever got into combat, but they were wonderfully photogenic on parade.

More than any of her overt operations, however, Mme. Nhu's greatest influence was exerted through her maneuvers inside the government itself. Her technique was all feminine. She simply issued orders, often on impulse by telephone, on virtually any subject to virtually anyone she wanted, from ministers and generals on down.

Under a family dictatorship it was the path of least resistance for the officials to assume that Diem and/or Nhu approved of the order, and to comply. Officials who tried to resist her seldom did so more than once. If an official appealed and managed to persuade Diem or Nhu that the order was wrong, Mme. Nhu would fight like a tigress to have her way, engaging family "face" in the issue, which was usually decisive. In the rare cases when one of her orders was overruled, the adventurous official would soon find that he had made a formidable and unforgiving enemy. Neither Diem nor Nhu, nor anyone else in Saigon including the U. S. Mission, was a match for Mme. Nhu, with eventual disastrous consequences.

(3)

In the admission office of the U. S. Air Force Hospital at Clark Field in the Philippines, which cares for U. S. Government employees from all over Southeast Asia, there is a chart recording arrivals of new patients by date, origin and ailment. When I was there one day early in 1963, the chart indicated that an average of three or four patients daily were being admitted with mental illnesses. Most of these were from Vietnam. This was one reason why the State Department rated Saigon as a "maximum hardship" post, and therefore paid an allowance of twenty-five percent above base salary to personnel stationed there.

Superficially, living conditions for official Americans in Saigon were fine. It was a tropical climate, permanently hot and steamy—the all-time recorded low was 57 degrees in 1937. But neither the temperature nor the humidity reached the extremes of other Southeast Asian posts, such as Bangkok or Manila. There was a risk of amoebic infection from drinking the Saigon water, or eating uncooked greens and vegetables, but this was a Foreign Service hazard all over the world. The city itself was lovely, with airy French colonial homes surrounded by coconut palms, excellent air-conditioned French and Chinese restaurants and good but cheap Chinese tailors.

Housing was free for U. S. Government personnel and usually good. Servants were plentiful and cheap. The Embassy recommended a maximum of thirty-five dollars a month for a cook, for example. The city had modern stores, often with fine French merchandise, as well as American and Japanese goods. There were first-class food markets with Western-style vegetables grown in the highlands at Dalat. The U. S. Navy ran a modern hospital and a PX and Commissary comparable with a small American supermarket. Saigon was a city of magnificent flowers, where two dozen roses could be had for something like three dollars at street markets. Even at the official rate of seventy-three piasters to a dollar (compared with black market rates of up to a hundred), most Americans in Saigon lived as well or better than they could at home.

For recreation, there were American bowling alleys, an American movie theater and several good Vietnamese theaters, a good golf course, American officers' clubs, a commercial American club called the Co-Co with hot dogs, hamburgers and slot machines. There was the famous Cercle Sportif, a private club with swimming pool and tennis courts established by the French and still noteworthy for its bikini-clad scenery. For riding, there was the Cercle Hippique, for sailing and water skiing the Club Nautique on the Saigon River, also inherited from the French. There was a Teen Club for dependent youngsters, an athletic ground called Pershing Field for baseball and Fourth of July picnics. There were innumerable nightclubs, ranging from whore-ridden dives to first-class establishments like the Baccara, Galère, and La Cigale with tantalizing Vietnamese and Chinese singers—and after the coup, dancing and imported floor shows.

There was certainly no "hardship" in American relations with the Vietnamese people. Under the circumstances, they were surprisingly good. There had long been a Viet Cong propaganda effort to stir hatred against Americans, and fear. One leaflet we picked up warned the people that Americans liked to eat "fried children's eyeballs." But the propaganda was always wiped out by personal contact. Repeatedly Americans found obvious fear, even panic, when they first established themselves in a village, and then watched it quickly vanish, usually with kids responding to proffered candy and chewing gum as the opening wedge. If there was a single main difference between the American approach to Vietnam and the way the French tried to do it, it was the Americans' built-in ability to make friends with the people—and to treat them sincerely as equals.

There were indications that a good many Americans also

felt a special affinity for the Vietnamese, as I did. Vietnam was the only place in my experience where there were large numbers of American troops yet no deprecating slang terms like "wogs" or "frogs" or "krauts" or "limeys" for the local people. The closest expression to something like this was "slant-eyes" for Asians in general, but there was no more rancor in this than the equally common expression "round-eye" for Americans and other Occidentals.

This was partly because military personnel assigned to Vietnam were mostly volunteers, with only a few draftees, and thus highly disciplined, high-grade men to begin with. Additionally they were enjoined repeatedly to watch their behavior and a troublemaker could expect to be sent home forthwith. The result was so good that one of the first units to be selected for withdrawal during the Pentagon's short-lived attempt to reduce forces for propaganda reasons in 1963 was a military police outfit. I do not recall a single instance of trouble of consequence between U.S. military personnel and Vietnamese civilians.

But there was also something special about the Vietnamese people themselves. Despite nearly two decades of war, or perhaps because of it, they were less corrupted than some of their neighbors by Western armies and Western ideas and technology. Unlike the Thai or the Filipinos, for example, they were seldom beguiled by fast cars or fast Western living. On the contrary, whether Christian or Buddhist, the Vietnamese observed exceptionally high moral standards. They seldom touched alcohol. There was surprisingly little crime—the streets of Saigon at night were safer for a stranger than the streets of many American cities. The family institution remained strong, and absolute. A wayward son or daughter faced punishment of a severity undreamed of in the West, including banishment. Vietnamese who attended the endless cocktail parties and dinners of Saigon's inbred foreign community usually did so as a duty rather than for pleasure, departing for home as soon as they could politely escape.

Their troubled history had made the Vietnamese at once wistful and intensely realistic. They did not smile as easily as the other peoples of Southeast Asia. There was little humor, at least by Western standards, in their character. I recall an occasion when we tested ideas for an anti-Communist comic strip on members of the Vietnamese staff at USIS. One strip was the old joke where a peasant covered a brick on the ground with a hat bearing an anti-Communist slogan. A Viet Cong bully then came along, kicked the hat and broke his toe. None of the Vietnamese thought it was funny. I asked what might be done to improve it. One of them replied: "Instead of a brick, why not put a hand grenade under the hat?"

It was regrettable that the explosive Mme. Nhu should become a symbol in the West of Vietnamese women. She was an exception. Vietnamese women had traditionally enjoyed a greater independence than in most Asian societies. The Trung Sisters who raised an army and temporarily ousted the Chinese in A.D. 39 were authentic national heroines, despite Mme. Nhu's attempt to make them symbols of her own ambitions. In the fifteenth century the Emperor Le Thanh Ton formally recognized this tradition by a decree giving women virtually the same legal status as men, including equal right to inherit property. The effect today was a quiet, confident, unmatched charm.

Urban Vietnamese women for centuries had worn a unique costume called the *ao dai*. Apparently an evolution of the Chinese pajama-like jacket and trousers, the *ao dai* was usually made of gossamer-thin, brightly colored silk or nylon, with loosely fitted but carefully tailored trousers topped by a high-necked, ankle-length tunic with slits on the sides reaching to the waistline. With long black hair falling in tresses and modern, open-toed, spike-heeled shoes, all this produced an impression of marvelously fluid beauty. The streets of Saigon were graced by the frequent sight of a Vietnamese girl riding her fragile Velox motorbike, weaving skillfully through the traffic, her gown fluttering in the wind, white-gloved hands on the handlebars, feet perched on the pedals, back straight, and usually a white, conical hat tied with a red ribbon under the chin—like a magic butterfly midst the oily, snorting turmoil of the traffic.

From their racial origins the Vietnamese seemed to have inherited the industry, resiliency and intelligence of the Chinese and the dignity and gracefulness of the Indonesians. They showed a rare reluctance to exploit foreigners who came to their country, just as their history showed a dogged refusal to be exploited by foreigners. They could hardly be called pro-American when millions of them were supporting a Communist effort to capture the country, but neither were they anti-American. Despite the continued presence of some six hundred full-time French teachers in Vietnam, compared with only a dozen American teachers (for lack of funds), English was gradually supplanting French as the second language. In Saigon alone, USIS was giving English lessons to more than five thousand Vietnamese students from every level of the community.

The Vietnamese did not bestow their friendship easily, but neither were they influenced by prejudice, and once given, their friendship was genuine and lasting. Many an American was so honored in Saigon.

What, then, was it that troubled so many Americans in Vietnam?

Partly it was certainly the element of physical danger because of Viet Cong terroristic attempts against Americans. In 1961 somebody threw a home-made grenade at Ambassador Nolting's car. It failed to explode, and the last I knew it was on display, along with other V.C. weapons, at the MAAG Headquarters. It was characteristic of Nolting that he ordered his bodyguard not to open fire—for fear of wounding innocent bystanders—as the would-be assassin escaped on a bicycle through busy traffic. One day in 1962 a twelve-year-old boy tossed another home-made grenade hidden in a loaf of bread into a station wagon with four U.S. officers. One of them picked it up, attempted to throw it back out the window and, to everyone's horror, missed the window. Fortunately the fuse was so slow that the officers still had time to dive out the doors before it exploded; nobody was hurt.

Several other bomb attempts were more successful. A handful of Americans were wounded in a half dozen instances of grenades tossed into bars and restaurants in 1962 and 1963. In June 1963 a massive charge, apparently attached to a bicycle, blasted a hole in a back wall of the MAAG compound, killing thirteen Vietnamese, and wounding forty-nine, plus one American. A friend of mine was standing in front of a window and moved away only a second before it was shattered to bits by the explosion. In March 1963 a grenade was tossed over a wall into the midst of a diplomatic garden party, killing a Frenchman and wounding two Americans and two Vietnamese. Worst of all were three outrages in 1964, after I had left: bombings of the American movie theater, of a crowd watching a softball game at Pershing Field, and of an officers' hotel in Saigon, with a total of eight Americans killed and more than one hundred wounded.

We took constant precautions against grenades. The Vietnamese Government closed the sidewalk cafés that had made Saigon famous—a symptom of fear to which the French had never succumbed despite a similar risk. Proprietors put steel grills over shop windows and doors all over the city, especially places patronized by Americans. Some American vehicles, especially buses, were fitted with steel netting on windows. A good many foreigners preferred to drive with windows nearly closed, despite the heat, rather than invite a grenade. Europeans often adorned their cars with signs and national flags to avoid being confused with Americans.

The Embassy Security Office reminded us repeatedly not to establish regular patterns in our movements, to leave home and office at different times and to follow varying routes to and from work. Packages of any sort, including ladies' handbags, were barred from all American installations unless they were first inspected by a U.S. Marine guard for concealed grenades. In USIS libraries around Vietnam, we maintained special vigilance against grenades, especially after we found a dud hidden behind a row of books. After the MAAG outrage, guards prevented Vietnamese civilians from parking bikes, scooters or even cars near American installations. The Vietnamese Government maintained a special network, or so it claimed anyway, of police spies to watch for suspicious persons around American homes (which later came in handy when the government also began tailing Americans). Drivers of official U.S. vehicles were rigidly forbidden to leave a vehicle unattended where it could be booby-trapped. Armed M.P. guards rode the buses carrying children to and from the American School in Saigon.

Grenades, furthermore, were only part of the threat, quite apart from the daily dangers faced by field personnel. There were repeated intelligence reports of diabolical plots against us. One was that scores of kids around Saigon were being equipped with poison-tipped needles with which they planned to jab Americans in crowds. The report said that death would follow within minutes. The Saigon police actually picked up some of the needles, but they were never used. Another report was that the V.C. were training some two hundred girls to pose as prostitutes, attract Americans to prearranged rooms and then run into the street screaming rape. The idea was that this would generate a mob which V.C. agents would provoke to attack the hapless and probably undressed American. Again it never happened.

We could never be sure whether this kind of report was authentic, or invented by somebody in the Vietnamese Government, or planted by the Viet Cong. We strongly suspected, for example, that the Nhus were behind the prostitute story, in the rather forlorn hope perhaps that this might keep Americans away from prostitutes and thus discourage Vietnamese girls from going into the business.

It was commonplace for military aircraft to be hit by Viet Cong ground fire—there was even an instance when a helicopter came back from a mission in Montagnard country with an arrow sticking in the fuselage. It was standard practice to fly at altitudes of at least two thousand feet, above the range of small arms. When the overcast was too low for this, military pilots often resorted to what they prosaically called "contour flying," i.e. a few feet above the tangled roof of the jungle. The theory no doubt was valid, that at this level both the plane and its sound were upon the guerrilla and beyond before he had time to unlimber his rifle, but an unbroken two or three hours of dipping into valleys and surging over hills while the water buffalo panicked only twenty-five or fifty feet below was a memorable adventure. Airmen also adopted the practice of sitting on flak vests as further protection against V.C. fire, which inevitably produced some eloquent scatological terminology.

It was quite another thing one day in 1963, however, when a Pan American jet airliner landed at Saigon with one engine dead from a V.C. bullet hole. It could only have happened within a mile or two of the airport, immediately raising the possibility that commercial airline service, our only tangible link with home, might be suspended.

The incident led to a grim little vignette of life in Saigon. Perhaps a dozen friends had gone out to the airport that same night to say goodbye to a woman who was leaving her husband, an American civilian official, rather than remain in Saigon for the rest of his tour. Her husband and her friends had pleaded with her for days to stick it out. They continued as they awaited her plane in the airport restaurant. In good humor but plainly fighting back the tears, she sipped her drink and parried the talk. Next to her sat her two small children, and next to them were two Pan Am cabin bags bulging with toys and treasures. The plane was late, and time hung heavier and heavier.

Then the airport public address system blared that Pan American had overflown Saigon. The pilot had been warned, erroneously as it turned out, that V.C. infiltrators had been observed near the end of the runway. The woman broke into sobs. The dreary party went back into town. She was forced to endure two more days of Saigon before the next plane.

Airline service was not suspended, but procedures for the Saigon airport were radically revised, requiring pilots to hold a minimum altitude until the final approach—often giving passengers a roller-coaster feeling as their plane suddenly nosed down to land.

Another aspect of the security problem in Saigon was the ban on unnecessary travel outside the city, creating claustrophobic problems for many Americans. This meant a family could not get to a beach except by air, no casual Sunday afternoon picnics, no walks in the countryside. The American Boy Scout troop of Saigon had its campouts in a military compound. There was one hole on the Saigon golf course where a bad slice would nearly put the ball in a strategic hamlet. The war was so close to the city that gunfire frequently could be heard at night, and sometimes from an upstairs balcony one could see distant flares being dropped to aid the defense of a beleaguered government position.

In the modernistic, air-conditioned bar on the eighth floor

of the Caravelle Hotel, one could look across the room almost any evening and see a young American captain or major chatting with Jacqueline, the pretty Vietnamese hostess. The same officer might die the next morning in an ambush ten miles outside the city.

But none of the foregoing, neither the personal physical danger of living in Saigon, nor the frustrations of trying to work with an inept, eccentric regime, gets to the root of the explanation of the psychiatric patients at Clark Field. There was another factor, perhaps the main one, and I think it had to do with the question, what were we doing there anyway?

This was a new undertaking for Americans, and it was indigestible. It was a brave commitment of American power and prestige, and a privilege to be one of the Americans entrusted to help make it work. But the reality of the struggle was ugly, mushy, indecisive. Nothing was moving, or so it seemed, but there was nobody clearly to blame, no villain to punch, no black-and-white challenge that could be solved by the U. S. Cavalry.

It was easy enough to accept intellectually that this was the nature of the struggle, that it would require patience and fortitude, and political courage. But it was not the persistence of a poker player or a trout fisherman that was needed; it was the will to stick with it for months, more likely for years, in a miasma of error that could not be easily corrected, if it could be corrected at all. Emotionally, many Americans found the task very nearly unacceptable.

Young American Army officers who came to Vietnam as advisors were set for hardship and extreme danger, and they accepted both with admirable spirit. But they were not prepared for a system where incompetents were given commands for political reasons, where a battle was lost because a company commander was a coward and was not then relieved, where there was no authority, and no possible action but to appeal to commanders who would not listen, because they had no authority from Saigon to listen, much less act.

There were no facts. For months, for example, the U. S. Mission wrestled with a problem that would seem ridiculously simple: How can we tell who is winning? It was never really solved—which was one reason for the repeated high-level missions to Vietnam from Washington, even before the Buddhist crisis, to try and try again to be sure of something. Casualty figures were meaningless. Each month the government claimed a thousand or more Viet Cong killed, yet intelligence estimates showed steady, relentless growth of V.C. strength. It was a quicksilver war and there was no sure way to measure its progress.

Intellectually it made sense to support the Diem regime, or this in any case was the considered judgment of U.S. policy-makers, including President Kennedy, who was deeply admired by most Americans in Saigon. This, in turn, meant in effect that it was near blasphemy to be critical of the regime, even in exclusively American company. Yet blasphemy there was, plentifully, with many a resulting guilty conscience. The bitter fact was that an overwhelming majority of all the Americans in Vietnam disliked the regime, and many of them hated it for its uniform abuse of so many principles Americans believe in, like free speech, even though that same majority kept telling itself our policy was right.

There were spies everywhere, telephones tapped, servants in the pay of the government or the Viet Cong or both. Often a Vietnamese friend would burst out in a bitter attack on the Diem regime, but an American was wise to listen without comment. The friend could be an *agent provocateur* planted by Nhu's secret police—which ingeniously called itself "The Service of Political and Social Studies" (SEPES)—to try to find out which Americans were unfriendly to the regime. There were at least a dozen cultured, English-speaking Vietnamese whom we suspected of this sort of thing.

American military outfits in the field were forbidden to fly the American flag over their headquarters because it would make the regime lose face, and help the Viet Cong make propaganda. General Harkins issued an order forbidding departing GIs to kiss their Vietnamese girl friends at the airport because it would displease the regime. Until a newsman wrote a story about it, Americans wounded in combat in Vietnam were even denied the Purple Heart medal because it was not officially a war.

As early as November 1962 resentment of all this had reached a point where an audience of American servicemen at the American theater in Saigon loudly booed when a newsreel of President Diem delivering a speech was thrown on the screen.

Of Americans whom I knew personally who could not take Saigon, there was a newly married wife whose symptom was repeated false pregnancies with resulting unacceptable emotional strain. Another young wife was evacuated after less than a fortnight yet was unable to explain months later what it was that troubled her. In the case of an officer who was similarly evacuated, the symptom was deep depression about duties to be performed as much as six months later, apparently because of the subconscious fear that they would prove impossible. The ultimate case was the story around town that an American psychiatrist assigned to Saigon had also been evacuated after a few months for psychiatric reasons.

A wife who went home after six weeks in Saigon tried to explain: "It was all so terribly, terribly hopeless." Another wife, who stuck it out but hated it: "It's so dreary. You expect the worst, and wait for it, and try to be set for it, but it doesn't ever happen."

Certainly it would be an inexcusable disservice to suggest that this kind of despair was in any sense typical of Americans in Vietnam. The vast majority faced up to it with good humor and stout heart. But it was never a happy community. It was a place of forced confidence, where an edge in a man's voice was normalcy, where tempers flared just a trifle too quickly, and moments of true, relaxed humor were hard to come by. We lived in the stress of deep crisis, and in the constant shadow of French failure only a decade earlier.

And many of us feared deep down that we too were losing.

(4)

Diem and Nhu were badly scared by the Viet Cong gains that led to the Taylor mission in October 1961. They were therefore uncommonly cooperative, at first, in the resulting new American effort to rally the Vietnamese forces and people. By the fall of 1962 there were indications of initial success.

The galloping deterioration that Taylor had found seemed to be stemmed. By the end of 1962 the Viet Cong were mounting only an occasional battalion-size attack, compared with two or three per week a year earlier. This was taken to mean they were reverting to small units which could be assembled and dispersed more rapidly to avoid government retaliation. Statistics on government weapons losses to the V.C., considered to be a key indicator of who was winning, showed gradual improvement. Night operation of the vital north–south railroad, which had been suspended because of V.C. attacks, was resumed in September 1962. South Vietnam showed a rice surplus for 1962, compared with a deficit in 1961, indicating more security in the countryside.

More than any other American action the V.C. appeared to be shaken by the introduction of troop-carrying helicopters, flown by U. S. Army and Marine crews. The total available jumped from a half dozen at the time of the Taylor mission to fifty by the end of 1962, and two hundred by mid-

1964, giving the war a dramatic new dimension. It became possible for the government to put down as many as two hundred men by surprise almost anywhere in the country. This was expected to deny the V.C. safe havens except in uninhabited jungle. Nothing like this had ever before been attempted anywhere in the history of warfare. The V.C. had neither the weapons, nor the tactics, to combat chopper-borne attacks.

Scores of U. S. Air Force and Army fixed-wing planes were brought in: liaison craft, transports, T-28 fighter-bombers (a World War II trainer fitted out with machine guns and rockets), B-26s (a World War II bomber now equipped with eight 50-caliber machine guns), reconnaissance craft. Most of these came with American crews who usually went into combat with Vietnamese observers or trainee pilots. Much of the U.S. air effort in Vietnam functioned under colorful code names like "Jungle Jim," "Farmgate" and "Mule Train." It gave the Vietnamese forces a degree of mobility undreamed of during the French era.

Simultaneously General Harkins rapidly seeded American military advisors throughout the Vietnamese armed forces. Boosting U.S. military strength in Vietnam from about six hundred in the fall of 1961 to twelve thousand by the end of 1962, this was a smoothly executed operation for which Harkins was not publicly given the credit he deserved. The U. S. had never before attempted a similar undertaking of this magnitude in conditions short of all-out war. It required tact to avoid ruffling Vietnamese pride, imagination to create new systems of procedures to fit the advisory relationship, and patience to overcome a thousand bureaucratic obstacles of both Vietnamese and U.S. origin.

If only by their own courage and example, American field advisors initially gave the Vietnamese forces new spirit, new aggressiveness, new confidence—and know-how that could never be acquired in a training camp.

One such advisor was Specialist Fourth Class James T. Davis of Livingston, Tennessee. Just before noon on December 21, 1961, he was riding with a detachment of Vietnamese troops in a truck that was ambushed by the Viet Cong ten miles west of Saigon. Davis and three Vietnamese were killed trying to fight off their attackers. He was the first American to die in the buildup that followed the Taylor mission.* By the end of 1962, combat deaths among advisors and helicopter crews and T-28 and B-26 pilots had climbed to twenty-one, by the end of 1963 to ninety-seven and by the end of 1964 to nearly two hundred and fifty. These were the first casualties the United States had taken in combat with a Communist enemy since the end of the Korean War ten years earlier.

U.S. training of the Vietnamese forces was dramatically expanded. An imaginative program was launched to recruit and train crews for a fleet of more than six hundred harmless-looking but well-armed junks to patrol Vietnam's coastal waters and cut off V.C. smuggling of arms, supplies and men from the north. Existing programs for training of ground forces were accelerated to boost combat-ready regular forces by 15,000 in 1962 to a total of 200,000; trained and armed rural militiamen jumped by 37,000 to 165,000. (1964 strengths, respectively, were 210,000 and 190,000.) Deliveries of equipment and weapons clogged the Saigon harbor. They included a major increase in artillery and introduction of newly developed items like the M-113 amphibious personnel carrier which could carry up to nineteen men at 40 mph on open terrain, at 10 mph across swamps and paddies.

---

*The only Americans to be killed in Vietnam by Communist gunfire between the end of the French war in 1954 and the Taylor visit in 1961 were Major Dale R. Buis and Master Sergeant Chester N. Onand who were watching a motion picture in a Vietnamese Army training camp in July 1959 when Viet Cong guerrillas broke in and opened up on the audience with submachine guns.

The strategic hamlet program got under way, with the total completed reaching more than a thousand by the end of 1962. Many of them were to turn out to be failures, but the initial impact on the Viet Cong was highly successful. Betraying their alarm, Communist propagandists concentrated their efforts on the hamlets, calling them "concentration camps." The theory of the strategic hamlets was to build fences around each community, train and equip part-time hamlet militia to fight off attacks until help could arrive, and to bolster morale by social reforms and economic assistance. Even if this was seldom achieved in full, the program was supposed to make it impossible for one or two armed Viet Cong to enter a hamlet at will, as they had previously done, to forage for food, recruit and/or kidnap young men and propagandize the inhabitants. In theory it now required an organized attack by a squad or more of guerrillas to enter the hamlet.

The program was supported by the installation in 1962 of hundreds of village alarm radios provided by AID. These were battery-operated transmitter-receiver sets that the village chief could use to summon help during an attack. Psychologically they were potentially of immense value to small, isolated garrisons. In the past resistance to V.C. attack had usually been useless because there was no way to call for reinforcements. Now for the first time there was hope, making it worthwhile to resist. In fact, typically, the radios eventually were discredited to some extent, because calls for help were so rarely answered, or answered so slowly as to be useless. But the principle was valid at the outset, with a resulting upturn in rural support for the government.

The U. S. began a crash project completed in early 1963 to install an ultramodern tropo-scatter communications system in South Vietnam. This was a high frequency radio net that operated by bouncing signals off the relatively low altitude electrical field in the troposphere. It provided military and civilian officials throughout South Vietnam with a reliable, instantaneous, high fidelity telephone system. As the system was completed, calls that once took hours—if they were completed at all, via shortwave radio—could now be put through in seconds, hopefully to the benefit of the government's reaction time to V.C. attacks.

USOM, the economic assistance agency, created a unique counter-insurgency division called Rural Affairs, headed by Rufus Phillips, a young, aggressive, highly imaginative administrator who had served in Vietnam as an Army lieutenant in 1954–55. This was the $20 million program mentioned earlier to apply "impact" economic assistance to the hamlets to help persuade the people to support the government and resist the Viet Cong—which should have been initiated years sooner. Phillips developed techniques for intimate coordination with military and propaganda operations so that creation of a strategic hamlet would immediately bring the people fertilizer, livestock, construction supplies and other benefits, along with physical security and information material explaining what it was all about.

USIS vastly expanded its field operations. By the end of 1962 we were showing motion picture films to more than one million peasants monthly, telling them about their country, V.C. outrages, and Free World support for Vietnam, in addition to numerous other informational activities in the rural areas.

Also during 1962 more than a hundred thousand Montagnards fled from the highlands of Central Vietnam to escape the Viet Cong, an encouraging demonstration of anti-Communist sentiment. CIA swiftly organized teams to arm and train Montagnard volunteers who then went back into the hills to defend their villages. In 1963 U. S. Army Special Forces detachments took over this mission, working under conditions of extreme hardship and danger. More than twenty thousand Montagnards were eventually organized and trained. By the end of 1962 this program was progressing so rapidly that there was hope the highlands could be denied to the Viet Cong, interdicting many of their secret jungle supply routes.

All of which made good reading in the U. S. Mission's dispatches to Washington—except that it was an illusion.

Subsequent evidence confirmed intelligence reports that the Viet Cong were surprised and in some instances staggered by the massive American intervention. We were wrong, however, to believe that they were seriously hurt. Instead what apparently happened was that they took time out to reassess the situation, decided that the Americans' hardware and free fertilizer had not brought anything dangerously new to the struggle, and proceeded to work out the necessary new tactics, such as training their men to "lead" helicopters just as a hunter aims ahead of a flying duck. In retrospect perhaps the most significant concession the Viet Cong made to U.S. intervention was a new accent in their internal policy directives on the line that the struggle would be long and difficult but patience would surely bring victory.

Post-mortem evidence indicated that 1962 and early 1963 was the time of decision for the Diem regime. Its failure to turn the tide with its new assets was fatal.

CHAPTER THREE

The Path at Binh Yen Dong

(1)

Just before ten o'clock one morning in June 1962, a detachment of the Vietnamese Army's battle-hardened 5th Division was moving in convoy along Route 13 near the town of Ben Cat thirty-five miles north of Saigon. Their seven vehicles—freshly washed American jeeps, scout cars and 2½-ton trucks—stretched along a black-top highway winding alternately through jungle and along the dikes of paddies that were just beginning to soak up the life-giving moisture of the early rainy season. All but an occasional patch of morning ground haze had already been burned away by a white-hot sun mounting an empty, neutral sky.

Of an instant came soul-crushing pandemonium. A mine exploded under a civilian bus ahead of the column, blocking the road. From positions hidden in tall grass, an unknown number of Viet Cong regulars opened fire, simultaneously, at savagely close-in range, with automatic weapons, rifles, pistols, shotguns, grenades. Soldiers who had not been hit in the first seconds dived for cover and bravely tried to fight back. They were hopelessly outpositioned, outgunned, outsmarted. The slaughter lasted only twenty minutes. The Viet Cong scrambled through the smoking ruins to seize weapons and ammunition, and then vanished.

The score: fifteen government troops killed, a score of modern American weapons lost, all seven vehicles burned out. Viet Cong casualties, if any, were carried away. Among the dead were an American captain and lieutenant, two of the advisors assigned to the 5th Division. Boots still shined, the captain's body was found slumped in a jeep, torn apart by Communist slugs before he could reach for his weapon. The lieutenant's body was found five hundred yards away. He apparently was wounded and tried to escape, only to be overtaken by guerrillas who killed him with a bullet in the head.

Nothing that happened that morning was new, nor even uncommon, to Vietnam. Communist guerrillas had used exactly the same tactics against the French, with exactly the same results, innumerable times, a decade earlier. (They were still using them with frightening effectiveness against the Vietnamese Government two years later.) But the ambush on Route 13 on that June morning was nevertheless significant.

For one thing it happened on the edge of the area of "Operation Sunrise," which had been launched a few months earlier with plentiful we're-off-to-victory publicity. Sunrise was the first of the so-called "clear-and-hold" operations which were to become basic to the government's strategy against the Viet Cong. The idea was that government forces would move massively into an area, drive out the Viet Cong, resettle the population in strategic hamlets, and keep out the Communists forever thereafter. The ambush on Route 13 suggested, correctly, that Sunrise was not working.

Secondly there was concern because several hours elapsed before reinforcements arrived at the site of the ambush and set out after the V.C., who would have been almost impossible to find even a half hour after the action. It developed that the only unit available had been part of the palace reserve—whose main mission was to prevent a coup d'état—and that Diem's personal permission had been required to move it. This was typical of the degree to which military operations against the Viet Cong were hamstrung by the regime's distrust—rightly as it turned out—of its own armed forces.

Thirdly there was the fact—perhaps most important of all—that the Viet Cong laid the ambush about three hours before their target arrived, that they must have been seen by dozens, perhaps hundreds of peasants, and that nobody warned the government authorities. In a dispatch to the New York *Times,* correspondent Homer Bigart asked poignantly: "Could this have happened if the peasants felt any real identification with the (Diem) regime? . . . The Viet Cong probably would never have undertaken this action without full confidence that the peasants were with them, or at least indifferent."

This kind of reporting made Bigart unpopular with both the U. S. Mission and Washington. In the context of the moment, midst all kinds of indications of gains against the V.C., what he wrote was almost unthinkable. If he was right, there was something awfully wrong.

Of course he was right. The unpleasant truth was that few of us in 1962 (nor two years later for that matter) really had faced up to the depth of our ignorance of the Vietnamese peasant and of the nature of the war in which he was of such pivotal importance.

Diem and Nhu talked of the peasants in intellectual jargon, but knew less about them than a Manhattan bartender knows about the Mexican wetbacks in Southern California. Top American officials mouthed platitudes about the peasants. It was a standard opening of official briefings, for example, that "this is really a war for the hearts and minds of the people." But they made little effective effort to find out what was happening in the hearts and minds of the people.

All of us, in truth, were long on eloquent pronouncements, but woefully short on knowledge of what we were talking about.

(2)

Vietnam was no China. It had not been racked by the population explosion. It was rich in fertile land which could comfortably sustain three times its present population. The Vietnamese peasant's life was not much worse than the life of peasants in other underdeveloped parts of the world, like Sicily or Egypt. But Vietnam nevertheless was part of the vast mass of land and humanity which was Asia, and Westerners had shrunk from confrontation with Vietnam no less than with the rest of Asia.

The United States engaged itself because Vietnam happened to be critical to global strategic considerations, not because of sympathy for the Vietnamese people. It was a harsh truth that Americans would be more likely—all other considerations aside—to allow a Vietnamese peasant to starve to death than a Sicilian or an Egyptian. The peasant of Asia, including Vietnam, was at the end of the line politically and emotionally. His problems were so immense and Asia itself so incomprehensible that Westerners preferred not to think about it.

Perhaps the Vietnamese peasant was aware of this, if only intuitively, and thus remained unswayed by fancy, one-shot American aid gestures. Like a GI medical team that came once to a hamlet and never returned, and thus could do little for the seriously ill but deepen the despair because of the new knowledge that a cure existed and was denied. The Viet Cong leaders were certainly aware of this, and they shrewdly exploited the knowledge. If the visiting American medic examined a cancer victim who subsequently died, for example, the V.C. would say the American poisoned him.

How to communicate a sensitive understanding of the Asian masses to Americans, as well as other Westerners, is one of the great challenges to twentieth century journalism.

Until this has been achieved, undertakings like Vietnam will remain immensely difficult for us, if not beyond our capability.

There was a glimpse of the depth of the chasm in the fact that the "have-not" Negro masses of America in early 1964 considered protesting their fate by stalling thousands of their *automobiles* on the access routes to the New York World's Fair, or by leaving their faucets open to create a water shortage. Many a Vietnamese peasant had never seen an automobile, much less ridden in one, and running water was unheard of. For millions of Vietnamese, wealth was ownership of a water buffalo that cost the equivalent of fifty dollars —or a year's income.

A Vietnamese hamlet (usually less than a thousand population) was a cluster of straw and bamboo huts with earthen floors and straw sleeping mats. The land between the huts was a quagmire of ankle-deep black mud in the rainy season, choking dust in the dry season. The peasant's wife or children often walked as much as three or four miles and then waited in line an hour or two for the daily drinking water. In the dry season the distance was often farther because the regular well became saline. There was seldom electricity, frequently no road of any sort to the outside world, and no communication except by foot.

He was beset by insects, by rats that could literally make a hamlet uninhabitable and become fierce enough to attack humans (in one province alone, some five million rats were killed in a two-month, U.S.-sponsored drive in 1962), by floods and by droughts. He was seared by the sun and whipped by the rain, and his bare feet became calloused, unfeeling boards. The beauty of his women was destroyed by their mid-twenties, and by the mid-thirties they were hags, wracked by years of merciless burden, and often by disease.

And forever there were the flies, cluttering the stinking

fish at the village market, swarming the open sores in the skin of his infant son, harassing his sleep. To survive his mind became numb, reconciled forever to submission and pain without end.

But these were the superficial aspects of the chasm. There were no reliable figures but perhaps as much as one half of the Vietnamese adult rural population was illiterate. Illiteracy is vastly more than simply being unable to read or write. It is human degradation, cutting off development of a man's mind, his birthright access to thousands of years of human civilization, human thought, human ingenuity, human enjoyment of this world.

The knowledge of an illiterate man is limited to what he has himself experienced or heard. His mind is untrained and therefore atrophies, like the shriveled leg of a polio victim. His vocabulary is limited to a few hundred words. His power of reason, the greatest of nature's gifts to mankind, develops only slightly beyond the level of an American six-year-old, again because it is never trained. This means that the simplest reasonable argument, e.g. that mosquitos bring malaria and therefore should be killed, is difficult to communicate. He is ridden by superstition, incapable of distinguishing between truth and falsehood, except at the most primitive level.

USIS in Vietnam made a study of peasant reaction to motion picture films in an area where movies had never been shown before. We found that even the simplest film, say a ten-minute reel on sanitation dramatizing the dangers of urinating in the well, should be shown at least four times to the same audience before it begins to penetrate. We experimented with giveaway matchbooks bearing the Vietnamese flag waving over the fence of a strategic hamlet and a six-word written message urging support for the strategic hamlet program. Our concern whether enough people could understand the message to justify the effort turned out to be a secondary consideration. The main problem was the fact that the peasants could not figure out how the matches worked because of the unfamiliar business of tearing one out before it could be scratched.

Once in 1955 I accompanied a Vietnamese Army patrol to a village deep in the mangrove bush of the Camau Peninsula at the southern tip of Vietnam. The village had been in Communist hands for some fifteen years, and had been used as a command post. Yet we found that the village headman, who was sixty-six, had never heard of the United States, Russia, China or France. He had never traveled more than fifteen kilometers from his own village. Everything beyond fifteen kilometers was "foreign." I was the first Occidental ever to visit the village. Children came in wonderment and pulled the hair on my arms (rare among clean-skinned Asians) as though I had escaped from a zoo.

Of the long French colonial war the old man expressed only one emotion: his hatred for "the big birds that spit fire from the sky," meaning the French napalm attacks which had twice burned out the village—and killed exactly one Vietminh soldier.

Similarly in December 1963 a USIS survey team visited the hamlet of Binh Yen Dong in Long An Province, less than one mile from the provincial capital and only twenty miles from Saigon. The team found eleven families there who had not yet heard about the coup d'état that destroyed the Diem regime eight weeks earlier.

Among most of the ten million people of rural South Vietnam, terms like democracy, Communism, imperialism and cold war were meaningless. The Vietnamese peasant was intensely aware of basic human relationships, like an unjust landlord, or common crime. But for generations he had accepted the system of his community as he found it, since he not only had no knowledge of any other system but seldom could even conceive of anything else. He was indifferent to the excesses of Mme. Nhu, if indeed he had ever heard of her, and equally uninterested in tales of Communist atrocities in China. His life revolved around the weather, the insects, the health of his family, the need for a new village well, and his dream of peace and security.

There was tragically little humor in his world, or romance. At the subsistence level of life, contentment is a full belly and untroubled rest.

For the Vietnamese peasant, even a proud history had been lost. Historians assert that the main reason the Vietnamese were able to throw off the Chinese yoke in A.D. 939 and maintain their freedom for nearly a millennium thereafter was the fact that resistance to the Chinese became a *popular* struggle. There was a powerful sense of nationhood in Vietnam, in other words, centuries before the idea came to Europe. Now even the concept of a nation was largely gone in the rural areas, much less of patriotism. Loyalties extended to family, and friends, and perhaps village, but seldom much further—and certainly not to the Saigon of the Diem regime.

Thus perhaps the most damaging of all the legacies of a century of French colonialism and colonial war: a great people reduced to an era of decadence. To date only the Communists had known how to stir a spirit of renaissance.

(3)

Just as Viet Cong combat tactics could be compared with the Indian wars in the United States, their political tactics resembled the familiar methods that American Communists had long used to infiltrate trade unions, or gangsters to corner control of vending machine businesses. Both techniques were so skillfully entwined in the life and character of the Vietnamese peasant, however, that they often confounded not only the U. S. Mission but also the aristocratic leaders of the Diem regime.

The Viet Cong military effort sought, on one hand, to demoralize the government forces by attacking only by surprise, only when victory was a certainty, and then dispersing so swiftly that retaliation was impossible. On the other, it sought to destroy the government's civil authority by assassination of local officials, harassment of civilian highway traffic by roadblocks which vanished before government forces could get there, and similar actions giving an impression that V.C. power was everywhere yet nowhere, and all-powerful, like the Mafia in Sicily.

Some twenty-five thousand to thirty thousand Viet Cong regulars—the so-called "hard hats" because of their conical, net-covered straw helmets—operated as full-time troops in standardized units up to battalion size (four hundred to five hundred men), attacking, dispersing and then regrouping at a prearranged rendezvous. They were based in jungle and mountain hideaways, or often in safe havens just across the Cambodian or Laotian frontiers, living in peasant-style huts that could be abandoned quickly. They were developed to a surprisingly sophisticated degree. They had jungle arms factories, radio nets, clandestine hospitals, propaganda printing presses. Survivors of ambushes even reported occasionally that they had seen V.C. cameramen filming the action.

Overall command was in Hanoi, under Ho Chi Minh's defense minister, Vo Nguyen Giap, the victor of Dienbienphu. There also were several regional headquarters, but the commanders were unknown, except sometimes to intelligence officers. The Communists themselves curiously did not identify any V.C. military leaders, much less try to promote anyone as a hero in their propaganda. This may have been insurance against internal political difficulties—there had always been friction between northern and southern Vietnamese—after the war was over. The Viet Cong were an army of faceless men.

The hard hats were supplemented by about a hundred thousand men in irregular formations: regional guerrillas who fought full-time but only in their native neighborhoods and militia who worked the fields by day and often took up arms by night—operating from their own hamlets, where they were indistinguishable from innocent peasants. Such hamlets often concealed a maze of underground tunnels (sometimes several miles long) and caves for hiding men and supplies and for fast escape from government raids. The regional units provided replacements for casualties among the regulars.

At this stage of the struggle the Viet Cong made no effort to take or hold territory, since this would only expose them to concentrated, overwhelming government attack. The primary objective was to capture the support of the people covertly and to blend themselves with the people, thus denying the government a target. This in turn tended to provoke the government, in its frustration, to turn its guns and bombs on the people, which seldom hurt the V.C. seriously yet always angered the people and turned them increasingly against the government. The idea was that eventually government influence would be driven from the countryside and isolated in the towns and cities.

Once this stage was achieved the V.C. would rapidly recruit reinforcements until they were strong enough to emerge in divisional strength, engage the government forces in open conventional warfare and destroy them, as they did the French at Dienbienphu.

On the political level the Viet Cong objective was the penetration and subversion of the peasants to separate them from the government. This was done initially by cells of secret agents. In 1962 the government captured the diary of one such agent telling how all the other members of his cell had been arrested or killed but he had managed alone to keep going and eventually rebuild an apparatus that brought the hamlet under control. As required, and circumstances permitted, the agents were backed up by ruthless, calculated terror. Inhabitants of a recalcitrant hamlet might awake one morning, for example, and find the head of a government official or known government sympathizer impaled on a fence post with a note saying that a "people's court" had found him guilty of "betraying the people's cause to the American-Diemist imperialists."

Or an armed V.C. unit might enter the hamlet at night, assemble the people at gunpoint, lecture them on the "people's cause"—it was part of the V.C. technique to behave as though they were the true government of the country—and then perhaps publicly try and execute a government sympathizer, or unpopular landlord. Reluctance of the government forces to fight at night helped make possible this sort of thing.

As they grew bolder the V.C. agents in a hamlet would seek to recruit more people by engaging them in crime, first perhaps in acting as a messenger, then as a porter carrying ammunition and supplies for a guerrilla unit, and finally perhaps in murdering a government soldier. Thereafter the man was trapped, an outlaw, and his loyalty assured, regardless of whether it was sincere. At the same time the V.C. agents associated themselves with the people's authentic grievances and tried to magnify them and create new ones. As the hamlet gradually became secure, whether by terror or persuasion, V.C. military units would begin to use it as a base, or perhaps only as a secret rest camp so as not to attract government attention. From this point on, all was sweetness and light, with the V.C. helping the peasants in the fields, building a new school and otherwise winning their affection.

It was fairly common for the V.C., in particularly difficult circumstances, to order their men to marry into local families in order to cement their support.

The V.C. also worked implacably toward a monopoly in intelligence, showing a respect for this vital factor in guerrilla warfare that regularly escaped the government forces. As soon as they achieved any kind of authority in a community the V.C. would impose the system of "positive loyalty" that prevails in China and North Vietnam—and is a frightening glimpse of the workings of Communist dictatorship. In effect this meant that a man was not only guilty if he saw something useful to the V.C. and failed to report it. He was also guilty if he had been in a situation where he *should* have seen it and failed to report it—if a stranger in the hamlet was found to have walked past his house during waking hours, for example. The stranger was presumed to be a government agent until proved innocent.

All this combined to turn the Vietnamese countryside into a world of spies, informers and terror, where no man was safe, and even indifference could be fatal. The problem was so acute that USIS in 1962 produced a motion picture to be shown to peasant audiences on how to inform on the V.C. It dramatized secret ways to pass information on the presence in the hamlet of a V.C. unit to the government authorities, like using a child messenger, or by prearranged signals such as a broken twig.

The problem that confronted the government forces in areas penetrated by the V.C. might be compared with the police problem in the slum district of a large American city, say, some parts of Harlem. Like the police in Harlem the government forces could go freely wherever they wanted throughout the countryside, as long as they moved in sufficient force. But a single Vietnamese Army vehicle, or a small patrol, invited sudden ambush, just as a single patrolman in Harlem risks being attacked in a dark alley. Also as in Harlem, reinforcements would arrive to find a neighborhood of blank faces. Nobody saw it happen. Nobody heard any shooting. Nobody ever, ever knew anybody who conceivably might be a Viet Cong.

Yet the commander of the government unit would know, and his men would know, that the peasant woman to whom he was talking might be the mother of the man who led the ambush. If a friend of the unit commander had been killed in the ambush, the temptation would be strong to take it out on the villagers who refused to talk. What the commander might forget is the fact that another of the woman's sons might be in the government forces, making her a tragic, helpless victim. He might also forget the probability that as many as half or even more of the people in the hamlet were secretly neutral or against the Viet Cong—like the overwhelming majority of decent people in a Harlem block contested by hoodlums—and would help him, if they dared.

They seldom did dare, like the people along Route 13 who failed to warn the men of the 5th Division. And every time the government forces were provoked by such silence to brutality against the people, their cause was damaged, for hatred is always a Communist asset.

(4)

An important part of Viet Cong psychological warfare among the peasants was the line that they were invincible, the wave of the future. The record did not support this. In the turbulence of awakening peoples that swept Southeast Asia after World War II, there had been four significant armed rebellions by Communist guerrillas using similar techniques (not counting desultory uprisings in Cambodia, Thailand, Burma and Indonesia that never amounted to much). The score to date was two failures (Malaya and the Philippines) against one success (North Vietnam) and one uneasy standoff (Laos).

The record did show, however, that in all four of these areas, the guerrillas were able to get started because the existing governments were weak and/or corrupt, already losing popular sympathy. They were defeated in the two areas where the government was strengthened and reformed, and the grievances that had led the population to support the guerrillas were removed.

In Malaya the British brought in imaginative, aggressive new leadership like General Gerald Templer and Malcolm MacDonald. They also moved rapidly to give the country its independence at the same time that they cracked down on the guerrillas. In the Philippines there emerged a great national leader, Ramón Magsaysay, who had himself fought as a guerrilla against the Japanese. He rallied the people against the Communist Huks as defense secretary and then defeated the inept regime of Elpidio Quirino at the polls in 1953 to become President. He died tragically in 1957 in a plane crash while still in office.

As a correspondent I watched Magsaysay in action against the Huks and among the people of the *barrios* (villages). There was a profound lesson in this man.

To all his people, including the Huks, Magsaysay offered "total friendship or total war." He delivered, in full measure, on both counts. To the uncommitted, harassed people of the *barrios,* he gave schools, security, medical services, economic aid—and justice. To the Huks who surrendered, he gave forgiveness and economic help toward a new, honorable life. Some of his most effective, intensely loyal lieutenants were former Huks who had been rehabilitated. To the Huks who chose to fight, he gave death. With the increasing support of a thankful people, his army tracked them down mercilessly until the movement was destroyed. This was exactly the policy that could win in Vietnam.

Paradoxically Diem himself may have been aware of this. He knew a great deal about Magsaysay and his methods. At one time he kept an autographed portrait of Magsaysay in his study (though the two men never met). But Diem was woefully unable to match Magsaysay's performance or even to bring himself to try.* This was the explanation of the people's silence on Route 13. This was also the explanation of the apparent Viet Cong conclusion in 1962 that American intervention could be overcome—because they saw that Diem, even with his new American assets, still was not threatening their vital base in the people.

Diem was incapable of friendship for the peasants, much less "total friendship." He regarded them—affectionately—as inferiors, and as mentioned earlier, expected their support as a "duty." The peasants—those who had heard of him—felt this. Diem was structurally unable to project himself in any other fashion. He was an introvert, as compared with Magsaysay, who was a slambang extrovert, never happier than in the midst of a jostling crowd—like the five thousand people who jammed themselves into Malacanan Palace, at his open invitation, on the day of his inauguration. Diem regarded this sort of thing as an indecency.

Contrary to the Western clichés about impassive Orientals, furthermore, there was nothing un-Asian about Magsaysay. Two of the most successful politicians in Southeast Asia, Soekarno of Indonesia and Sihanouk of Cambodia, surely ranked among the noisiest, most extroverted demagogues in the trade, yet they also enjoyed the affectionate

---

* The Diem regime repeatedly rejected American suggestions that a team of Filipino veterans of the war against the Huks be invited to Vietnam in an advisory/training capacity. We heard that Nhu thought the Filipinos were "too Americanized." For equally fuzzy reasons Washington vetoed suggestions from Ambassador Nolting and others that Major General Edward G. Lansdale be transferred from a Pentagon desk job to become a special advisor to Diem, who had welcomed the idea. Lansdale was a friend and advisor to Magsaysay and later won Diem's confidence as an advisor in 1954–55. High officials in Defense and CIA were down on Lansdale, one of the United States' ablest experts on counter-guerrilla operations, because of his tendency to break bureaucratic crockery to get things done.

loyalty of their peoples. The Communists had tried to generate guerrilla movements in both countries and miserably failed. Soekarno and Sihanouk ran two of the most inefficient, chaotic, irresponsible governments in the world, but it made no visible difference to their popular support.

Almost everything the Diem regime did, by contrast, seemed to accentuate its isolation from the peasants. Preservation of the Mandarin psychology in the public service encouraged petty pretensions among local officials, who looked down upon the common people and withdrew from them, while at the same time often milking them for kickbacks. We repeatedly discovered cases of local officials who refused—often from snobbishness as much as fear—even to live in the hamlets for which they were responsible. Despite U.S. objections Diem ordered doctors in the armed forces not to treat civilians wounded accidentally in government battles with the Viet Cong. He explained that there was a shortage of doctors and the armed forces' morale must come first.

Even this was capped in at least one area where we found tax collectors attached to military units. The idea was that this was a convenient way to collect back taxes for absentee landlords in hamlets where government authority had totally collapsed, often several years earlier. For the peasant in such hamlets, "liberation" from the Viet Cong meant a demand at gunpoint for payment of taxes that he probably did not know he owed.

The Vietnamese peasant was born to grinding poverty, backbreaking toil in the mud of the paddies, and usurious claims on his crop. He accepted that as part of the scenery. He had no dreams about the dawn of a new democratic Vietnam, as many a Western idealist insisted. Democracy, like Communism, was meaningless to him. With its essential requirement of a knowledge of public affairs, a national democracy in the Western form would hardly make much sense anyway in a land where it took eight weeks for news of the assassination of the chief of state to travel twenty miles from Saigon to the hamlet of Binh Yen Dong.

But the peasant did have a strong sense of social justice as it applied within a framework of centuries of immutable hamlet living, where seemingly little things were everything. The Viet Cong understood this. The Diem regime did not. And in the absence of such understanding, American aid had little more lasting value than a bandage on a malignant tumor.

"There are three principal paths in the hamlet," said the USIS survey of Binh Yen Dong (in the stilted English of a Vietnamese employee). "The one which leads to the river edge, where V.C. infiltration would be a problem, is impaired by a bad bridge which the people would like to see repaired. The people would also like to see the path straightened. It now takes an irregular course due to land of a rich landlord."

Another USIS team visited the hamlet of Binh Co, also in Long An Province. "Complaints," said the report, "revolved around the antics of the hamlet council. Although elected, the council's selection was actually forced upon the people. The council collected fifty piasters (about sixty-five cents) from each family, giving no receipt, for a hamlet office. As yet there is no hamlet office and the people wonder where the money went. Ten piasters was collected from each family for numbering of the houses. As yet this has not been done. The people would like to reelect the hamlet council."

There was no further background on either case. It was likely, however, that Diem's local authorities had brushed aside the complaints because the rich landlord in Binh Yen Dong and the hamlet council members in Binh Co were all Diem supporters. It was equally likely that the Viet Cong in Binh Yen Dong had said: "Support us and we will repair the bridge and straighten the path." And in Binh Co: "Support us and we will punish the hamlet council, and return your money. We will also build the hamlet office and we will place numbers on the houses."

Not only did the Viet Cong understand what the people really wanted, what would count with them *now*, but in most cases the wants were so simple that even the V.C. guerrillas had the means to fulfill them immediately. The U. S., by contrast, had spent some $4 billion in Vietnam, but failed to find a way to straighten the path at Binh Yen Dong.

(5)

The Diem regime's failure to mount "total war" against the Viet Cong was equally dismal. Its military performance often did more damage to its own relations with the people than it did to the V.C.

The regime talked all-out war. Perhaps it genuinely believed that such moves as the ban on dancing and sentimental music and Mme. Nhu's paramilitary women were stirring the nation to maximum effort. In fact it was a siestas-as-usual effort, just as it had been for the French a decade earlier. Like the French the regime seemed to think that somehow a guerrilla war was not quite a real war and that therefore there must be a cheap solution.

This was most obviously evident in the fact that it fielded only about half, or a third, of the armed forces that the job required.

The French committed the same error. Many experts believe that if they had brought in the same strength in 1950 that they did so futilely in 1954, they could have defeated the Vietminh. If reinforcements had been available at Dienbienphu to expand the perimeter and destroy the Communist artillery, the battle could have been a French victory of immense importance, instead of an argument for the myth of Asian guerrilla invincibility. At the peak of their strength, about 350,000 men of mixed nationality, the French still had an advantage of less than two to one over the Vietminh.

Apologists for Western failure in Vietnam react indignantly to comparisons with British success in Malaya. They argue, among other points, that almost all of the Malayan rebels came from the Chinese half of the population which was cordially disliked by the Malay half. They also argue, correctly, that the guerrillas there were relatively easy to defeat because there was no contiguous Communist-controlled territory where they could obtain supplies and safe haven. In contrast, they argue, South Vietnam had 60 miles of common frontier with the North, plus 780 with Laos and Cambodia where Communist supply routes operated freely.

This argument overlooks the fact that the British at the peak of their "easy" crisis in Malaya mounted a force of about 100,000 men against a guerrilla strength that never exceeded 8000, or a ratio of 12½ to one (or 35 to one if 180,000 special police are included). This was subsequently accepted as a rule-of-thumb ratio for effective antiguerrilla warfare. The explanation is the combined requirement of men to guard critical installations against terrorist attacks, and also of forces large enough to hunt down the elusive guerrillas throughout the country. The government, in effect, must be ready for a fight everywhere, while the guerrillas can choose their own place and time to concentrate their strength. The Malayan experience presumably was the basis of President Kennedy's remark at a 1962 press conference that "you need ten to one, or eleven to one." At the time he said it, the ratio in South Vietnam was about three to one (about 350,000 regulars and militiamen versus about 120,000 Viet Cong regular and regional guerrillas). The ratio did not change appreciably in the following two years.

Proportionately the Diem regime at the height of its effort was fielding about one-fourth the manpower per guerrilla that the British fielded in Malaya, where conditions were much more difficult for the rebels anyway. What was needed to defeat the Viet Cong, especially in the absence of effective political work to win popular support, was an army approaching one million men.

Even the forces that Diem did field were outclassed by the Viet Cong.

The officer crops was demoralized. Inept officers were given commands for political reasons, mainly because Diem trusted them not to stage a coup. Good officers (such as Duong Van Minh, who led the coup of November 1, 1963) were relegated to meaningless jobs because they were politically suspect. Generals manipulated colonels for political (or worse) reasons. The colonels did the same to majors and so on down to the platoon level. There were petty jealousies everywhere, impairing efficiency. Performance in battle was often irrelevant to promotion. Indeed a successful action could damage a man's career. Diem was possessed by the idea that casualties should be avoided—despite repeated American efforts to explain the classic military principle that casualties taken in a fast, successful action usually avoid far greater losses later—and repeatedly relieved officers who took losses, regardless of the reason. Many a unit commander understandably reacted to this by avoiding combat as much as possible.

Officers were so fearful of reprimand that they frequently hoarded ammunition and other supplies because they did not dare ask for more. One American advisor got around this by requisitioning supplies himself through American channels so he would lose face instead of his Vietnamese counterpart if it were refused.

The same psychology made unit commanders unwilling to deviate from advance combat plans to exploit unexpected opportunities to get at the Viet Cong. If the plan were to move from Point A to Point B, for example, no amount of wheedling could persuade the commander to attack a V.C. position observed at Point C. The Americans eventually persuaded the regime to prepare "alternate" plans permitting limited flexibility, but it was a half-baked solution at best.

Almost everything the regime did, in short, tended to discourage initiative—in a fast-moving, fluid struggle where initiative was vital.

Most of the senior Vietnamese officers had been trained by the French. The result in some cases was simply to superimpose French arrogance upon their own ignorance. There was the case, for example, of an American-trained C-47 pilot who refused to take off with a load of Vietnamese colonels one day in 1962 because the manifold pressure in one engine was dangerously low. He was court-martialed, demoted from captain to lieutenant, and ordered thereafter to fly only as co-pilot, on grounds of "insubordination."

Frustrated, humiliated and often disgusted, unit commanders tended to lean on their new American equipment like a crutch, just as the French had, hoping that machines and gadgets would bring easy victories with minimum danger and physical hardship.

They demanded helicopters, or M-113 personnel carriers, for jobs that their troops could have performed more effectively on foot. There was less patrolling, still further reducing the government's presence in the hamlets.

Commanders were reluctant to attack without artillery and air support, and often did not press home attacks on the assumption that bombs, napalm and shells would do the job for them. There were a few lucky occasions when V.C. units were caught in the open and this worked. But as any war veteran knows, air and artillery are of marginal value against experienced, dug-in troops. Much of the time the victims were civilians caught in barrages, or burned to death by napalm in their homes.

There was less wanton killing and property destruction

than the French had indulged themselves. American airmen and field advisors did their best to prevent this sort of thing. But there was no question that abuses were multiplying, with serious damage to the government's efforts to win popular support. A good many Americans in Saigon felt that the occasional military profit from air and artillery attacks on inhabited areas was more than outweighed by the psychological damage.

The regime, with American encouragement, tried repeatedly to force the Viet Cong into combat on its terms—just as the French had tried so futilely—by "sweep" operations. The idea was to trap and annihilate V.C. formations whose whereabouts had been reported through intelligence channels. In a typical sweep the government would use American-piloted helicopters to put down several hundred troops, hopefully by surprise, in positions surrounding the V.C. and then close in by foot. Occasionally they were successful. More often the V.C.—tipped by agents—were gone when the helicopters arrived.

It was argued that sweeps were useful psychologically, even if they failed militarily, as a show of government strength. There may have been some merit to this, but it was often lost because the troops would steal chickens from the people, and otherwise abuse them, especially in hamlets known to be V.C. hideouts. There was frequent torture to try to get information on the V.C. This was tragically stupid. The peasant under interrogation knew that the raiding force would soon leave, that the V.C. would immediately return to the hamlet and that any help he gave to the government would be quickly found out.

For the average peasant, even if he secretly sympathized with the government, a sweep through his hamlet brought only fear and destruction, and renewed pressures afterward from Viet Cong propagandists—the exact opposite of the peace and security for which he yearned. In effect these operations often tended to make the V.C. look like the established authority and the government forces like the outlaws, especially in the many areas where there had been no government authority for years.

The "clear and hold" operations were the most sensible government effort. These were based on the "spot of oil" theory, which the British had used successfully in Malaya, wherein the government would move into an easily defended position, usually on the coast, and then expand its authority outward on a permanent basis by establishment of strategic hamlets. The idea was that in such areas the arrival of government troops would mean the end of V.C. penetration forever, just as the appearance of Allied troops in European villages in World War II meant the end of the Nazis forever.

Several such operations were undertaken. They worked well at the outset, but regularly came apart because of poor administration, or corrupt officials, or failure of the military to provide the security that had been promised. There was one major operation that collapsed because the military commander was feuding with the civil administrator and refused to do anything that might make the civilian look successful. Also the Viet Cong concentrated on wrecking such operations. Their technique was to introduce agents into hamlets in clear and hold areas, subvert one or two of the hamlet militiamen, and then arrange for a traitor to open the hamlet gate so V.C. raiders could murder the loyal militiamen and the hamlet civilian officials in their sleep.

The regime's attitude toward prisoners and defectors from the Viet Cong was maddening. In contrast to Magsaysay's offer of "total friendship," and a new life, Diem insisted moralistically that the V.C. were "criminals" and should be treated as such. After months of pleading, the U. S. Mission persuaded him to modify this to the extent of an appeal to the guerrillas to surrender and be rehabilitated, but it was not very successful. Instead of exploiting defectors to lead government troops to V.C. hideouts and to make propaganda appeals to their former comrades, the regime wasted most of them in camps where they were lectured on Personalism.

It was characteristic of the regime that American advisors, including our intelligence specialists, could obtain access to prisoners and defectors only with difficulty, presumably because it feared loss of face as their stories came out on why they had joined the V.C. in the first place—for example, disgust with Mme. Nhu.

With their helicopters, their artillery, their M-113s, their advisors and their air support, the Vietnamese armed forces were, in short, musclebound.

The ultimate indictment of the Diem regime, however, was the fact that man for man the Viet Cong was a better fighter than the government soldier, better prepared to die for his cause, where the government soldier was more likely to run short of guts at the critical moment.

There were no instances to my knowledge of government troops refusing to obey an order. The statistics showed conclusively, and tragically, how often they died, so often uselessly in attacks that were not followed up, in ambushes that should have been avoided such as Route 13. There were, however, numerous instances when their officers found ways not to give the order to attack. The Vietnamese forces undeniably lacked what the psychologists call "motivation," that elusive spark in the human spirit that makes a man go the extra, seemingly suicidal ten yards that it takes to overrun an enemy position. As our field advisors put it, the government forces, officers and men alike, were convinced that the Viet Cong were "eight feet tall."

In an article published by the *New Republic* (May 4, 1963), Correspondent Jerry A. Rose reported the bitter remarks of an American helicopter pilot who had taken some

Vietnamese troops on an "assault" mission against the Viet Cong. "Yesterday," said the pilot, "I dropped a whole bunch of these Vietnamese troops into a field. Today I went back to the same field with another load and you know what I saw? That first group was still there in the field, tents up and cooking lunch. They hadn't moved a damn inch."

Two thousand years of struggle against the Chinese, apart from the remarkable Vietminh performance against the French, precluded any suggestion that this was a fault in the Vietnamese character. The Vietnamese simply would not fight for Diem, or Nhu, or Mme. Nhu.

Diem's troops developed subtle ways to avoid a fight. One strategy, to the despair of their American advisors, was to fire their weapons needlessly and talk and shout to each other during combat operations to alert the Viet Cong to their presence. Units assigned to lay an ambush outside a hamlet would deliberately let the word get around the hamlet so agents could warn the V.C. Or they would take up their positions in daylight when V.C. agents could see them. This sort of thing happened mainly with irregular forces, especially the Self Defense Corps or hamlet militia, but the regular forces were capable of it too.

American field advisors reported instances where government troops succeeded in flushing major V.C. concentrations but then failed to close off their escape route, again apparently to avoid a fight.

In 1962–63 the Diem regime admitted defections from its regular forces at rates sometimes running as high as a thousand per month, occasionally to the Viet Cong, often simply to go home. The true figures probably were higher than those reported to the U. S. Mission. Resistance to the government's military draft ran high in the rural areas. There were reports of young men who cut off one or more of their own fingers to avoid it.

The government forces were afraid of the night. This was

true a decade ago of the French in Vietnam. It was also true today of the white man in Harlem. Night is the friend of minorities, enemy of the gutless, and friend of the man with confidence in his cause and the support of his neighbors. The Viet Cong asserted their power at night, just as the Nazi bully chose the night to rap on the door of a victim. The night gives cover to the fugitive, help to the sudden assailant, and confuses caution. But to surrender the night to an adversary is to give him a tremendous advantage. In a struggle as critically in doubt as it was in Vietnam, it was inexcusable.

The U. S. Mission made some effort to correct this, but the resistance was insurmountable and the U. S. failed to persist. On May 17, 1964, more than six months after the overthrow of the Diem regime, the Associated Press carried excerpts from the letters to his wife of Captain James P. Spruill, of Suffern, New York, an advisor who was killed in Vietnam a month earlier:

"I have a project. It is a proposal to train . . . men in night combat and that they be employed as a mobile strike force at night. It is in the night that the myth of the invincible guerrilla must be destroyed. The people are afraid then. I can feel it. When the night becomes more ours than theirs, events will take a dramatic turn.

"To continue to fight in the day is foolish, for the day is ours for all intents and purposes. It is in the night that they are strong and it is in the night that their back must be broken. Choppers (helicopters) do not and cannot fight at night, but soldiers can and will, and it is soldiers who will win this war, not choppers.

"I still maintain that we can beat them in a year or less if we fight them at night and maintain constant pressure on them at night. *Little emphasis is given to this aspect."* (Italics mine)

The Diem regime did not adopt the French practice of

posting signs on key roads saying that they were secure only until such-and-such time (usually 6 P.M.) when the road security patrols went home. But the effect was the same. At nightfall virtually every government unit in South Vietnam withdrew to the cities and towns, or camped where they were with sentries, leaving the people in the hamlets to their own defenses. This seldom consisted of more than a few scared militiamen armed with carbines, shotguns and grenades. It was a common practice for government forces to break off a battle at nightfall, even when they were winning, allowing the V.C. to escape.

Also like the French, Diem compounded this by insisting that fortified outposts be maintained in areas dominated by the Viet Cong. Like the French, Diem wanted to maintain the government "presence" in such areas, even though this was little more than flying the flag. The V.C. attacked and overran such outposts so regularly and easily that our advisors began calling them "Viet Cong PX's", meaning that the guerrillas used them for supplies and weapons with almost the same ease as an Embassy wife shopping at the Saigon post exchange.

Diem's attitude was Maginot Line thinking. On one hand the V.C. moved about the countryside at will after dark, choosing their own time and place to attack a government encampment, or hamlet, or outpost. On the other the government attempts to build up defenses of critical positions tended to pin down more and more forces in fixed guard duty, reducing its own capability to seek out and destroy the enemy. It did not work anyway. The V.C., having complete freedom of movement at night, could attack whatever target they selected with superior strength, overrun it and be gone before reinforcements arrived, especially if the government waited until daylight to send help, as it often did.

Compounding things, furthermore, the V.C. usually knew where the reinforcements would come from—the government positions being static—so they would lay an ambush and shoot up the relief column, too. This happened hundreds of times in Vietnam (and was still happening a year after Diem's death). The government forces could not get the point that one cannot fight a mobile war from fortresses.

The absence of government authority in the hamlets at night made the people easy prey of the Viet Cong. In a community filled with spies, it was suicidal to try to cooperate with a regime whose police protection ended at 6 P.M. At the very least it was unrealistic to expect the simple, illiterate peasants in the hamlet militia to give battle to a superior V.C. force when they knew that there was little hope of help until dawn.

Most of all, the villagers knew why they were abandoned this way. They knew that the government troops were afraid, reluctant to meet the V.C. on even terms, in the chaotic pandemonium of hand-to-hand fighting at night when their ultramodern weapons and equipment would be useless. The people tended to bestow their loyalty accordingly.

CHAPTER FOUR

"Meck the Knife"

(1)

As public affairs officer of the U. S. Mission, I was the Ambassador's chief advisor on relations with the newsmen in Vietnam. I was also assigned to advise the Vietnamese Government on press relations. I can hardly claim success. Ambassador Nolting went home under a barrage of press attacks such as few if any American diplomatists had experienced. The Diem regime collapsed cursing the American press with its dying words.

The so-called "press problem" in Vietnam was overshadowed by the "newsmanagement" furor resulting from the Kennedy Administration's treatment of the Cuba crisis, but in many ways our problem was more significant. It contributed to a breakdown of dialogue between the U. S. Government and the American people on our policy and operations in a critical area at an exceptionally critical time. It was partly responsible for the public confusion, and suspicions, about Vietnam which became an issue in the 1964 presidential campaign.

The newsmen who worked in Vietnam in 1962–63 charged that the U. S. Mission deliberately lied to them about the war and the Diem regime.

Charles Mohr of *Time* (who later resigned to join the New York *Times*) complained that the Mission attempted to portray defeats as victories and otherwise was "deliberately misleading." Stanley Karnow of the *Saturday Evening Post:* "It became part of American policy to camouflage the shortcomings of the Diem oligarchy." David Halberstam of the New York *Times:* "The U. S. Embassy turned into an adjunct of dictatorship. In trying to protect Diem from criticism, the ambassador became Diem's agent." Neil Sheehan of *United Press International:* "A tremendous amount of misinformation (was) put out."

"The harsh facts of the war in South Vietnam," said a New York *Times* editorial on May 21, 1964, "were only brought to public notice through the enterprise of American newspapermen on the spot." Despite its look-ma-no-hands tone, this was true, but the case against us was more complex than the sin of falsehood.

The root of the problem was the fact that much of what the newsmen took to be lies was exactly what the Mission genuinely believed, and was reporting to Washington. Events were to prove that the Mission itself was unaware of how badly the war was going, operating in a world of illusion. Our feud with the newsmen was an angry symptom of bureaucratic sickness.

Part of the explanation was simple bumbling, and inexperience with this kind of war among some of our top people. We made the error of basing critical judgments of both the political and military situations on information provided mainly by the Vietnamese Government. This was sometimes prettied up to keep the Americans happy. Mostly it was just plain wrong. Indeed one of the main reasons the Diem regime was losing the war was the fact that it never understood what was happening in the countryside.

The U. S. Mission made little effort to distinguish between information provided by Vietnamese sources and the reports of American advisors in the field. If the V.C. attacked a hamlet, for example, information on what happened would be reported initially by the hamlet chief, who quite possibly heard about it from an illiterate, teen-age peasant militiaman, who was as terrified of the hamlet chief as he was of the Viet Cong. From the hamlet chief it would pass through a succession of military commanders who were often political appointees, who owed their jobs to the continued pleasure of the palace, and who knew that Diem frequently fired commanders who reported unpleasant news, or took too many casualties. The U. S. Mission often accepted this kind of information as fact. Much of it was material that even an unscrupulous gossip columnist would regard as doubtful.

The government figures on Viet Cong casualties—which the Mission accepted—became a joke around Saigon. It was a V.C. practice—like other high-caliber fighting men, such as the U. S. Marines—to try to carry away not only their wounded but also their dead, even at great hazard, during a battle. This made it easy for government forces to claim victories when they had only three or four V.C. bodies to show, on the grounds that dozens more were "carried away." Similarly the fact that V.C. guerrillas often masqueraded as simple peasants made it easy to claim as "V.C." the innocent civilians killed by the government forces through indiscriminate bombardments of hamlets.

The Mission was equally sanguine about the casualty claims of Vietnamese and American pilots who attacked supposed V.C. concentrations. These were usually labeled PI-REPS (pilot reports) but nevertheless accepted as reasonably accurate. Many a "victory" thus was based on the claim of a pilot flying at 150 or 200 mph over a battlefield, often under fire from the ground, that he had counted 50 or 100 "V.C." bodies.

In the field of political information the Mission's shortcomings were more consequential, and revealing of a basic error in our approach to the problem of Vietnam. This was our inclination to treat the problem like any other war. There was a commendable effort to keep track of political developments on the enemy side, e.g. such questions as the effect of the Sino-Soviet split on the Vietminh leaders in Hanoi. But our knowledge of what was going on inside the Vietnamese Government, and among its officials in the provinces, was casual and incomplete. In effect we treated the Diem regime like any other ally—for example, the British in World War II—whose effectiveness and determination were beyond doubt, and who therefore should not be spied upon. A heart-warming glimpse of American good faith perhaps, but unrealistic in the circumstances.

Similarly there was little effective effort to keep tabs on the political attitudes of the Vietnamese people, despite the known fact that our adversary gave first priority to this. The Mission paid lip service to the fact that the objective in this kind of war was the support and control of the people, instead of the control of territory which determines the outcome of classic warfare, but failed to mount a reliable watch on popular opinion. This was no less inexcusable than neglecting to find out where the enemy forces are located geographically in conventional combat, or a political party neglecting to find out what the voters think.

Instead we made a heroic effort to fit the problem into the standard military mold, expending countless man-hours and reams of paper to reduce the question of who controls what to charts and graphs. One result was a "measles" map of South Vietnam purporting to show this by different colorings. Another exercise was a line graph to show the progress of the strategic hamlet program in terms of numbers of hamlets under the regime's control. Both efforts turned out to be meaningless because of the basic fallacy in assuming that the war could be profiled in geographical terms.

General Harkins was not unaware of the problem. One of his favorite acts with visitors was to tap his head with a finger and say "the real strategic hamlet program is up here," meaning that what counted was what the people thought about it, which was certainly the fact. Yet American advisors in the field operated under standing orders not to raise political questions with the villagers or even with their Vietnamese counterparts—for fear of annoying the Diem regime. Instead the U. S. Mission accepted the judgment on such things of a government that had so desperately lost contact with its own people that its very survival now depended on U.S. aid.

Inexperience with this kind of war and poor intelligence were, however, only part of the explanation of the illusions inside the U. S. Mission. There was another and perhaps more significant factor—our own psychological blinders.

There was truth in the remark of one senior official, long after he had left Saigon, that "we were too involved subjectively." This was often blamed on Ambassador Nolting and General Harkins as the dominating personalities of the Mission. They were indeed "subjective," but so were most of the top people in Washington, including the men who gave orders to Nolting and Harkins—McNamara, Taylor and Rusk, for example. It was a euphoria that went far deeper than individual officials.

The root of the ailment was the fact that the U. S. had bet all its chips on Diem. There was no alternate, fall-back policy if Diem failed us.

This was not as inexcusable as similar one-crop policies that the U. S. had attempted elsewhere. It could not be compared, for example, with our stubborn, unimaginative and needless support for Premier Adnan Menderes of Turkey in 1958–59 when he was unmistakably running his country into the ground. In Turkey there was an immediate, responsible, anti-Communist alternative in Ismet Inonu and his Republican Party, who eventually did come to power to the distinct betterment of U.S. interests. In Vietnam there was no visible Inonu.

On the contrary, even the severest critics of Diem conceded merit in the argument that "dumping" him would not necessarily produce a successor regime that would be an improvement. The Communists had long since drained off many of the ablest Vietnamese leaders. The French and/or Diem had suppressed many of the remainder, or driven them into exile. The senior officers in the armed forces—the only people who could overthrow Diem, as they eventually did—were mostly political appointees of uncertain character and intelligence, in many cases unthinkable as candidates for national leadership.

There was very real danger that collapse of the Diem regime could lead to a power vacuum and an immediate threat of a Communist victory. This, in turn, would confront the U. S. with two equally unpalatable choices: (1) to seek a "neutral" solution on the pattern of Laos, which probably would only delay a Communist takeover and thus would amount to a step toward surrender, or (2) to bring in American combat forces to continue the fight, which would be unpopular with the American public—and might not work anyway. This was almost exactly how things developed after Diem was ousted in the coup d'état of November 1, 1963.

U.S. support for Diem thus was not a whim, nor based in ignorance. It could be argued that the Mission persisted too long in this support, in the face of mounting evidence that Diem was a failure. But our critics were equally at fault in concluding that Diem had to be unseated long before there was adequate evidence that this critical gamble was justified. Whether he should have been unseated at all, in fact, was still a political issue more than a year after Diem was gone.

The psychology behind U.S. policy was compounded by special emotional considerations that were unique to Vietnam. As mentioned earlier, a large portion of the American community in Vietnam privately disliked and distrusted the Diem regime, and doubted that it could prevail. Among those of us who felt that we nevertheless should keep trying, in the absence of an acceptable alternative, this tended to create a complex of defensiveness. I hope it is not presumptuous to suggest that this in turn created an underlying feeling, perhaps subconsciously, of guilt vis-à-vis the American people because we were politically bankrupt, failing to serve their interest well in a critical situation. This, in any case, was the way I felt. Failure became unthinkable.

At the Washington end, all this was further convoluted by the recent spectacular failure at the Bay of Pigs, and President Kennedy's resulting sensitivity to any suggestion of a similar outcome in Vietnam. Washington was also acutely aware that it had seriously damaged the security of South Vietnam by accepting the "neutralization" of Laos at Geneva in mid-1962, more or less removing all hope of effective action against Viet Cong infiltration through Laos. The possibility of still another retreat in Vietnam thus was political dynamite.

We were stuck hopelessly with what amounted to an all-or-nothing policy, which might not work. Yet it *had* to work, like a Catholic marriage or a parachute. The state of mind in both Washington and Saigon tended to close out reason. The policy of support for Diem became an article of faith, and dissent became reprehensible.

In its dealings with newsmen, the U. S. Mission thus was often wrong about the facts, in a situation of utmost importance to the U.S. national interest, in support of a controversial policy that was costing the lives of American servicemen. Even if conditions had otherwise been normal, this was incompatible with the inquisitive, skeptical nature of American journalism, and trouble would have been inevitable. Unhappily conditions were not otherwise normal.

(2)

The breakdown of communication between the U. S. Mission and American newsmen, and thus the American public, was further exacerbated by the special political considerations that enveloped our operations in Vietnam like a terminal-care oxygen tent.

For one thing the U.S. decision in 1961 to intervene massively in Vietnam amounted to outright abrogation of the Geneva Agreement of 1954. (The U. S. was not a signatory but it pledged itself unilaterally to honor the agreement.) The agreement provided that there be no increase in foreign forces in Vietnam above the level at that time. In the case of the U. S., this was some 685 men. There was also a provision limiting introduction of armaments which was similarly dumped in the trash can of history.

It was characteristic of the schoolbook morality that so often inhibits U.S. foreign policy that the Kennedy Administration was extremely uneasy about this, despite the fact that the Communists flagrantly violated the agreement years before we did.

Secondly Washington was worried about the propaganda and diplomatic ammunition that U.S. intervention in Vietnam would provide the Communists, not only in Southeast Asia but globally. This no doubt resulted in part from the fact we had been so badly burned so recently in the Bay of Pigs, but it was an unrealistic concern. Any increased American effort in Vietnam was certain to stir a storm of Communist talk about American "imperialism," and so on, and there was nothing we could hope to do about it—except to make it work, which would more than cancel out the damage of any amount of Communist propaganda.

Thirdly the Kennedy Administration knew that U.S. support for Vietnam had never been popular among American voters, and it feared that increased "involvement" might lead to damaging domestic political repercussions. President Kennedy was one of the most politically sensitive men who ever occupied the White House, making this consideration particularly important.

The problem was further compounded by the attitude of the Vietnamese Government toward the press. Columnist Joseph Alsop described it as "idiotic." The Diem regime reacted to newsmen as though they were a foreign substance in the bloodstream, in uncontrollable convulsions.

Ambassador Nolting called the problem a "clash of cultures," as indeed it was. It was also a clash of centuries: the twentieth versus, let's say, the sixteenth. To the Ngo Dinh family with its Mandarin background, and its feudalistic form of government, the average freewheeling American newsman seemed both incomprehensible and dangerous. The family could not understand why the American press would publish anything that was derogatory to an ally locked in battle against an enemy who was also an American enemy. It demanded the same blank-check support from the press that it was receiving from the U. S. Government.

After a good many years of trying, the Americans persuaded Diem early in 1961 to hire a professional public relations consultant. The contract went to a New York agency, at a reported fee of $100,000. An American expert turned up in Saigon, but the experiment fizzled. One reason was a morass of financial complications. Another was the suspicion among some newsmen in Saigon that one of the expert's functions was to keep track of their activities for the palace.

This was all before my time, but I suspect the expert also failed because the palace regarded him as a form of technical assistant, expected to make the newsmen be good, just as an insecticide specialist would wipe out malaria. The root of the trouble was beyond the reach of specialists. This was the Ngo Dinh family's unshakable belief in its own infallibility. It regarded public relations as the mere process of communicating the word. Newsmen were expected to listen and be swayed, like the audience of the Saigon radio, which turned out to be equally unswayed. Diem and the Nhus sincerely believed that it was not only insulting for newsmen to seek information from sources other than the palace, but that such information could not possibly be accurate in any case.

The regime was not malicious, nor particularly self-seeking about this. The palace seldom lied intentionally to the press. It often tried to persuade reporters to accept absurdities, but it usually believed them itself—and regularly tried to sell the same absurdities to the U. S. Mission, often, unhappily, with greater success.

Almost nothing was done to provide essential working facilities for newsmen. Vietnam was a nation at war, yet the only official spokesman for the Vietnamese armed forces was an obscure Lieutenant Bang, who could seldom be found. Military developments were reported in a daily communiqué, but it was regularly three or four days behind the news, and always played down setbacks. It was largely ignored. There were three or four relatively competent civilian information officers, but they too were difficult to find, especially when the news was bad.

The newsmen, of course, found other sources for the news, and increasingly treated the regime's communiqués with the contempt they invited. This, in turn, outraged Diem and the Nhus, who tended to blame the U. S. Mission. Like politicians all over the underdeveloped world, they believed that the U. S. Government controlled the American press, just as they controlled the Vietnamese press. No amount of patient explanation could persuade them of the reality that the American newsmen not only were wholly independent of government control but in fact regularly transmitting dispatches that the U. S. Mission considered to be damaging to the U.S. interests.

This created a dangerous vicious circle. The Diem regime, recognizing that it could not persuade the newsmen, sought to control them. It tried to limit their movements around the country, to block their sources, and to keep them under surveillance. It lifted their dispatches out of the cable office —in violation of international communications codes—and had them translated for private circulation inside the government. And it protested vigorously to the U. S. Mission about everything it disliked in the newsmen's reports, sometimes calling us on the carpet for dispatches that had not yet been published in the newspapers to which they were addressed. The protests would often interfere with negotiations between the Mission and the regime on more important issues.

This still further poisoned the Mission's attitude toward the newsmen. We rationalized our attitude like this:

1. Success of the struggle against the Viet Cong depended importantly on persuading the Diem regime to heed U.S. advice.
2. The regime believed, however wrongly, that the U.S. press reflected the views of the U. S. Government and therefore blamed the U. S. Government for press reports that it disliked.
3. Such reports angered the regime and made it reluctant to accept American advice on matters of importance to the war effort.
4. Newsmen who wrote such dispatches were therefore damaging the U.S. national interest. To put it another way, it became unpatriotic for a newsman to use an adjective that displeased Mme. Nhu.

Completing the vicious circle, this kind of thinking led the Mission to react with sympathy to the regime's complaints, in the understandable human hope that by doing so we could get on with other business. Occasionally it worked that way. More often our sympathy simply tended to encourage the regime to more complaints. This also tended to identify the Mission with the regime's hysterical attitude toward the press, including eventually even its physical reprisals against newsmen.

Together all these special considerations led to an official U.S. policy on press relations that attempted on one hand to discourage publicity of any sort about our operations in Vietnam, and on the other to pamper the Diem regime.

At the outset, in 1961 and early 1962, the American buildup was treated like a clandestine operation, producing some memorable absurdities. When the aircraft carrier *Core* tied up at a dock in the Saigon River, for example, newsmen at the rooftop bar of the Majestic Hotel across the street could almost flick a cigarette down among the helicopters cluttering her flight deck. Yet if one of them asked if that was an aircraft carrier across the street, the official reply was supposed to be "no comment." The Mission was forbidden to discuss arrivals of military personnel or materiel of any sort.

This kind of foolishness quickly stirred the wrath of newsmen working in Vietnam, especially when the Viet Cong began killing Americans who were clearly engaged in combat missions. Excessive American secrecy became a news story in itself and was widely reported, with the implication that the U. S. Government was cheating on its own people, trying to fuzz up a policy that was costing the lives of American servicemen. The main result of the secrecy was considerably more publicity than the U.S. buildup would otherwise have generated. It also provoked indignant editorials and, more importantly, queries from congressmen.

By early 1962 difficulties with the press had reached a point where Washington ordered a reexamination of information policy. The result was a new directive, State Department cable No. 1006 of February 21, 1962—two months before my arrival—which was supposed to "liberalize" the policy. It was "liberal" in the sense that it recognized the right of American newsmen to cover the war in Vietnam, but it was otherwise little more than codification of the errors the Mission was already committing.

The text of the cable, which was classified, was not released, but it was shown to members of the House Subcommittee on Foreign Operations and Government Information headed by Rep. John E. Moss, Democrat, of California. The Subcommittee's report on October 1, 1963, paraphrased the cable as saying:

News stories criticizing the Diem government "increase the difficulties of the U.S. job."
Newsmen "should be advised that trifling or thoughtless criticism of the Diem government would make it difficult to maintain cooperation" with Diem.
Newsmen "should not be transported on military activities of the type that are likely to result in undesirable stories."

The Subcommittee's report commented: "The restrictive U.S. press policy in Vietnam . . . unquestionably contributed to the lack of information about conditions in Vietnam which created an international crisis. Instead of hiding the facts from the American public, the State Department should have done everything possible to expose the true situation to full view."

Cable No. 1006 was the policy I was expected to carry out as public affairs officer.

(3)

Feuds between newsmen and government officials had long been commonplace. During a World War II press conference, for example, President Roosevelt contemptuously presented a Nazi Iron Cross to an unfriendly reporter, implying that his reporting had been helpful to Hitler. Conflict was built in under the American system of checks and balances—the clash of the people's fundamental right to know versus the government's duty to guard secrets that would help the nation's enemies.

In Vietnam the feud reached a degree of bitterness such as I had never before encountered in some twenty years of foreign duty.

I was treated to a disconcerting glimpse of the official attitude toward newsmen on my first morning in Saigon. My advice was invited on a press conference to be given later that day by two American sergeants who had just been released after several weeks in the jungle as prisoners of the Viet Cong. The Communists had given them a fistful of propaganda leaflets to distribute among their comrades —the standard claptrap appealing to peace-loving Americans to cease participating in this dirty imperialist war against the peace-loving Vietnamese people and go home.

To my surprise an American military officer suggested that the sergeants be ordered not to tell the press about the leaflets. "Why should we help the V.C. circulate their propaganda?" he asked. He seemed to be saying that he thought American newspaper readers might be swayed by it. I objected and argued that, as a matter of principle, the sergeants should be instructed to withhold only sensitive military information of possible help to the V.C. In any case, I said, Americans don't take that kind of propaganda seriously, just as we all had laughed at Tokyo Rose and Axis Sally during World War II.

Came the press conference. After the sergeants had recounted their adventures, Peter Kalischer of the Columbia Broadcasting System asked: "Did the V.C. give you anything to bring out?" One of the sergeants looked Kalischer in the eye and replied: "No, sir."

It was an evident falsehood, obviously on orders, in equally obvious disregard of my recommendation. As is usually the case, the lie didn't work. Kalischer had visited the spot where the sergeants had come out of the jungle, talked to the American authorities there and heard about the leaflets. He even had a copy of one of them in his pocket when he asked the question. The lie was duly reported by newspapers, TV and radio all over the United States the next morning.

For some officials of the U. S. Mission, misleading a newsman was almost instinctive, if only as a way to get rid of him. It was a curious phenomenon, not necessarily malicious. These officials were men of high personal integrity, who would never dream of deceiving their wives or a colleague, or a friend. They seemed to regard a journalist as a natural adversary who was deliberately trying to sabotage the national interest, or as a child who would not understand and should not be asking about grown-up affairs in any case. Once in a press statement, for example, a senior American officer—I think inadvertently—used a figure on Viet Cong casualties that was absurdly inflated. I asked one of his aides to consider issuing a correction. "That would only draw attention to it," he replied, closing the matter.

To the best of my knowledge, no responsible U.S. official in Saigon ever told a newsman a really big falsehood. Instead there were endless little ones. They were morally marginal and thus difficult to dispute.

One day in 1962 a delegation of angry newsmen came to see me to complain that the U. S. Mission had been lying to them. I asked for examples. They could think of only two. One was our report that an American soldier was drowned when he fell from a boat on an "outing," when in fact the boat had been fired on by Viet Cong. The second was an official announcement that Vietnamese forces had rescued the American crew of a downed aircraft, when in fact they had been rescued by an American search party. I explained that in both cases our initial reports had been based on erroneous information from our own people, and I said I thought these were poor examples to support an accusation of lying.

What I did not say, could not say in my position, was that I understood their point exactly, that there had been so many little deceptions that they no longer believed anything we said on any subject.

A man from Mars admitted to official inner circles in both Vietnam and Washington could have been excused if he got the impression that the newsmen, as well as the Viet Cong, were the enemy.

At a meeting in Saigon one day it was reported that a V.C. bullet had missed the foot of a reporter riding in a helicopter by only an inch or two. A senior officer snapped his fingers in disappointment, like a man who had missed a putt on the golf course. Everyone laughed. At a meeting in Washington, a "negative" story by Homer Bigart in the New York *Times* was under discussion. A senior official cracked that "Mr. Bigart spells his name wrong," meaning that it should be "bigot." Everyone laughed. Among newspapermen, Bigart was one of the most respected men in the trade.

There was a patronizing, holier-than-thou tone in the official attitude toward the press. We repeatedly received cables from Washington using expressions like "tell the correspondents" to do so and so, or "explain how they were wrong" to write such and such. This was like trying to tell a New York taxi driver how to shift gears. Newsmen the world over are extraordinarily jealous of their prerogatives, often suffer from an inferiority complex, and react violently to any kind of pressure on their reporting.

Still worse was the frequent official suggestion that a "negative" reporter was somehow un-American. Visiting Saigon on one occasion, Admiral Felt was asked a difficult question at a press conference. "Why don't you get on the team?" he snapped at the offending reporter. The local press corps was outraged. Similarly Ambassador Nolting once asked a newsman to "give President Diem the benefit of the doubt," implying that the press had been slanting its dispatches against Diem. The point was not entirely unjustified, but Nolting was never forgiven the remark.

This was characteristic of the whole sorry mess. Neither Felt nor Nolting was deliberately trying to needle the newsmen, nor even aware that what he said would be so strongly resented. With one or two exceptions the same insensitivity was true of the other senior officers in Saigon. There was a self-righteous witlessness about the official attitude toward newsmen that was hard to explain in men of such long and varied careers in the public service.

The Mission persisted in the practice of excessive classification, under the secret fraternity doctrine of State Department Cable No. 1006, to a degree that denied newsmen access to whole segments of U.S. operations in Vietnam. During the time I was there, whether or not napalm (jellied gasoline) was being used against the Viet Cong was technically classified, despite the fact that *Life* Magazine in early 1962 published a cover photograph in color of a napalm attack in Vietnam. The classification presumably was removed after Secretary McNamara, in a press conference on April 24, 1964, admitted that napalm was being used, though he insisted this was only "very rarely."

Newsmen were forbidden (until mid-1964) even to visit the airfield at Bien Hoa, outside Saigon, where an important part of the U. S. Air Force effort in Vietnam was based. (This was the same base so disastrously hit by Viet Cong mortars in November 1964.) This was part of a near total ban on publicity about the Air Force. Inevitably it backfired.

Much of what the Air Force was doing was "blown" by Captain Edwin Gerald ("Jerry") Shank, a T-28 fighter-bomber pilot who was killed in Vietnam, in letters to his wife that were widely published in the spring of 1964. There was eloquent comment on the U. S. Mission's policy toward the press, and how it affected many of the Americans out there, in this passage (*U.S. News & World Report,* May 4, 1964) of a letter dated January 20, 1964:

"What gets me most is that they won't tell you people what we do over here. I'll bet you that anyone you talk to does not know that American pilots fight this war. We—me and my buddies—do everything. The Vietnamese 'students' we have on board are airmen basics (raw recruits). The only reason they are on board is in case we crash there is one American 'advisor' and one Vietnamese 'student.' They're stupid, ignorant sacrificial lambs, and I have no use for them. In fact, I have been tempted to whip them within an inch of their life a few times. They're a menace to have on board. . . ."

Surely it would have made more sense to invite the press to report the life and activities of Captain Shank and the other American fliers in Vietnam, and thus to give them some of the credit they so richly earned, than to have the story appear in this bitter, sensationalized form, coupled with an accusation from a dead hero that the U. S. Government had misled the American public about his work. Shank's letters were dramatic proof of a basic reality, that secrets don't keep in a situation as confused and controversial as Vietnam.

Excessive classification infected newsmen with distrust of everything we did and said on the understandable assumption that we probably were not telling the whole truth.

One of the spectaculars of the American performance in Vietnam was the compulsive official optimism about the state of the war. This was partly explained by the common ailment of "career involvement," a man's natural inclination to make his work look good. It was partly caused by the fact that Diem liked to be praised, and was inclined to regard as an enemy anyone who failed to praise him. Praise became part of the "advisory" technique. Mainly, however, the unrealistic optimism about Vietnam in both Washington and Saigon was defensive, a silly effort to counter hostile press reporting—in some ways like the losing candidate on election night who keeps pleading for everyone to wait for the upstate returns.

There were some memorable extravagances. Lyndon Johnson, who visited Vietnam in 1961 as Vice-President, compared Diem publicly with Winston Churchill. Secretary McNamara called him "one of the great leaders of our time." After a visit in 1962 General Taylor claimed to have found "a great national movement" that was crushing the Viet Cong. Ruefully I must confess helping to draft a speech by Ambassador Nolting in 1962 forecasting that "the Republic of Vietnam will take its place in history as the country where the tide of Asian Communism was reversed and the myth of Communist invincibility forever shattered." McNamara, Felt and Harkins repeatedly predicted publicly that the war would be in hand by 1964 or 1965, often coupling their remarks with disdainful references to "slanted" or "irresponsible" press reporting from Saigon.*

In early 1963 Senator Mike Mansfield visited Saigon and departed *without* commenting on the war at all. Things had

---

* A ditty, sung to the tune of "Twinkle, Twinkle, Little Star," circulated through American field messes in Vietnam. I can recall only the first two verses:

> We are winning;
> This I know.
> General Harkins told me so.
>
> If you doubt me,
> Who are you?
> McNamara says so too.

reached such comic opera proportions that the newsmen regarded this as news and reported it widely.

Way-out official optimism and public abuse of the press often led the newsmen to look for more bad news to justify their previous reporting, further outraging the VIP optimists. Official restrictions on fresh, unedited news, under Cable No. 1006, similarly led the newsmen to look for private sources of their own. They were plentiful, and many of them were malcontents: resentful aircraft crews who were taking most of the American casualties, incompetent officials seeking recognition that had been denied in the public service, neurotics whose vanity was massaged by the attention of reporters from big-time organizations, or sincerely indignant officers who believed the Kennedy Administration was leading the U. S. to disaster in Vietnam and were willing to risk a jail term (by compromising secrets) to appeal their case to the U.S. public.

To protect such sources as these the newsmen used terms like "informed Americans" or "American observers" or "knowledgeable American sources" in their dispatches. Just as regularly each such story would provoke a protest from the Vietnamese Government, or Washington, or both, and the Mission would receive instructions to prevent any further stories attributed to "American sources." This was roughly like trying to prevent a reporter visiting a city of twenty thousand population from talking to anyone, yet some very important people in Washington apparently believed it could be done. The usual result was, first, a massive security investigation which always failed to uncover the source of the story; second, a directive reiterating previous instructions on how to talk to newsmen without saying anything; and third, a rash of indignant stories accusing the Mission of trying to "intimidate" news sources.

There was a particularly spectacular leak in late February 1963. It concerned a change in the rules of engagement for helicopter gunners. The principle was that they could open fire only in self-defense. Previously this had been interpreted to mean they could only fire when fired upon from the ground. The new order said that gunners now could fire if they observed the V.C. preparing to shoot, i.e. the Americans could shoot first in self-defense. It was a sensible but also sensitive order, first because the change would be of great interest to the V.C. and, second, because it suggested further U.S. "involvement" and thus invited political repercussions.

It leaked so rapidly that stories appeared in the press before the new rules had even taken effect. This was hardly surprising. The order had to be circulated among something like a thousand persons, most of them young, embittered helicopter crewmen who had lost buddies to V.C. fire, and many of whom were close personal friends of newsmen. It should have been obvious from the outset that it could not be suppressed and that the only hope for avoiding page-one headlines was to call in the newsmen, tell them about it and appeal for it to be played down. Most of them would have cooperated. Instead the attempt to keep it from them led to sensationalized publicity all over the world.

Altogether the Mission's press policy tended to encourage soreheads while it outraged the newsmen. Its gumshoe investigations of leaks poisoned the American community with doubt and suspicion of colleagues, further depressing morale in an extraordinarily difficult situation. And it was unworkable anyway.

(4)

In the judgment of some of their peers the newsmen in Vietnam were far from guiltless themselves in their feud with the U. S. Mission and the Diem regime. Indeed in recent times there had seldom been so much invective in the public print against a group of relatively junior-grade working newsmen.

In a scathing article (September 20, 1963) that led to the protest resignation of Charles Mohr, its chief correspondent for Southeast Asia, *Time* asserted: "The press corps on the scene is helping to compound the very confusion that it should be untangling for its readers at home. . . . They pool their convictions, information, misinformation and grievances. . . . They have covered a complex situation from only one angle, as if their own conclusions offered all the necessary illumination."

Columnist Joseph Alsop (September 23, 1963) accused the Saigon newsmen of "carrying on another of these egregious crusades" comparable with the campaign against Chiang Kai-Shek by some of the correspondents in China in 1944. "It is easy enough to paint a dark, indignant picture, without departing from the fact," Alsop wrote, "if you ignore the majority of Americans who admire the Vietnamese as fighters and seek out the one U.S. officer in ten who inevitably thinks all foreigners fight badly. . . . The repertorial crusade against the government has also helped mightily to transform Diem from a courageous, quite viable national leader, into a man afflicted with a galloping persecution mania, seeing plots around every corner, and therefore misjudging everything."

Columnist Marguerite Higgins, who was then writing in the New York *Herald Tribune*, asserted: "Reporters here would like to see us lose the war to prove they're right."

This, however, was a minority opinion in the news-gathering profession. Members of the Saigon press corps dominated the 1963 awards for journalistic excellence.

The Pulitzer Prize for international reporting was awarded jointly to Malcolm Browne of the Associated Press and David Halberstam of the New York *Times*. The Louis M. Lyons award for conscience and integrity in journalism went jointly to Halberstam, Browne and Neil Sheehan of United Press International. The Sigma Delta

Chi award for foreign correspondence went to Browne. The Overseas Press Club of America gave no fewer than five awards and citations to members of the Saigon press corps: Browne and photographer Horst Faas of Associated Press, correspondent Peter Kalischer of the Columbia Broadcasting System, photographer Larry Burrows of *Life,* and author Richard Tregaskis for his book *Vietnam Diary.*

Altogether too much heat and partisan fog were injected into the debate about the press role in Vietnam. It seemed likely that there was a defensive factor, for example, among the award committees (composed largely of newsmen) to counter official attacks on the correspondents. Pro-Diem partisans tended to place excessive blame for his fall on the newsmen. The newsmen were vigorously supported by the vast power of their own employers. They had the sympathy of Americans who tend to favor the underdog, and who often are instinctively suspicious of the government in any case. And most importantly Foreign Service regulations prohibited the officials who clashed with the newsmen in Saigon from defending themselves effectively.

To try to put things in focus it was unlikely that anything the newsmen wrote during that hectic period 1962–64 would be memorialized in journalism schools for literary excellence or brilliant analysis. The newsmen involved were professionally no worse, and not much better, than the average in comparable "boondocks" assignments elsewhere. There certainly was truth to the charge that they allowed themselves to become involved emotionally in the story.

What will be remembered is the furor itself that revolved around the newsmen, and its considerable significance in the evolution of the role of the press in U.S. foreign policy. The personal courage, doggedness and professional sense of duty of the Saigon newsmen in the face of exceptional difficulties will also be remembered, and for this the prizes were richly deserved. (By this standard incidentally it was regrettable that Neil Sheehan of UPI was passed over for all but one lesser-known award. His energy, ingenuity and personal integrity were outstanding.)

This was particularly evident in their persistent refusal to be swayed from their own judgments by the obsessive optimism of the official U.S. line. One of the main reasons for the crisis of press relations was the fact that the consensus among the newsmen throughout 1962 and 1963 was that the progress of the war was at best marginal, which turned out to be unpleasantly close to the truth. In refusing to be intimidated the Saigon press corps performed a distinct public service.

The issue reached beyond the quality of the reporting from Saigon, and into the institution of American informational media as such. Whether the reporting was good or bad the American people got just about what they were willing to pay for, or anyway what the media editors believed the people wanted.

Here was a war, the only war at the moment involving the United States, with an American investment of nearly twenty thousand military and civilian personnel, costing the U.S. taxpayer a half billion dollars a year. The outcome was vitally important to U.S. national security. Yet only three American organizations—Associated Press, United Press International and the New York *Times*—maintained full-time staff correspondents in Vietnam. Malcolm Browne of AP was thirty-two in 1963, Neil Sheehan of UPI was twenty-six and David Halberstam of the *Times* was twenty-nine. Their salaries ranged as low as perhaps $150 a week. They were all intelligent, able, well educated, and they all came to Saigon after successful overseas assignments elsewhere. But their pay, age and experience nevertheless paralleled junior officers in the armed forces.

Also resident in Saigon were a number of "stringers"—part-time correspondents who worked on a piecework basis, often for several publications—who were even less experienced for the most part. Among the publications they represented were *Time-Life, Newsweek,* CBS, NBC, ABC, the New York *Daily News* and the Mutual Broadcasting System. There were staffers in Vietnam for Reuters and Agence France Presse, and stringers for a number of other European and British organizations.

Once a major story broke, however, we were regularly inundated with newsmen from regional bases like Hong Kong, Bangkok, Singapore and even Tokyo. For really big developments they came from as far as London, Paris and the United States. On several occasions Saigon's journalistic population rose as high as a hundred or more, to the considerable benefit of the local hotels, bars and the Vietnamese cable office. The visitors ranged from first-rate professionals to neophytes who displayed astonishing ignorance and incompetence. Like the Britisher who once belabored me for a half hour on the theme that the Viet Cong leaders were not really Communists. Or the American free-lancer who thought Viet Cong was the name of a country that had invaded Vietnam.

Under this system it worked out in practice that the fast-breaking, unexpected and often most significant news was usually left to the young men who were resident in Saigon. In despair Nolting, Harkins and other officials frequently asked why more "mature" correspondents could not be assigned to live there. The answer was, first, the judgment of editors back home that Vietnam was a good story but that it did not generate enough reader interest to justify ordering a high-priced man to move to Vietnam. Second, "mature" newsmen usually were beginning to get ahead in the profession, verging on middle age, and simply did not want to bring their families to a place like Saigon. It was difficult to persuade career Foreign Service officers to go there, if given a choice, for the same reason.

The arrangements for press coverage of Vietnam thus were relatively normal for news from such an area, but they nevertheless contributed significantly to the feud between the newsmen and officials. For the most part the policy-makers in Washington and Saigon were fifteen or twenty years older than the resident newsmen. They had devoted their careers to military or diplomatic service in a good many countries, through a good many crises. They were understandably resentful of the brash young newsmen who presumed the right to sit in judgment.

This, however, was the nature of the species. American newsmen, whatever their age, are often brash and hard to live with. This is one reason why Americans are the best-informed people in the world. The burden of the blame for the mess in Saigon must therefore lie with the officials who tried to reform the American press from the other side of the world instead of learning to live with it, who were old enough and who should have been sophisticated enough to know better. This was particularly true in view of the subsequent evidence that the "immature" newsmen were better judges of what was happening in Vietnam than the supposedly seasoned officials.

Which is not to suggest that the newsmen in Saigon were lovable, much less faultless.

If there ever was a place that needed a light touch, it was Saigon. Unlike the usual case, there were a good deal more people with a sense of humor on the official side than among the resident newsmen. For the most part the resident newsmen were intense, earnest, unbending puritans—who failed, as far as I can recall, to report, much less coin, a single good joke about Vietnam. In retrospect, perhaps the dismal absence of humor in Saigon was one of its most depressing aspects, and the correspondents contributed to the absence. With one or two exceptions they were so simon-pure that it was painful, always with basketball-size chips on their shoulders. Their solemn, self-righteous, unceasing complaints, however justified, became boring.

They were given to ultimatums. On the occasion of one particularly noisome official action, for example, the reporter for one of the world's most illustrious organizations telephoned me and announced that if our sin was not corrected within forty-eight hours, "we'll blast the —— out of you."

Once a delegation of three newsmen descended upon Ambassador Nolting's office and demanded an immediate session with him on a "very urgent" matter. Nolting broke a previous date to give them an appointment an hour later. Only one of them showed up, and he was a half hour late. On another occasion a reporter arrived at Nolting's office and demanded to see him immediately. A secretary explained that he was out of the building until after lunch and suggested that the newsman talk to another Embassy officer. "All we ever get from him is lies," said the newsman to the helpless secretary.

Then there was the correspondent who brightened up the annual July Fourth reception at the Ambassador's residence. When Nolting offered the traditional toast to the chief of state of the host country, President Ngo Dinh Diem, the correspondent clutched his glass to his chest and said in a voice that at least a dozen of the ambassador's American and Vietnamese guests could hear: "I'd never drink to that son of a bitch."

The inquiring, open mind of the fearless reporter was not always in evidence. There was one newsman who had been in Vietnam for some time and never even tried to interview President Diem. One day I suggested that I might use such influence as I had with the palace to try to arrange an appointment. The reporter rejected the idea. "If I had an interview," he explained, "Diem would just talk a lot of crap and we would have to print it." This particular reporter ranked among the noisiest critics of the U. S. Mission for giving the press one-sided information.

Since most of the routine news from Vietnam related to military operations the principal target for press complaints was General Harkins' public information officer. Initially this was Lieutenant Colonel James G. Smith, an easy-going Air Force officer from the South. Seldom had any PIO anywhere been so badgered, insulted, shouted at and otherwise worked over. One day he told me about fourteen telephone calls from newsmen the night before between midnight and 7 A.M., none of them courteous. He took to calling the correspondents "the friendlies." The name stuck inside the U. S. Mission.

One of Smith's chronic problems was reluctance of the friendlies to be up and ready at 5 or 6 A.M. when they had applied to go along on combat helicopter missions. One day he sent me a wry, one paragraph memo about that morning's effort. One correspondent, a lady, failed to show up and telephoned to explain that she had overslept. Another failed to show and also failed to telephone. A third turned out to have departed for Hong Kong the night before. Three more, a television team, canceled out on grounds of "illness." Six places wasted on a combat mission.

Saigon was unique among overseas posts I had known for the absence of social contact between the resident newsmen and senior officials. One day I took a poll of the country team members. Not one had ever been invited for lunch, or even a drink by a local reporter. Rather than try such time-honored therapy the newsmen preferred to spend their leisure hours with each other, or their secret sources, talking themselves into a persecution psychology that reached the state of Pavlov's dogs.

A visitor to Saigon told me one day in wonderment about riding through the city with a resident correspondent. The car went by the home of a senior official. The correspondent broke off an amiable conversation, shook his fist savagely at the house and shouted: "That's where the son of a bitch lives." Then he returned to the original conversation as though nothing had happened. Said my friend: "It was kind of unnerving."

The professional ethics of some of the Saigon newsmen occasionally were at least debatable, weakening my efforts to persuade officers of the Mission to take the newsmen into their confidence.

On one occasion we had received a preliminary report indicating that the Vietnamese police had used some kind of "blister gas" against a Buddhist demonstration in Hue. Since this could provoke serious repercussions, I persuaded the chargé d'affaires, William Trueheart, to call in the newsmen, tell them all we knew, and then appeal for omission of references to the "blister gas" until the report could be investigated. The newsmen agreed, but one of them immediately filed a dispatch that was widely published in the U. S. accusing the government of using "blister gas." As we had hoped, investigation revealed that the burns had been caused by deteriorated tear gas grenades, but by then the damage had been done.

Similarly one day a visiting American general asked for a private meeting with two newsmen to hear their grievances, with the specific understanding that nothing about the meeting would be reported and that even the meeting itself would be treated confidentially so as not to arouse resentment among other newsmen who were not invited. After a good discussion of the reporters' problems in covering Vietnam, the conversation touched on the state of the war. The general, honoring my advance reassurance that he could speak freely, remarked that another helicopter company would soon arrive. Within twenty-four hours: (1) one of the reporters had published a story about the helicopters; (2) somebody had leaked the fact of the meeting itself and I was besieged by complaints from other newsmen; and (3) the general was on my neck demanding an explanation of the whole sorry affair.

In another case an American newsman reported that an autopsy had been ordered on the body of an American sergeant who was killed on a patrol with a Vietnamese unit to determine whether he had been "shot in the back." It implied that he had been murdered by men of his own patrol. The story was absurd per se because a man could easily be shot from any direction in the confusion of a jungle ambush and an autopsy would be meaningless. If the reporter had checked he could have learned that another American survived the action and there was no question of treachery in any case. This story infuriated both Washington and the Mission in Saigon because of its potential effect on morale, especially after it appeared on page one of the Pacific edition of the armed forces newspaper *Stars and Stripes.*

During the Buddhist crisis a newsman embarrassed the Mission politically by reporting that American planes had been used to ferry Vietnamese police reinforcements to put down an anti-Diem demonstration at Hue. The fact was that the Vietnamese had asked for planes and been refused, which the reporter could have checked with a phone call. Of all the way-out stories, however, perhaps the fanciest was the one reporting "simmering hostility" between Vietnamese and American troops. After it had been widely published we established that the reporter's "evidence" was the fact that somebody had thrown a stone at a newsman's jeep.

The way things were going in those days it could easily have been thrown by an American foreign service officer.

(5)

The Diem regime's bitterness against the American press built up imperceptibly but massively, like a rainy season thunderhead in the Mekong Delta. It became uncontainable at some point in the spring or summer of 1962.

Some of the blame for this critical event, which grievously embarrassed the Kennedy Administration's support for the regime, must rest with the U. S. Mission. The regime's false confidence, which emboldened it to act against the newsmen, was produced in part by repeated American pronouncements that the war was going just fine. Similarly Diem and the Nhus must have been heartened by frequent U.S. reassurances that the Mission shared in the regime's resentment of the newsmen.

The first sign of real trouble came in March of 1962 (six weeks before my arrival) when Diem advised the Mission that he had decided to expel the correspondents for two major American publications: Homer Bigart of the New York *Times* and François Sully of *Newsweek*. Ambassador Nolting dissuaded him, arguing that the resulting uproar in the American press would be unacceptably damaging.

The "negative" dispatches continued, in defiance of the official U.S. line of "steady progress" and "cautious optimism," and the regime's anger mounted. In May, Bigart coined a term that became a theme of press attacks on the regime and the U. S. Mission. American policy, he wrote, was "sink or swim with Ngo Dinh Diem." In July, Bigart was transferred back to New York where he wrote a prophetic essay on the Vietnam situation. "Victory is remote," he reported. "The Vietnamese president seems incapable of winning the loyalty of his people. . . . Should the situation disintegrate further, Washington will face the alternative of ditching Ngo Dinh Diem for a military junta or sending combat troops to bolster the regime."

To the acute embarrassment of both the regime and the mission an American television network acquired movies of a Viet Cong prisoner being tortured, while an American officer looked on. There was a protest from the regime because *Time*, in an otherwise friendly story, reported that Diem had been "prodded by the U. S." to launch a campaign to win support of the Montagnards. It made Diem lose face. Cables flew like shuttlecocks between Washington and Saigon because of an enterprising UPI story reporting, correctly, that the U. S. had inaugurated a $10 million program to direct aid to the peasants "bypassing slow-moving Saigon bureaucracy." More face lost.

In retrospect, however, it seems likely that what most alarmed the regime during this period was a little-noticed event back in the U. S. in June. This was a speech by Senator Mike Mansfield at Michigan State University. Despite Diem's good qualities, said Mansfield, American aid to Vietnam had not reached the people and had created the wrong kind of military forces. "There is no longer any escaping the fact," he said, "that after years of enormous expenditure of aid in South Vietnam, that country is more rather than less dependent on aid from the United States. Vietnam's independent survival is less rather than more secure than it was five or six years ago."

This one could not be shrugged off as "irresponsible reporting." Mansfield had been an early, invaluable supporter of the regime in the mid-fifties and now seemed to have turned against Diem. Because of Mansfield's position as Senate majority leader, Diem and Nhu assumed (erroneously) that the speech had been cleared with President Kennedy and thus reflected high-level American opinion. Diem and Nhu also indicated to the U. S. Mission that they believed

Mansfield, and by implication Kennedy, had been misled by the American press.

The regime reacted to all of this by intensified harassment of the newsmen in Saigon. They were shadowed by the police, their telephones tapped. One reporter's Vietnamese girl friend happened to be a Roman Catholic; a Vietnamese priest, presumably at the request of Nhu's secret police, attempted to get her to tell about the reporter's activities when she came to Confession. Transmission of unfavorable press cables was delayed deliberately as long as twenty-four hours, on grounds of "technical difficulties."

In the field, newsmen encountered increasing difficulty in hitching rides on military aircraft, including planes with American pilots under Vietnamese operational control.

On August 7, 1962, AP correspondent Malcolm Browne wrote to General Harkins listing the newsmen's complaints and appealing for a "general reassessment of press policies as they relate to the military."

"Military officers and men, both Vietnamese and American, who formerly were helpful to reporters," Browne wrote, "are now unable to disclose even trivial details. . . . A chance at a helicopter mission comes up about once every two months. . . . More often than not, the correspondent who does get out finds he is confined to some field command post miles from the actual engagement. . . . Correspondents are no longer permitted access to field maps or briefings. . . . Photographs of 'touchy' subjects usually are prohibited. These include battle casualties, Americans flying Vietnamese planes, prisoners and a number of other things. . . .

"None of us expects the government of Vietnam to pay much attention to the press, except as a potential propaganda organ. But we are not gathering news for Vietnam. Our primary concern is for Americans.

"Like soldiers, we, too, have our traditions, in the light of which this is a strange war. The AP has been covering wars for 100 years, and has had its share of battle casualties. An AP correspondent died with Custer at the Little Big Horn (an ambush remarkably similar to some of the fights here) and there have been many others since. Somehow or other, we have managed to keep the people accurately informed. And we are proud of this tradition."

Nothing came of it.

Then came the issue of *Newsweek* for August 20, 1962, with a long article by correspondent Sully. Under the title "Vietnam: The Unpleasant Truth," it called the war "a losing proposition." It quoted Author ("Street Without Joy") Bernard Fall, who had just visited Hanoi, as saying the Americans were ineptly teaching the Vietnamese conventional military tactics that were useless against guerrillas, and that the Vietnamese Government lacked adequate leadership. It also quoted an unnamed Vietnamese officer as saying the war was being lost for lack of political action among the peasants. The article was accompanied by a photograph of some of Mme. Nhu's paramilitary women captioned "Female militia in Saigon: The enemy has more drive and enthusiasm."

The regime was incensed.

Mme. Nhu launched the counterattack by publishing an open letter attributed to her paramilitary women (I heard later that she harangued their central committee with five hours of vitriol in preparing the letter). It expressed "profound indignation," implied that Sully had been "bought" by the Viet Cong, dismissed Fall as a "café strategist," charged that all the regime's critics were "cowards" living off "defeatist rumors" collected in backroom bars, and demanded Sully's expulsion "on behalf of the women who have been tortured and murdered by the Communists."

The letter was followed by a series of violent attacks on Sully in the Saigon press, often under eight-column, page-one headlines. No fewer than three secret police agents were assigned to shadow Sully and inspired rumors were circulated suggesting that he was an opium smuggler, V.C. spy, French spy, and patron of sex orgies.

At a dinner one night during this period Dr. Tran Kim Tuyen, chief of the secret police, and two other senior Vietnamese officials told me in all earnestness that Sully was indeed a French agent, and that he had probably helped promote the bombing of the palace in February 1962 by two renegade pilots. They said this was proved by the fact that one of the pilots had told interrogators that he was inspired to the attack by an article in *Newsweek* indicating that the U. S. Government wanted the regime destroyed. "We must show the world that we have dignity," said one of the officials. They indicated that Sully would momentarily be expelled from Vietnam.

It was an incongruous problem for the U. S. Mission. We had long regarded *Newsweek* as an implacably hostile critic. Sully, moreover, was not a regular staff correspondent and he was a French citizen. He first came to Vietnam in the French Army and remained as a journalist after his discharge in 1947. Technically his welfare was the responsibility of the French Embassy, but the French Embassy was not interested.

Sully himself was a personable man, whom I had known for nearly ten years. He was young, energetic, and brave in the face of physical danger. The Mission discounted the regime's line that he was a French agent, but the French sour grapes attitude toward Vietnam sometimes showed up in his reporting. Sully's reportorial curiosity was otherwise directed toward flashy generalizations and offbeat detail rather than probing thoughtfully for balanced judgments. It was unfortunate that events were to make Sully a symbol of intrepid American journalism.

But that was only part of this miserable problem. It was

not unusual for American newsmen to be expelled from countries like Vietnam. It had happened to me several times in other parts of the world—for example Jordan and Iran, both of which were also dependent upon American aid for survival. The U. S. Government, like other big powers, normally deplored, protested and forgot such expulsions. The reasoning normally was that nothing more could be done without forcing a crisis in our relations with the offending regime of proportions that were not justified by the offense. The right to control information, and the activities of foreign citizens, is an attribute of sovereignty.

Examined in the abstract, it would seem that honoring this aspect of sovereignty was more important in Vietnam than elsewhere. The U. S. was already infringing on the Diem regime's independence in a thousand ways through our "advisory" function, to the profit of Communist propagandists. It was the nature of our shotgun marriage with the Vietnamese, however, that we could not make a gesture to the regime's pride in the case of Sully. The gesture would be taken as kowtowing to Mme. Nhu, further confirming the "sink or swim with Ngo Dinh Diem" charge against us, with resulting uproar back home, including perhaps damaging domestic political repercussions. Emotions were so inflamed among all three parties—press, Mission and regime—that reasonableness was an anachronism.

The Mission therefore went to bat for Sully. Ambassador Nolting on August 30 called on Diem to request, for a second time within six months, that no action be taken against Sully. Diem produced a dossier on Sully as thick as an unabridged dictionary, talked at length about Sully's sins, but promised to consider Nolting's appeal. In fact the appeal apparently was the ultimate, unforgivable, face-losing indignity. Four days later Sully was ordered to leave the country forthwith.

The appeal thus made everything worse. There was nothing further Nolting could do short of sanctions which would have damaged the war effort. Yet we now stood accused of weakness in permitting Diem to defy us.

The Sully affair provoked some equally painful agonizing among the newsmen. A dozen of them argued until 3 A.M. in a room at the Hotel Caravelle. They were torn between those who wanted to fight back with a strongly worded protest, and those who feared that they too might be expelled if the protest angered the palace. There were numerous epithets, e.g. "coward." The dispute reached a McCarthyesque moment when Sully was formally required to say whether he was (1) a French spy, or (2) a Communist. He replied no to both questions.

The meeting broke up without agreement. Next morning six newsmen (AP, UPI, CBS, NBC, New York *Times, Time*) signed a letter which was sent to both Diem and Kennedy. It said Sully's expulsion would be a propaganda weapon for Vietnam's enemies, raise "serious questions" among Vietnam's friends, and could "only be interpreted as an attempt to intimidate the others (correspondents) and can only be regarded as contrary to the interest of free people everywhere." Unwisely it also noted: "The United States alone is spending here more than one million dollars a day and has stationed ten thousand of its finest young men in Vietnam to aid in this struggle"—implying that therefore the Vietnamese Government had better do what the United States wanted.

Predictably the letter was useless. The regime angrily called it "iniquitous blackmail" and reiterated that Sully must leave. The letter to Kennedy was equally futile. White House Press Secretary Pierre Salinger replied that Kennedy "appreciated" the newsmen's concern, and that "our officials abroad will continue to assist you in every way feasible to carry out your all-important task." The newsmen appeared to be pleased. In fact it was a brush-off.

Sully departed on September 9, with most of the press corps at the airfield in a show of solidarity. In Hong Kong he straightaway put together a what-it-all-means article for *Newsweek* (September 25, 1962). It said Diem was "reddish and bloated . . . a virtual prisoner in his own palace . . . a confused philospher . . . almost completely out of touch with the mainstream of Vietnamese life . . . the whole apparatus of the nation seems paralyzed." It said Nhu was "a vicious political in-fighter with an unquenchable thirst for power" and that Mme. Nhu was "grasping, conceited and obsessed with a drive for power . . . the most detested personality in South Vietnam."

(Sully then proceeded to Harvard where he put in a year, sponsored by *Newsweek*, at the Nieman Foundation. He returned to Vietnam for *Newsweek* after the 1963 coup, and soon resumed reporting that the war was going badly.)

As I had feared, the regime observed that Sully's expulsion had not been followed by bolts of lightning from Washington. It redoubled its offensive against the newsmen, cluttering the Saigon newspapers with invective. There was a lively rash of stories charging that the New York *Times* had accepted a forty thousand dollar bribe to publish an interview from Moscow with a Viet Cong leader, Nguyen Van Hieu. When the New York *Times* omitted a few words from a letter she had written to the editor, Mme. Nhu proclaimed that the paper was part of "an international Communist-inspired conspiracy aimed at slandering Vietnam." She told an American network correspondent that American newsmen were "intoxicated by Communism. They believe whatever the Communists say and they speak for them, but in a Western tone. That's why it's worse." To another American reporter she railed that Vietnam was not required to observe "your crazy freedoms."

On the evening of October 25, 1962, the other shoe dropped. James Robinson, NBC correspondent for Southeast

Asia, telephoned me at home, reported that he had been ordered to leave the country "within the shortest delay," and demanded that the U. S. Mission do something about it. He was accused of a technical infraction of Vietnamese visa regulations.

It was a steaming rainy-season night, just after one of those tropical downpours that whip the land and the people like a thousand firehoses, tossing the coconut palms into wild, flailing disarray. As I began dialing Phan Van Tao, the director general of information, to ask for details, I heard the crunch of a car on the gravel driveway outside. It was Tao himself and his deputy, Dang Duc Khoi, uninvited, sport-shirted and in a state of alarm such as Asians seldom display.

Tao described the Robinson order as *une catastrophe,* revealing for the first time that somebody on the Vietnamese side was as worried about the press problem as I was. They said the order had been issued by Nhu, that they had just come from a ninety-minute session with him and that they had begged him to rescind it, futilely. They quoted Nhu as saying he could no longer tolerate newsmen treating Vietnamese regulations with "contempt." They were more upset than Robinson had been. It was a rare inside glimpse of what it was like to work for the Ngo Dinh family. We agreed to ask Robinson to write a letter of apology for the visa infraction to see if that would mollify Nhu. Robinson did so, but it failed.

We soon learned of course that the visa complaint against Robinson was a subterfuge. This time it was Diem himself who was outraged. Reason No. 1: After a rambling three-hour interview with Diem some months before, Robinson injudiciously had remarked to the interpreter that it had been a "waste of time," which was duly reported back to Diem. Reason No. 2: In a broadcast Robinson had once used the term "family clique" with reference to the Ngo Dinh, which Diem took as an insult.

We proceeded with what was becoming a familiar routine. Ambassador Nolting called on Diem and appealed for reconsideration of the Robinson order. Among other points during the ninety-minute session, Nolting asked Diem to make concessions to American domestic political considerations, just as the U. S. Government was doing for Vietnam. This was particularly appropriate at that moment, which happened to coincide with the Cuba crisis. Diem was adamant, again producing a fat dossier, backing down only to the extent that he granted Robinson another three days before he would have to leave.

Next step of the ritual was a protest to Diem from the Saigon newsmen, this time signed by nine of them. They asserted that Robinson's expulsion was "an unjustifiable infringement of traditional principles of freedom of the press. We respectfully request that you reconsider." It was ignored. Robinson left for his home in Hong Kong on November 5.

"We in Vietnam," said an official statement, "have had enough of the calumnies and insults that the unscrupulous and unreliable heap upon our Chief of State, our Government, our Army and our youth while we are fighting a ruthless war." Translation: Three hours with Diem is never a "waste of time."

A few days later Nhu told an American visitor that the regime intended to expel any correspondent thereafter who dared to deprecate any member of the Ngo Dinh family, or the war effort against the Viet Cong. Having now been kicked in the teeth twice, the Mission took this too. Again there was no choice short of provoking a crisis that would surely help the Viet Cong more than NBC.

Then came Thanksgiving Day, November 22, 1962. Residents of the area around the Saigon airfield were awakened at dawn by the throbbing of forty-five American helicopters loaded with Vietnamese troops. They were heading for an assault against a Viet Cong stronghold in the jungle north of Saigon known as Zone D. At that time it was the biggest combat helicopter operation in the history of warfare, with at least two hundred American fliers and infantry advisors aboard. No American newsmen had been invited to go along, much less advised that the operation was going to happen. Still worse, neither General Harkins' headquarters nor the Vietnamese would discuss the operation for several days. It was classified "secret." There was a security investigation to find out who told the newsmen that forty-five helicopters participated—called off when the sleuths found out that one of the reporters had simply counted the copters from his bedroom window.

As usual with such massive operations, relatively little damage was done to the Viet Cong, but the newsmen were apoplectic. David Halberstam of the New York *Times,* who had been in Vietnam less than three months, stormed into my office, slammed a letter addressed to Ambassador Nolting on my desk, and sat shaking with rage while I read it. It began by announcing that he, Halberstam, had been converted from "a neutral bystander into an angry man" and proceeded:

"Two hundred Americans risked their lives. Yet we were not allowed to cover—a story that would have been a fine opportunity to show Americans just what their fighting men were doing here, what our involvement is and why. And our people—from General Harkins on down—went along with this.

"The reason given is security. This is, of course, stupid, naïve and indeed insulting to the patriotism and intelligence of every American newspaperman and every American newspaper represented here. Let me point out that we, as our predecessors in times of conflict have been, are fully prepared to observe the problems of security, to withhold printing classified information. . . .

"Let me also point out that from the moment that fifty helicopters landed at a given point in Zone D, certain aspects of the operation lost all classified status. You can bet the V.C. knew what was happening; you can bet Hanoi knew what was happening. Only American reporters and American readers were kept ignorant. . . ."

Some weeks later the Moss Committee in Washington investigated the Zone D episode. Assistant Secretary of State Hilsman testified that the Vietnamese "excluded reporters on ground they were afraid one of the newsmen was going to get killed. . . . (This) was against our policy. The decision was made by the Vietnamese military commander." If the exclusion was against U.S. policy, nobody told the newsmen at the time in Saigon—or me either. Nor was there any talk at the time about saving newsmen's lives. In Saigon it seemed clear that the newsmen were barred at the vindictive whim of the palace. And again the U. S. Mission took it.

By the end of 1962 relations between the Vietnamese Government and the U. S. Mission on one hand and the newsmen on the other were indescribably bad. Ironically it remained for *Newsweek* to compound the shambles.

Apparently shaken by the Sully affair, and particularly by what must have been an avalanche of complaints about Sully's reporting from Washington officials, *Newsweek* sent a new man, columnist Kenneth Crawford, to Vietnam for what it called "a fresh look at the struggle." Crawford was a respected, long-time professional reporter with experience in difficult stories all over the world. He came to Saigon with an open mind. The fresh look produced an about-face.

In a cover story (December 10, 1962) Crawford reported that "Diem's position has taken a turn for the better in the last few weeks. . . . (He) is promising and promoting a social revolution for the benefit of the villagers. . . . There are evidences that the villagers are responding to Diem's program. In the opinion of Diem's responsible American advisors, his strategy is right and he has made a promising start. . . . Reforms are slow in coming but results are beginning to show." Sully's "detested" Mme. Nhu now became "the beautiful, strong-willed sister-in-law of the President." Sully's "bloated" Diem became a man who "talked earnestly about the importance of the strategic village concept." In conclusion Crawford said of Diem: "Whatever his shortcomings, confidence in his ability to hold out against Hanoi is growing. His well-wishers, whatever their feeling about the President and his family, see no preferable alternative."

The palace was pleased. In effect the story seemed to prove that if you have an unfriendly correspondent, all you do is kick him out of the country and his employers will then send a friendly one.

(6)

One day in July 1962 the *Times of Vietnam*, an English-language daily often used as an outlet by Mme. Nhu, printed an article asserting that the United States had fallen into a "Communist trap" in accepting the Geneva settlement on Laos a month earlier. That evening an American newsman charged into my office and demanded comment from the U. S. Mission. I said we had none. The newsman thereupon exploded: "Doesn't the United States have any dignity left at all?"

Dignity, according to Webster's New World Dictionary, means "calm self-possession and self-respect." This would suggest that the way *not* to be dignified would be to make a fuss about the *Times of Vietnam*. Indeed tolerance of that kind of pinprick is a requirement of world power, just as the British in their day had tolerated obscure potentates who "twisted the lion's tail." The British had discovered a century or two earlier, moreover, that such tolerance often had a cathartic political usefulness.

In many ways the whole press relations crisis in Vietnam was a crisis of pinpricks, if examined against the importance of the stakes—though I certainly did not regard it as such at the time. The newsmen—meaning perhaps the American people?—were not sophisticated enough about the obligations of big-time power politics to permit Mme. Nhu to play out her prideful fancies. On the contrary they lost their temper almost as easily as she did. Less excusably the same could be said about the senior officials of the U. S. Mission vis-à-vis the newsmen. There was a failure of tolerance, and abdication of dignity, by all parties.

As a bright-eyed newcomer to all this in 1962, my initial thought was that perhaps I could persuade the Vietnamese Government to change its ways. There was a chance that my good relations with the Ngo Dinh family as a newsman a decade earlier might be helpful. I began by sending a five-page letter to Nguyen Dinh Thuan, secretary to the presidency and the U. S. Mission's best channel to the family, appealing for better facilities for the foreign press. It concluded:

"You may ask quite understandably what the foreign press will do for its part to improve relations. I can assure you that with improved facilities, the newsmen will certainly include more of the GVN (Government of Vietnam) side in their reports of controversial situations. But it would be futile to invite them to make any kind of a 'bargain.' This is contrary to the nature of the species—as officials of all nationalities the world over have discovered to their despair.

"It is a characteristic of the Anglo-Saxon way of life that freedom of the press be honored to the point where even a hint of pressure is regarded a near blasphemy. The reporter is assumed to be responsible and thus privileged to sit in judgment on all things and all men. It is this kind of inviolability that has made possible the great newspapers of the Anglo-Saxon world—but that, admittedly, doesn't make the reporter any easier to live with. . . .

"However, most of the foreign newsmen in Vietnam are honorable men, who will react intelligently and warmly to a GVN initiative to reach a happier mutual understanding. I think you will find it more than worth the effort."

Thuan was sympathetic, but the letter was a waste of time. I also discussed press relations with Diem, Nhu and Mme. Nhu perhaps a dozen times, and with lesser officials innumerable times, along essentially the same lines. It was all to no avail, like begging an American teen-ager to think about geometry instead of drag racing.

In September 1962 I was invited to make a speech on the subject of "Credibility" to one hundred and twenty Vietnamese Army officers attending a psychological warfare school in Saigon. I tried to make the point that truth is the only propaganda that works. I told about the time I was an escaped prisoner of war hiding with the French underground in 1944 and how we listened at great risk to the British Broadcasting Corporation because we knew it told the truth. I told about the German radio set we captured during World War II with a warning stamped over the dial that listening to the enemy was punishable by death. I noted that the Soviet Union spends more money on jamming transmitters than the global budget for the U. S. Information Agency because it is afraid of truth. I pointed to the fact that it was the youth of Hungary who staged the rebellion of 1956, despite nearly a lifetime of Communist indoctrination. The evidence was overwhelming, I said, that truth would always prevail, and so on.

When I had finished, a young Vietnamese lieutenant stood up and said: "What you say may be right in other countries, but you clearly do not understand the situation here in Vietnam. How can we tell the truth in wartime?"

I was soon convinced that there was no hope—or in any case that I lacked the ability—of persuading the Vietnamese Government to improve either its attitude toward the foreign press or its propaganda to its own people, though of course we kept trying.

I decided to concentrate on relations between newsmen and the U. S. Mission. It was essential, I thought, to change the Mission's rules vis-à-vis the correspondents and to tell them about virtually everything we were doing, if only on a not-for-publication basis, i.e. to trust them. There was nothing shameful or reprehensible about our activities, I argued. On the contrary, we could justly be proud of our effort to help this small and tortured country stave off Communist envelopment. Our present policy, under Cable No. 1006, made it look as though we, not the Viet Cong, had something to hide.

To anyone who would listen I told about a World War II incident which I had always regarded as an example of intelligent press relations. In July of 1944 General George Patton, the U. S. Third Army commander, personally briefed fifty or sixty war correspondents, including myself, on plans for Operation Cobra, the offensive that broke us out of the Normandy Beachhead. Several correspondents immediately traveled down the beach to the First Army headquarters to coordinate plans for coverage of the offensive with colleagues. The First Army correspondents had not been briefed and of course complained. That evening Patton called us all back to the briefing tent.

"You men have been briefed on a top secret operation involving the lives of tens of thousands of American soldiers," he barked. "Now somebody has blabbed." Then he launched into a four-letter tirade such as only Patton could deliver. When he finished, he said: "It is not my intention, however, in spite of this incident, to change my policy of telling you everything I know." For this and many other reasons our relations with Patton were excellent, and there was no more "blabbing." His policy was just what was needed in Saigon.

I tried every additional argument I could think of. Among them:

The American press is far from perfect, but it cannot be reformed from Saigon, so let's stop lecturing the newsmen and trying to tell them how to do their jobs, which only gets their backs up. The press is like the weather; we can't change it and we have to live with it, including occasional "irresponsible" stories.

We may be headed toward what I called "a crisis of public opinion" in the U. S., which could endanger congressional votes for our policy of support for Diem. It is therefore becoming more important to appease American opinion than to avoid offending the Diem regime's sensitivities.

Instruct American field advisors to cease condoning Vietnamese efforts to obstruct newsmen, and to use all possible influence to persuade the Vietnamese to be cooperative. If necessary, American helicopters should be denied to operations like Zone D from which newsmen are barred.

The U. S. Mission should bring direct pressure on Diem to remove the Nhus from all authority in press relations.

Public statements excessively praising Diem should cease, as well as optimistic forecasts on progress of the war. When the war in fact begins to shift undeniably in favor of Diem, the newsmen will report it—in effect ending the press "problem" —and until then official brave words are useless.

Cease official security investigations of "leaks." They are never successful and serve only to demoralize the community and further antagonize the newsmen, who (correctly) see the investigations as efforts to cut off their sources.

Cease reacting publicly to unfavorable stories, which serves mainly to draw attention to them and to enlarge the egos of the offending newsmen. I cited the example of President Eisenhower's reputed reply when he once was asked to give battle to Senator McCarthy: "I won't get into the gutter with that guy."

Occasionally some of this was heeded. More often my pleas tended to estrange me from the official family, and to stir doubts about my loyalty to Mission policy. Closed minds on the principle of credibility, in short, were no monopoly of Vietnamese psychological warfare lieutenants.

Vis-à-vis the newsmen, my position was equally difficult. Many of them were old friends and all of them expected me, as a long-time foreign correspondent, to repair their grievances. Such influence as I had at the outset declined in direct proportion to my inability to do so, especially since I felt it would be both dishonorable and counterproductive to become a "leak" myself. An old Washington public affairs hand told me long afterward that this was probably the most unimaginative, and damaging, of all my mistakes. "In this business," he said, "if you don't leak, you're dead." Perhaps, but he had never worked in the troubled world of the U. S. Mission in Saigon.

In any case, over those dreary months I devised a line for newsmen which I hoped was loyal to the policy and the ambassador but not so empty as to be ignored.

Its gist was that U.S. support for Diem was preserving the option of the Vietnamese people to install another, non-Communist regime later if they so chose, and that this of course would be impossible if the Viet Cong won control. I said it was contrary to American principle and tradition to "play God" by using our power to make and break the governments of friendly countries, and that the Communists in any case would immediately and effectively tag any such regime as a "puppet." I argued that without U.S. support, Vietnam would long since have gone under, and that as long as we maintained our present effort the Viet Cong could not win, even if it turned out that Diem could not win either. I said it could even be argued that a permanent American expenditure at the present rate of $500 million annually was justified, and indeed a cheap price compared to the losses that would follow a Vietnamese collapse. I conceded that Diem had many weaknesses, perhaps too many to survive, but I insisted that sufficient evidence was not yet in to gamble on any other policy.

This approach worked once or twice with newcomer newsmen who wanted an A-B-C briefing on what the U. S. was trying to do in Vietnam, but seldom with old hands. Like my good friend Denis Warner, an able Australian journalist whom I had known well during the French war in the early fifties. One day he remarked: "The place has the smell of Dienbienphu, doesn't it?" It did, but I tried to duck by saying that if this was true, then the judgment of some of the best people in the U. S. Government was incredibly wrong. Said Warner: "The French thought they were winning too. Remember?" I said I just work here and let's have a drink.

It was a frustrating position. In February 1963 I discovered in spectacular fashion that it was also untenable.

A visiting VIP from Washington asked me to prepare a background memorandum about the press problem in Vietnam. It was an ideal opportunity to register my ideas where they would count, and I worked on the paper deep into the night. It was an attempt to be urgently eloquent about the need to level with the newsmen, but to be persuasive I also included a report on the Mission's grievances against them and a personal assessment of the quality of the reporting from Saigon. It was a classified memo, so I was candid.

A day or two later I was obliged to leave for what was expected to be minor surgery at the U. S. Air Force Hospital at Clark Field in the Philippines. To my dismay the doctors there discovered that I required major chest surgery for removal of a tumor which possibly was malignant. They arranged for it to be performed at the Naval Hospital at Bethesda, Maryland. I flew back to Saigon for a few days to tidy up my affairs in anticipation of an absence of two or three months, if not permanently, arriving in a state of considerable emotional disarray.

It soon got worse. I learned that somebody had shown parts of my memo on the press to several newsmen. Who did it remains unknown—a score of Mission officials had access to it—but it evidently was done maliciously. We knew that the newsmen had seen a passage saying that some of the reporting from Saigon had been "irresponsible, sensationalized and astigmatic." They apparently had not been shown the portions of the paper—indeed the bulk of it—which had been a plea in their behalf.

The newsmen were not pleased. Word got back to me that I had been boycotted forever. I had become known as "Meck the Knife." I heard that one correspondent, upon learning that I faced surgery, had remarked: "I hope the s.o.b. dies."

Assuming that he would be disappointed, it was a convenient moment to be sick. And the long flight across the Pacific was a convenient time to think. With the newsmen's Pavlovian reflex now extended to me, should I go back to Saigon, if I could go back? The forthcoming long absence would be a reasonable excuse to ask for reassignment. It was tempting. Still mulling, I pulled an unfinished novel from my briefcase. The place marker happened to be a thank-you note from a friend who had visited Saigon a few weeks earlier. The note closed with some homemade Latin: Illigitimi non carborundum (Don't let the bastards wear you down).

Then came Diamond Head, etched against a sparkling blue-green sea, as the plane banked to land at Honolulu. A drink at the airport with a friend from CINCPAC. Then Washington, the first traces of spring, the azaleas splashing beauty. The agonies of Saigon were wonderfully remote, if not unbelievable. Somehow distance made it all seem easier, too. I decided that I would go back, if I could.

During the long weeks that followed I tried to sort out the

shambles I had left in Saigon. It seemed clear that my primary error, so dramatically proved by the compromised memo, had been to temporize, to try to please both sides in the feud. This had certainly failed, leaving me in dead center.

There was the argument that I was a government official, that I was therefore obligated to accept Mission policy, to take the taunts of the "friendlies" like everyone else, and to stop trying to rearrange the scenery. But this kind of passive time-serving was not why I had volunteered for government service. Our rift with the press was more than an unpleasant spat that we could learn to live with. It had become a breakdown of communication with the American people so serious that it threatened our whole policy in Vietnam. It was mandatory to keep trying to do something about it or to turn in my suit.

Where then was the critical fault? There were many, on all sides, but one seemed to me to stand out. This was the unrealistic official idea that American newsmen somehow could be persuaded, or tricked, not to report unfavorable news. All else related to this central illusion, which had been codified by Cable No. 1006. I resolved to concentrate on this, even though it might lead to my removal from Saigon. The way things stood anyway, it was not a particularly heroic resolution.

Under the magnificent care and skill of the Navy surgeons and staff at Bethesda, the operation was successful. By late April I was engaged in a bureaucratic minuet called "consultations" which is required of officers about to go overseas. I used these meetings to speak my piece on the press problem. The problem had continued to deteriorate during my absence, stimulated by the report of a special congressional committee headed by Senator Mansfield expressing "deep concern" about the progress of the war. I thus found ready listeners. One of them was Pierre Salinger, the White House press secretary, who suggested that I tell my story to President Kennedy.

The appointment was on April 29. There was a two minute wait in Salinger's office. I said I hoped I could make my report without appearing to criticize people who were a lot more important than I. "If you don't level with the President," said Salinger, "he doesn't want to talk to you at all." Then we were in the Oval Office. Kennedy sat down in his rocking chair and motioned me to a sofa. He was disarming, calling me by name and asking about my health. But that was the only small talk. "Why are we having so much trouble with the reporters out there?" he asked. Then he listened intently while I recited for about ten minutes.

The gist of what I said:

It is futile to blame individuals. The newsmen in Vietnam compare favorably with newsmen elsewhere. They are bitterly frustrated and angry at both the U. S. Mission and the Diem regime. There are two ways to achieve more favorable coverage, by undeniable gains against the Viet Cong, and failing that by telling the newsmen more about our activities with the hope of winning at least a sympathetic understanding of what we are trying to do. This is admittedly difficult because of the Diem regime's sensitivities but there is no other choice. Under existing policy we are helpless to correct the problem in Saigon. Washington should change the policy.

Kennedy asked what specific action I recommended. I said I thought he should personally instruct Washington agencies and the Mission in Saigon to cease excessively optimistic public statements, to stop complaining about unfavorable stories which only exacerbated the Mission's reluctance to level with newsmen, and most of all to take the newsmen into their confidence. I said this should apply particularly to events which the newsmen would find out about anyway. I cited as a horrible example the attempted secrecy about the change in the rules of engagement for American helicopter gunners.

I said the newsmen had accused us of doubting their patriotism, in refusing to trust them with confidential information, and that we should prove to them that this is not true, and in effect appeal to their patriotism by just such trust.

Kennedy appeared to be skeptical but willing to try. One result was a cable from the State Department to the U. S. Mission not long afterward. It was classified but the Moss Subcommittee report revealed that it was sent and that it "did advise cooperation with U.S. correspondents." It was a distinct improvement over No. 1006.

Back in Saigon at the end of May I was pleased to find that the top people in the Mission had learned that Kennedy was behind the new instructions, at my instigation, giving special new weight to my point of view. I hoped that this might be the beginning of a bright new era. Instead we were submerged immediately in the Buddhist crisis—and problems that probably could not have been solved if Kennedy himself had come out to buy the newsmen a round of beers at the Caravelle bar.

CHAPTER FIVE

The Buddhist Flash Fire

(1)

The Buddhist crisis in Vietnam began with a government blunder comparable with a presidential proclamation in the United States outlawing carol singing at Christmas. It banned public display of religious flags during the festivities on May 8, 1963, celebrating the 2527th anniversary of the birth of The Buddha. In Hue, a sleepy town at the northern tip of South Vietnam, there was bitter Buddhist resentment because only a few weeks earlier there had been no objection to widespread display of Roman Catholic flags honoring the twenty-fifth anniversary of the promotion to bishop of Diem's brother Ngo Dinh Thuc, Archbishop of Hue. There was a protest demonstration by several thousand Buddhists.

The Saigon error was then compounded by the local authorities. They called out troops equipped with armored vehicles to break up the demonstration. The crowd had gathered in a narrow street with no escape routes. In the ensuing melee nine Buddhists were killed and fourteen injured. Exactly what happened was never clarified. The Buddhists charged that the troops opened fire on the crowd and brutally crushed some of the victims under the wheels of their vehicles. The government initially claimed that a Viet Cong agent had thrown a grenade into the crowd, sparking a stampede in which some of the victims were crushed. (A post-coup court agreed with the Buddhists and sentenced the officer in command of the troops to life imprisonment.)

The event touched off a chain reaction that produced one of the unlikeliest political upheavals in modern times, climaxed by the regime's destruction six months later.

Not even the government claimed that the initial demonstration was a Buddhist conspiracy, or any kind of conspiracy. There probably was truth to the government claim that the flag ruling was meant to prohibit all flags in wartime except the national flag, that the Roman Catholic flags for Thuc's anniversary had been an oversight, and that the regime had not meant to be provocative.

It seemed likely that the clash was accidental, unpremeditated by either side.

As fate would have it, however, Hue not only was Thuc's diocese but also the semiautonomous political domain of a second brother of Diem, Ngo Dinh Can. Family prestige was involved. The palace reacted on the basis of "face" rather than common sense. Instead of swift action to apologize, to help the victims and to punish the responsible authorities, which possibly could have ended the whole affair, its only gesture of conciliation was to promise to "investigate."

The Buddhists next day staged a mass demonstration, estimated at some ten thousand persons, in front of the province chief's house in Hue. It was peaceful but the Hue authorities promptly banned any further demonstrations, adding to the Buddhists' anger. Thich (Venerable) Tam Chau, a prominent Buddhist leader in Hue, reacted with an open move to make it a national dispute. In a letter addressed to "all Buddhists in Vietnam," he appealed for action "to protect our religion in an orderly, peaceful, non-violent manner." He asked Buddhists to be "ready to march the road to martyrdom."

On May 13 the Hue leaders submitted five "aspirations" (demands) to the government: (1) Lift the ban on religious flags; (2) Give Buddhists the same legal standing as Roman

Catholics; (3) Give the Buddhists freedom to preach their religion; (4) Compensate victims of the May 8 riots; and (5) Punish the officials responsible for the May 8 incident.

The government stuck to its line that appropriate action would be taken after its investigation of the incident was completed. The Hue Buddhists then began a series of hunger strikes by nuns and bonzes (monks) inside their pagodas. They also called meetings in Hue on May 21 and again on May 28 of Buddhist leaders from other parts of the country.

On May 30 mass protest fasting by about a thousand bonzes and nuns began in pagodas at Hue and, for the first time, in Saigon. On the same date several hundred bonzes demonstrated peacefully before the National Assembly in the heart of Saigon. From USIS we could see them in their saffron robes squatting silently in the attitude of prayer, drawing the casual attention of passersby until police shooed them away. It was now undeniably a national issue.

Diem reluctantly began to take notice, more than three weeks after the Hue rioting. On May 31 he received a Buddhist delegation and promised vaguely to consider the five "aspirations." The response next day was a silent protest procession by some four thousand Buddhists in Hue. On the day after that there was violent rioting in Hue. About sixty persons were burned by tear gas grenades which troops used against the mob, exacerbating popular emotions.* Alarmed at last, Diem now dismissed three government officials in Hue, including the officer who commanded the troops on May 8, and created a special committee of ministers headed by Vice-President Nguyen Ngoc Tho, himself a devout Buddhist, to try to settle the dispute.

Three weeks earlier this might have been an adequate

---

* This was the "blister gas" incident mentioned earlier.

response. Events proved swiftly that it was now almost useless.

With astonishing speed the Buddhists had organized to the point where they could orchestrate demonstrations at will in every major city in South Vietnam. Command posts were set up in pagodas, especially the Tu Dam Pagoda at Hue and the Xa Loi Pagoda in Saigon, only a few blocks from Ambassador Nolting's house and next door to the USOM (economic aid) headquarters. The Buddhist leaders also began cultivating the American correspondents, providing English-speaking monks in the pagodas and arranging for demonstrators to carry English signs for television cameramen. In late May they began hinting to newsmen that if the government continued to reject their demands, there would be "protest suicides."

On the morning of June 11, at a street corner near the Xa Loi Pagoda, an old sedan pulled up. A monk in saffron robe got out and squatted cross-legged on the pavement. Two other monks poured a can of gasoline over his head and robe while he fingered his prayer beads. Then the squatting monk calmly lit a match. Instantly he was enveloped in billowing flame and smoke. Except for involuntary muscular twitches, he sat impassively in the Buddhist attitude of prayer, palms pressed together under his chin, until—after three or four minutes—his charred body toppled on its side in the street. He was later identified as Thich Quang Duc, seventy-three, a lifelong Buddhist priest. He was the first of seven suicides by burning in protest of the Diem regime.

Quang Duc's death was spectacularly not in vain. A photograph, taken by Malcolm Browne of Associated Press*

---

* Several American newsmen were tipped in advance by telephone calls that something might happen that morning, but there had previously been a number of false tips, and Browne was the only one who responded. Buddhist tips were seldom ignored thereafter.

an instant after the flames erupted, was published throughout the world. It had a shock effect of incalculable value to the Buddhist cause, becoming a symbol of the state of things in Vietnam that a thousand rosy, statistics-laden speeches could never undo.

(2)

From a Western viewpoint the Buddhist upheaval was a tangle of contradictions. Buddhism was a religion of withdrawal, of inward-looking meditation, of passive indifference to world affairs. Except for resistance to Western encroachment by the Buddhist emperors at Hue, it had never been a primary force in Vietnamese political affairs. Its leaders for the most part were men who had spent their lives in their pagodas. Yet their campaign against the Diem regime was executed with such sophisticated skill as to suggest that they had been trained on Madison Avenue.

The explanation related in part perhaps to the fact that Vietnam, unlike its neighbors, was occupied by the Chinese for a thousand years. The waves of Buddhist culture and philosophy that swept over much of the rest of Southeast Asia were diluted and corrupted in Vietnam by Confucianist, Animist and Taoist ideas from the north. In Cambodia, Laos and Thailand, Buddhism became a fundamentalist religion, dominating the life of the people. In Vietnam it became an orthodoxy competing with the day-to-day requirements of an essentially materialistic society inherited from China.

This could help explain why the Vietnamese were a more vigorous people than their neighbors. It could also be a clue to the fact that Communism had made more progress in Vietnam, like China, than elsewhere in Southeast Asia—perhaps because there was less spiritual resistance. And it would suggest that a Vietnamese Buddhist leader might have fewer philosophical problems in using his religious influence over the people for political objectives.

It was a question that needed exhaustive, expert study beyond my competence. Long after achievement of its initial objective, to topple Diem, Buddhist political power in Vietnam was clearly establishing itself as a permanent and important fact of life.

The U. S. Mission in Vietnam was criticized for failing to anticipate the Buddhist eruption. The same could be said about all the other foreign diplomatic missions in Saigon, the Diem regime and the American newsmen. There were one or two scholarly experts on Buddhism in the U. S. Mission who lectured occasionally to uniformly tiny audiences on topics like the differences between the Greater and Lesser Vehicles and the significance of the Noble Eightfold Path to Nirvana. They had a number of good friends among the senior bonzes in Saigon and Hue, but the experts were no less surprised than the rest of us when the Buddhists went into politics so spectacularly.

The Diem regime charged that the Buddhist leadership was a skillfully camouflaged front for the Viet Cong. On the basis of circumstantial evidence it was tempting to believe this. If Ho Chi Minh had planned the upheaval himself, it could hardly have been more helpful to his interests.

For years it had been a standard Communist technique throughout the world secretly to infiltrate legitimate organizations, like American labor unions, to work into key positions of leadership, and to push openly for Communist objectives only when conditions offered the maximum chance of success. The Buddhist rebellion exactly fitted this pattern, and the Buddhists in Vietnam had long been vulnerable to exactly this kind of penetration.

Their leadership was fragmented among a half dozen major organizations, plus innumerable local splinter groups. Half the Vietnamese people were already under total Communist control in the North, and another two or three million were under varying degrees of clandestine Viet Cong control in the South, providing an ideal base for the placing of agents in any organization. Unlike other faiths, moreover, there was no distinct Buddhist hierarchy, or anything resembling the discipline of the clergy in most Christian denominations. It was relatively easy to pass as a Buddhist monk, requiring little more than a shaved head, a robe and an attitude of humility.

The Buddhists were also vulnerable to Communist exploitation because of their legitimate grievances against the Diem regime. There was a violent controversy about this during the 1963 crisis, stimulated by extravagant Buddhist charges of "persecution." This was absurd. Better than two thirds of the generals in Diem's armed forces, and of the ministers in his cabinet, were Buddhists. For years Diem's innumerable enemies had dredged up every possible charge against him, but it was only after the May 8 incident at Hue that they discovered that he was also guilty of oppressing the Buddhists.

The Diem regime did, however, discriminate against the Buddhists. There was a Vietnamese law inherited from the French—Point 2 of the "aspirations"—which treated the Roman Catholic Church as a religion and the Buddhists as an "association." It was loosely applied, affected only such legal matters as forms of property ownership, and did not interfere with Buddhist teachings, but it was nevertheless unjust. Catholic communities generally received more government help. Catholic civilian officials and military officers tended to get ahead faster than Buddhists, so much so that a good many of them decided to be "converted" to Christianity in the interest of their careers. Mostly the discrimination was unthinking and arrogant rather than malicious, like the flag ruling at Hue, but it was real enough to be exploited.

The Vietnamese Buddhists, in short, offered a classic opportunity for a Communist sleeper play. In a country whose every sinew had been diseased to some degree by the Communists, that was divided against itself and tottering on collapse, it simply did not make sense to accept that the Viet Cong had overlooked the Buddhists. This was further suggested by the extraordinary speed with which the Buddhists organized themselves, as though they were receiving secret professional advice. There was similar ground for suspicion in the fact that the movement swiftly changed from simple protest to a deliberate effort to unseat the government.

Apart from this kind of speculative reasoning, however, not a scrap of hard evidence of Communist penetration of the Buddhists turned up during the 1963 crisis. This was the fact, moreover, despite frantic efforts by the Diem regime's considerable intelligence apparatus to find such evidence to discredit the Buddhists. United States intelligence also tried and failed.

The conclusion was therefore inescapable that the Buddhist upheaval primarily was just what it looked like, an accidental flash fire.*

The main reason that it ignited was universal unrest and discontent with the regime among the politically conscious elements of the South Vietnamese people, meaning the urban population for the most part. (The upheaval stirred relatively little interest among the peasants.) This was a long-standing condition. It had been deepened, however, by the failures of successive military coup attempts, suggesting that there was no hope that the military could unseat Diem. There also was growing disillusionment because

* Communist influence among the Buddhists was still an unknown more than a year later when Buddhist mobs had again taken to the streets for political objectives. Some of the Buddhist leaders were showing neutralist inclinations, but so were a good many other people, like the editorial writers of the New York *Times*.

the massive new American intervention, now eighteen months old, was not bringing about speedy victory over the Viet Cong, if indeed victory was assured at all. The nation was ripe for almost any kind of opportunity to express its resentment of the Diem regime, while at the same time rejecting the immediate Communist alternative.

The regime's ineptitude was incredible in picking a fight with the Buddhists. They were the only mass movement in the country, apart from the Viet Cong, that the regime did not totally control, and therefore the only non-Communist force in the country that could polarize opposition to the regime—which was exactly the way it worked. Through the months that followed, the regime compounded the original blunder by what seemed like a compulsion to do everything else wrong, too. It never really understood what was happening, revealing such political insensitivity as to clinch the argument that it was also incapable of winning the much more difficult political struggle against the Viet Cong.

It was a rule of thumb that about fifteen percent of the Vietnamese people were Christians, another fifteen percent members of such eccentric sects as the Cao Dai and Hoa Hao, and most of the balance, or about seventy percent, at least nominally Buddhist. Of these only a small minority were practicing Buddhists, just as only a small minority of American Christians regularly go to church. As the crisis developed, however, and Buddhist propagandists spread the word that the faith was under attack, hundreds of thousands of normally apathetic Vietnamese Buddhists flocked to the pagodas, just as millions of Americans who never go to church would rally if they thought the Christian faith was in jeopardy. Vietnam's Roman Catholic leaders, Diem, Nhu and Mme. Nhu (herself a convert from Buddhism), did more to bring new life to Vietnamese Buddhism than any other event in modern times.

The Buddhist leaders themselves emerged in the same

accidental fashion. Some were motivated by genuine religious considerations. Others were opportunists who disliked Diem, recognized that a chance to unseat him had been thrust upon them and reacted accordingly.

This balance of opportunism and sincere religious protest prevailed throughout the crisis. Obviously, for example, the suicides were motivated by extreme religious fervor, if not fanaticism. The same was true of the thousands of politically unaware monks and nuns who fasted and chanted prayers in their barricaded pagodas. It was equally obvious that the advance telephone tips to foreign newsmen to publicize the suicides were politically motivated. The dichotomy was so subtle and harmonious that it baffled the regime, the U. S. Mission, and the Western world.

Still another unlikely aspect of the Buddhist upheaval was the probability that it could not have succeeded without the help of the American press and radio/TV. Expressed more bluntly, American news coverage of the upheaval contributed directly to destruction of a national U.S. policy of direct importance to the security of the United States, in an area where we had deployed nearly twenty thousand Americans, where we were spending some $500 million a year, at the only point in the world where we were engaged in support of a shooting war against a Communist enemy.

This was not, however, a malicious achievement. There were individual newsmen in Vietnam, and editorial writers and columnists back home, who hated Diem and enjoyed writing about his difficulties. But the reporting on the Buddhist crisis, for the most part, was straight. There was little sensationalism. None was necessary.

What happened perhaps could best be compared with the role of American news media in the short-lived headline strutting of the late Senator Joseph McCarthy. Mal Browne's photograph of Quang Duc's suicide no doubt produced an exaggerated impression of what was going on in Vietnam, for example, especially in view of the fact that the Buddhists planned it that way. Yet the burning was certainly news and Browne could hardly be accused of distorting his photograph. Similarly McCarthy's reckless accusations misled the American public on the degree of Communist penetration of the U. S. Government, which was the way McCarthy planned it, too. Yet McCarthy was a senator, chairman of an important committee, and the press had no choice but to publish what he said.

In both cases the newsmen simply did their job. If there was damage, it arose from public reaction to knowledge which would otherwise have been denied. The issue, if there was one, was the American system itself, not the reporting of the news. In the McCarthy case the press was vindicated in the sense that it was continued publicity, revealing the man as he was to the American public, that led to his downfall, as well as his rise. A good many people believed the Buddhist upheaval, and the press role in making it count, did the United States a favor in discrediting a policy that was becoming untenable anyway.

The Buddhists' liaison with the newsmen developed accidently. Their first hope was for help from the U. S. Mission. They quickly discovered that the Mission seemed to side with the government. American officials were not even permitted to establish contact with the Buddhists, except through clandestine channels, for fear the regime would suspect us of helping them. The Buddhists were unaware of the considerable pressure that the Mission applied to the regime secretly on their behalf. They turned to the newsmen as the only Americans to whom they could tell their story.

The newsmen were no second-best channel, and the Buddhists soon recognized a good thing. They had found an open line to the American people and the rest of the world over the heads of both the U. S. Mission and the Diem regime. What was more, the newsmen also became a channel to the Vietnamese people. It was this unexpected development that made the role of the newsmen so dramatically important in keeping the Buddhist rebellion going.

The explanation was radio. There had always been a good audience in Vietnam for foreign broadcasts because Diem's press and radio were so heavily censored and so cluttered with dreary Personalist propaganda. Now the word quickly got around that uncensored reports from newsmen in Saigon on the Buddhist crisis could be heard regularly on news programs beamed to Vietnam, in both Vietnamese and English, by the Voice of America, the British Broadcasting Corporation and Radio Australia. The Buddhist upheaval was mainly an urban phenomenon and it was the urban population of Vietnam that had radio receivers.

By the fall of 1963, as a result of this, VOA was reaching Vietnamese audiences of unprecedented size, performing a function that could be compared with the BBC broadcasts to occupied Europe during World War II. Students in Saigon, as a symbol of rebellion against the regime, began using a Vietnamese phrase with a double meaning in greeting each other. One meaning was: "What do you have to say for yourself?" The other was: "What does the Voice have to say?"

The Diem regime quickly realized that this was happening and complained to the U. S. Mission. VOA practice, under the direction of Edward R. Murrow, was to give foreign listeners access to the same news that was available to Americans, regardless of its good or bad effect on U.S. policy. The reasoning was that any other practice would weaken VOA's credibility, and that American policies in any case were good enough to stand on their own merits. We continued relaying news reports from Vietnam.

In a land where almost everyone had been against them,

the newsmen suddenly found themselves being treated like heroes at pagodas all over the country. Occasionally they were even applauded in the streets by Buddhist demonstrators. The Buddhists obtained mimeograph machines to crank out press releases, installed special telephones, bowed and scraped and served endless cups of tea to visiting newsmen. They were shrewd enough not to lie very often, and they seldom criticized stories they disliked. They made a point of finding out what the newsmen wanted, and how they wanted to be treated, and did their best to comply—in diametric contrast to the palace and the U. S. Mission.

The Buddhists also trusted the newsmen. While General Harkins' headquarters continued to refuse them advance tips on military operations, the Buddhists made sure they were advised well in advance of demonstrations, public statements, messages to Diem, and burnings. Harkins refused the minuscule risk that advance tips might somehow get back to the Viet Cong. The Buddhists accepted the large risk that tips on their plans would leak to the palace, with disastrous results from Diem's police—arrests, beatings and worse. They were not betrayed.

On the contrary the newsmen refused even to pass on such tips to the U. S. Mission on a confidential basis. One reason was their general bitterness toward the Mission. Another was their fear that the Mission would tell the palace. Their fear may have been justified. Thus the Mission's astigmatic treatment of the newsmen over the previous year or two was repaid in kind. The press had suddenly become a factor of vital importance in a crisis threatening basic U.S. policy, yet we found ourselves with close to zero influence on how the newsmen covered it. And now it was *we* who had become the bad security risk.

Just about everything seemed to be going for the Buddhists. The Diem regime found itself caught between twentieth-century public relations techniques and mass emotions rooted in the misty depths of Asian history.

The Buddhist maneuvers became increasingly political, unmistakably directed far beyond the five "aspirations" set forth at Hue. By midsummer they were verging on general insurrection. Yet the leaders remained the same, all of them legitimate Buddhist bonzes. The command posts remained the pagodas. The movement continued to be known as a "Buddhist" phenomenon. Whatever the Diem regime did, even in the legitimate interests of its own security, invariably appeared to the world as action against "the Buddhists" and thus as shameful religious repression.

Like the civil rights forces in the United States—whom the Buddhists may have copied—the bonzes for the most part limited their tactics to passive demonstrations. They could summon crowds of ten or fifteen thousand, but they seldom attacked anything. Instead they confronted the regime with thousands of people, most of them poorly dressed coolie classes and students, along with monks and nuns, kneeling in prayer in the streets while their leaders heaped insults upon the government, including vulgar jokes about Mme. Nhu, over blaring public address systems that could be heard for blocks. Inevitably the police reacted. Inevitably the result was a new crop of television film of Diem's police brutally beating up defenseless Buddhists, and all too often hauling them away in trucks bearing the clasped-hands emblem of American economic assistance.

This would then be capped from time to time by a fiery suicide, shocking both the world and the Vietnamese people into emotional spasms.

A definitive explanation of this phenomenon also required scholarly research beyond my scope. It was a well-known fact that Asians had a different attitude than Westerners toward suicide as such. It had been dignified sometimes by ritual such as Japanese hara-kiri and the kamikaze pilots of

World War II. It was more commonly invoked in Asia than in the West in the wake of political or military failure. Vietnam's Trung Sisters, for example, leaped to their deaths in a river when the Chinese invaders returned and defeated their armies. It may also have been relevant that Buddhism teaches defiance of pain and idealizes self-sacrifice for others. But my superficial research revealed no evidence of Buddhists, in Vietnam or elsewhere, previously resorting to multiple suicide as a means to a political objective.

What happened in Vietnam in 1963 apparently was unique, a bizarre product of endless war and desperation, of television cameras and ancient superstition, of Western ideas clashing with Asian mystique.

The suicides knifed into the Vietnamese psyche no less dramatically than they unnerved Westerners. A servant in an American home, a middle-aged Vietnamese Buddhist who had worked for foreigners all his life and never before volunteered an opinion on anything, met his employer at the door on the evening of the first burning. His eyes wide, more with fear than anger, he said: "I have always believed in President Diem. But now this has happened. This proves that the President is bad." Events were to prove that millions of other unsophisticated Vietnamese, as well as foreigners, were persuaded by the same illogic. Nor was the servant alone when he added as a foregone conclusion: "America will know now that President Diem is not good."

This kind of reasoning was multiplied a thousandfold a few days later when the body of Quang Duc was cremated. The bonzes announced that his heart had not been reduced to ashes, and this was regarded as a miracle. A charred object, said to be the heart, was placed in a glass casing and installed in a prominent position in Xa Loi Pagoda, where it became an object of veneration.

Quang Duc acquired an aura akin to sainthood. The powerful emotions of horror and dread of the unknown somehow became linked with a sense of absolute rightness of the Buddhist cause in the minds of the people. At the same time, Quang Duc's act and the posthumous fame that it brought to him sparked a chain reaction of imitators. The Buddhist leaders by midsummer were claiming to newsmen that dozens of bonzes all over the country stood ready to burn themselves to death and were in fact being restrained with difficulty. They staged a grotesque press conference with the eighty-year-old mother of a prominent government official who said she had volunteered.

Saigon was like a mental institution. Neither the Vietnamese nor the Americans understood what was happening, nor what to do about it, nor even what to say. There were Americans who made jokes about "bonze fires" or "hot cross bonzes" or "Buddhist cookouts," almost as an escape mechanism. There was also something hypnotic about the mood. One day the young son of an officer of the American Embassy poured gasoline on his clothes and struck a match. He was seriously burned before the fire was put out. His only explanation: "I wanted to see what it was like."

(3)

There was a personal drama behind the scenes of the American reaction to the Buddhist upheaval. It arose out of the coincidence that Ambassador Nolting had left Saigon on a well-earned home leave with his family just before the crisis developed. His escape was a cruise with his family through the Greek Islands.

It was a last-straw touch to Nolting's anguished tour of duty that in his absence the U. S. switched back to a "tough" policy with Diem and it failed miserably. It will remain one of the unanswerable "ifs" of history that Nolting's low-key way, at the moment of ultimate challenge, might have been more effective.

Unlike our attitude toward the state of the war, there were no U.S. illusions about the Buddhist upheaval. The U. S. Mission, like everyone else, was surprised by the crisis, but quickly recognized its gravity. On orders from Washington, Trueheart applied direct, relentless, table-hammering pressure on Diem such as the United States had seldom before attempted with a sovereign, friendly government. For a period of weeks Trueheart averaged nearly a call a day on Diem, plus innumerable visits and telephone calls to lesser officials.

He urged Diem to repair all the Buddhist grievances forthwith, to accept responsibility for the May 8 killings, and to indemnify the victims and apologize, perhaps by visiting Hue himself to do so. The campaign developed such heat that Trueheart was soon protesting, almost hourly, such trivial details as the placing of a police barricade in front of the Xa Loi Pagoda.

If Diem had immediately heeded Trueheart's advice he probably could have stopped the upheaval before it got started. It was beyond his capacity. Instead he made token gestures, always too slowly, too little and done so grudgingly as to waste the psychological effect. On the question of compensation for the Hue victims, for example, Diem ordered that generous payments be made but tried to keep them secret on the ground that they might be taken as a government admission of guilt for the killings. After the Quang Duc suicide the rebellion reached such proportions that nothing the government might have done would have made much difference.

In mid-June the Buddhist leaders agreed on a "settlement" with the Tho Committee, and then abrogated it the next day with rioting in the streets of Saigon. Police resorted to tear gas and dozens of arrests to break up the demonstration.

Thereafter American pressure probably was counterproductive, serving mainly to make Diem and Nhu even more intractable. The regime bitterly resented Trueheart, both because of what he said and because its pride was hurt by the fact that he was only a chargé. It reasoned that there was no true "persecution" of the Buddhists and that therefore their actions were no more than another political conspiracy to destroy the government. In a sense this was true. What the regime failed to recognize was, first, the fact that Trueheart spoke for the U. S. Government and, second, that the Buddhists were attracting overwhelming mass support from the Vietnamese people. The requirement was swift political action appealing to the people, not just repressive police measures.

Almost compulsively the regime repeatedly provoked the Buddhists in public statements, defying Trueheart's pleas for conciliation. Mme. Nhu told interviewers that the Buddhists were Communists, or Communist dupes. She remarked to an American TV correspondent that "all the Buddhists have done for this country is to barbecue a monk." On another occasion she said if she had her way the Buddhists "should be beaten ten times more." The *Times of Vietnam*, probably on Mme. Nhu's orders, reported that Quang Duc had been "drugged" before his suicide. Nhu told visitors that Buddhism was "an international neutralist conspiracy."

In its own contorted fashion the regime apparently read Trueheart's pressuring as evidence that the United States Government was really on the side of the Buddhists. Why else did we urge making concessions to them? Mme. Nhu publicly said the United States attitude was "blackmail." Nhu began dropping hints that there were too many Americans in Vietnam and that three or four thousand should be sent home.

In despair Trueheart in June resorted to a formal warning to Diem that if he continued repressive measures against the Buddhists the United States would be forced to "dissociate" itself publicly from such actions, as indeed we did two months later. The warning was a momentous step. It amounted to a direct, official command from the United States. Public dissociation could have disastrous results, encouraging the Buddhists, heartening the Viet Cong, strengthening the regime's foreign critics, perhaps even stimulating the Vietnamese Army to try another coup.

The regime regarded the warning as an insufferable humiliation, and such influence as Trueheart may still have possessed was dramatically weakened. The warning also was the beginning of a split inside the U. S. Mission that was subsequently to attract considerable unfriendly publicity.

One faction, including Ambassador Nolting when he returned a few weeks later, contended that the warning was an ultimate affront, provoking the regime to defy all U.S. wishes, to intensify repression of the Buddhists out of spite, and thus to wipe out all hope of preventing eventual disaster. "No government in the world can take this kind of treatment," said one officer at the time. "Diem could well declare Trueheart *persona non grata.* I hope he does." The other faction argued that the regime was headed for disaster anyway, that the warning therefore could do no harm, while there was an outside chance that it would shock the regime into corrective measures.

Inevitably all this was further exacerbated by the American press. Trueheart tried to keep his negotiations secret, but details soon began leaking. They led to a series of hostile, told-you-so dispatches. Neil Sheehan of UPI, for example, reported on June 10 that "the United States is at present in a curious dilemma where it is unable to do anything to retrieve the situation because it lacks any real influences over Catholic President Ngo Dinh Diem. . . . American officials here are visibly rattled. . . . Although the United States will inevitably share in the outcome of the dispute between Diem and the Buddhists, it finds itself in the impotent position of having the Diem regime refuse its advice on the Buddhist issue, just as it has on so many other issues in the past. . . . One American official describes the U.S. position this way: 'We have been playing chicken with Diem for years and he knows he can tell us to go to hell and get away with it.'" It was all true.

Four days later, on page one under a Washington dateline, the New York *Times* reported in detail just about everything that Trueheart had been doing, including the "dissociate" warning. The story read as though the reporter, Max Frankel, had been shown the file of classified cables from Saigon. The palace was outraged. The effect on Trueheart's negotiations was like putting a plate of watery mashed potatoes into a deep freezer.

In its mounting frustration and anger the Diem regime turned almost by habit upon the foreign newsmen again. Diem suggested to a visitor that the Associated Press had "bribed" Quang Duc to burn himself so that it could make a profitable photograph. The Frankel story reinforced the regime's suspicion that much of what the newsmen were writing secretly reflected the true opinions of the U. S. Government. It was becoming increasingly aware of the degree to which publicity was helping the Buddhists, and suspected the newsmen of deliberately plotting against the regime. This no doubt was reinforced by the fact, which surely was being picked up by the regime's intelligence apparatus, that some of the newsmen were talking openly about the possibility of a coup d'état and obviously hoped for one.

On the morning of July 7 several newsmen were watching a Buddhist procession in an alley outside a Saigon pagoda. Suddenly they were surrounded by a gang of Nhu's plainclothes police. There was a scuffle. One of the policemen smashed a camera with a rock. Malcolm Browne and Peter

Arnett, both of AP, were roughed up and possibly would have been seriously injured but for the intervention of David Halberstam of the New York *Times,* a powerful six-footer who held off the thugs until they could all escape. It could have been an accident, but the evidence was persuasive that the police deliberately attacked the newsmen.

Trueheart instructed me to protest to Information Director Tao, which I did. Tao said it was an unfortunate case of somebody "losing his head." The newsmen bitterly rejected this. In a stormy session in Trueheart's office they demanded a formal diplomatic protest to Diem. Trueheart refused on the grounds that he lacked adequate information on what happened. This was true, but it also implied that we doubted the newsmen's account, adding to their anger. That evening they fired off a protest cable to President Kennedy, including a complaint that the U. S. Mission was indifferent to their problems.

(Kennedy responded a few days later that the U. S. Embassy in Saigon had reported "the full measure of our concern to the Government of Vietnam." He also said that Robert Manning, Assistant Secretary of State for Public Affairs, would visit Saigon to investigate the situation further.)

On the day after the scuffle the police called in Browne and Arnett and interrogated them for four hours, politely but insistently, on the line that they had "attacked" the plainclothesmen. The possibility loomed of two AP correspondents being arrested, jailed and formally charged with assault. Trueheart appealed to Nguyen Dinh Thuan, secretary to the presidency, to stop anything like that. Thuan said Diem was pondering what to do.

That evening a delegation of eight correspondents came to my office and demanded to be told what, if anything, the Mission was doing. On Trueheart's orders I said I could not discuss it. Thereupon the newsmen exploded in such a tumult of four-letter invective on the theme of American "gutlessness" that an officer next door came in to see if I needed physical protection.

It was during this period that word reached Saigon that Ambassador Nolting was returning for a month or two only and would then be succeeded by Henry Cabot Lodge. There was no explanation of what this was all about, but there was immediate speculation in Saigon that it meant a change, at long last, in U.S. policy.

(4)

Ambassador Nolting, meantime, continued his vacation in Europe. He knew from an occasional newspaper that the Diem regime was having trouble with the Buddhists, but he was unaware of the gravity of the crisis. He learned from a news bulletin on a ship in mid-Atlantic that Lodge had been appointed to succeed him within a few weeks.

When the ship docked, Nolting went immediately to Washington to be briefed, canceled the rest of his leave and proceeded to Saigon, arriving on July 11.

It was a sweltering rainy season morning, humidity and temperature both near ninety. The awkwardness of Nolting's position was compounded by the coincidence that Diem happened to be returning from a trip at the same hour. All his ministers were there to meet him, but only one even said hello to Nolting, whose plane pulled up fifty yards away. Since Diem was using the VIP terminal, Nolting had to receive some twenty to thirty newsmen in a small waiting room that soon was unbearably hot and smoky.

Dripping with sweat in the blinding white glare of TV lights, Nolting read a prepared statement which gently implied U.S. dissatisfaction with press and religious repression in Vietnam and concluded: "But victory, in my judgment, is well on its way in Vietnam—provided only that unity of purpose and perseverance in action are not weakened by internal dissension." The newsmen immediately opened fire. Did he still believe, as he had said some eighteen months earlier, that the Vietnamese people should cease criticizing Diem and get on with the war? Nolting managed to duck most of the thrusts, but it was a sour morning.

Nolting was not the kind of man to reveal his personal emotions on an issue such as this, but there was no question that he was deeply upset by what he found in Saigon—two years of work in a shambles.

Saigon was a city of nervous uncertainty and rumors. Gia Long Palace, where Diem and the Nhus lived and worked, was isolated by police and barb wire for a radius of at least two blocks.* On occasions of particularly urgent rumors of Buddhist demonstrations the radius was extended several blocks farther, creating monstrous jams of fuming, sweltering people and vehicles. Special additional jams were frequently created when Diem or one of the Nhus made a trip to the airport, or even to a social function, because the police would clear all traffic from the route they planned to use, forcing hundreds of vehicles into narrow side streets. So often that it seemed deliberate the family regularly chose to make such outings during the rush hours. It was infuriating, intensely uncomfortable, insulting to the people. Being Asians they took it impassively at the idle pleasure of the Ngo Dinh family.

The regime's relations with the U. S. Mission were near breakdown as a result of our pressure tactics. Just after Nolting's return, President Kennedy appealed to the regime in a

* The family moved to nearby Gia Long after Doc Lap (Independence) Palace was bombed in February 1962. The regime undertook complete reconstruction of Doc Lap, which was badly damaged, but little more than the skeleton had been completed at the time of the coup d'état. Among Americans in Saigon the project became known as "the last strategic hamlet."

press conference to "respect the rights of others," meaning the Buddhists. The U. S. thus was already verging on "dissociation." Nhu's censors cut the President's remark out of the version of the press conference circulated to the Saigon newspapers. This was an unprecedented affront to the United States.

Nolting set out quietly but urgently to try to set things right, working twelve and fourteen hours daily seven days a week. His first problem was Browne and Arnett. On the day after his return we received an intelligence report that the Nhus were demanding that Diem order their arrest and prosecution. This would certainly have stimulated such an outcry in the United States that Kennedy would have been forced to public protest, with incalculable repercussions in Vietnam. The press problem was threatening to become a flashpoint of American revulsion at the Diem regime.

It was at this juncture that Assistant Secretary Manning arrived as Kennedy's special emissary to the newsmen. He was greeted by a Buddhist demonstration in front of Nolting's residence. Next day there were three clashes in Saigon between Buddhist demonstrators and Diem's police. In one of these the police charged a gathering of several hundred Buddhist nuns and bonzes squatting in prayer in front of a pagoda. It was witnessed by newsmen and publicized the world over. After the rioting the police laid siege to the Xa Loi Pagoda, surrounding it with barb wire and armed men. The Buddhists exploited this by tossing a letter, appealing for help, over the wall of the USOM compound next door, and it too received worldwide attention.

Manning listened to the newsmen's grievances at length. He also conferred with Nhu and Diem, attempting to persuade them not to bring charges against Browne and Arnett, to readmit NBC's Jim Robinson and otherwise to accept the realities of living with American newsmen. A highly perceptive, experienced newsman himself, Manning tried to make the point to Diem that free, critical news reporting, even if not always friendly, was better than no coverage at all of such a difficult situation because it reassured the American people that they were not being deceived about their commitment in Vietnam. Nolting, who attended the meeting, recommended a gesture of good will to permit Manning to reassure President Kennedy that Vietnam regretted its troubles with the newsmen as much as we did.

Diem replied that the newsmen were conducting a "cold war" against the regime, that they were "low caliber" and "insulting," and that they should be "objective" (translation: pro-Diem). He did, however, drop the charges against Browne and Arnett, and soon afterward he permitted Robinson to reenter Vietnam. The Manning visit thus was successful in a limited sense. Not much else came of it. Not much else could have come of it, short of replacing not only Nolting, but also Harkins, the Ngo Dinh family, and the newsmen—all of whom were hopelessly incompatible.

Nolting was able to reestablish communication with the regime, but his efforts to persuade Diem to make peace with the Buddhists made little progress. The main reason was the Nhus. In late July I attended a dinner where the guests included Nolting, several other top American and Vietnamese officials, and Nhu. For five hours we listened to Nhu talk, a rambling, nearly incoherent monologue. It was particularly memorable because Nhu allowed himself one or two extra brandies. There was a trace of thickness in his speech, and he joked wryly several times about "*in vino veritas*" as he launched into new tangents.

The substance of what he said was so fuzzy that we could not even compose a meaningful report to Washington on it. But there were numerous glimpses of absolute intransigence —and worse. Among my recollections:

Diem was inept and "weak," an incompetent leader because he tried to compromise with the Buddhists. He, Nhu, was ready to quit the government if Diem failed to be tough, and indeed he had already submitted his resignation if Diem wanted to accept it. The Buddhists were neutralist plotters working for Sihanouk and other "fools" among Vietnam's neighbors. The police had attacked the bonzes only because they were "tired and separated from their families" and therefore could not control themselves. The American newsmen in Vietnam were "disgusting." They had insulted Mme. Nhu by reporting that she had outlawed taxi dance halls because the girls had refused to pay big enough kickbacks to her. (A charge none of us had heard before.)

As he was leaving, well after midnight, Nhu remarked: "If the Buddhists wish to have another barbecue I will be glad to supply the gasoline and a match."

During his last weeks Nolting also attempted to reestablish communication with American newsmen through a series of individual interviews. His idea was a last-ditch effort to counter the mounting damage to U.S. policy that press coverage of the Buddhists was inflicting. He made the mistake of trying once again to be defensive about Diem and the Nhus. Once again it backfired, loosing a new storm of merciless criticism.

The error was a casual remark to an interviewer that there had been no "persecution" of the Buddhists. Semantically he was right, at least with regard to Vietnamese history prior to May 8. But Nolting made the remark less than a fortnight after photographs of Diem's police attacking the bonzes in front of Xa Loi Pagoda had been published all over the world.

The Buddhists reacted instantly and skillfully. They issued a communiqué asserting that Nolting's remark had been his "last gift to Ngo Dinh Diem," and charging that he knew nothing about the Buddhist cause in any case because he had never been inside a pagoda. A desperately earnest American correspondent telephoned to ask me if this was true. I said I did not think it was particularly relevant. His voice taut with emotion the reporter said: "This is a formal demand for an official statement. Has or has not the American Ambassador ever been inside a pagoda?" The tone was exactly like an attorney for a congressional committee asking a witness if he had ever belonged to the Communist Party. I solemnly declared that yes the Ambassador had visited a pagoda.

In this deadly humorless atmosphere everything Nolting touched seemed to turn to sand. In early August the palace telephoned the Embassy and announced that it had been decided to name a strategic hamlet after Nolting as a symbol of appreciation for his work in Vietnam. Nolting tried to duck by saying he was busy. The palace trapped him by saying the ceremony could be held on whatever day the Ambassador suggested. It was a bad idea, if only because the Viet Cong would surely feel it mandatory to attack any hamlet named after the American Ambassador. But Nolting felt he had to go through with it.

Everything went wrong. Nolting wanted to keep the ceremony secret, but news of it leaked to the press well in advance. Then on the day before the affair an American gunner on a helicopter accidently triggered a machine gun, spraying the hamlet with bullets and wounding six inhabitants. That evening a Vietnamese Army jeep struck and injured a small boy in the hamlet. Reports to Saigon on what happened were garbled. A news agency reported erroneously not only that both incidents occurred in the Ambassador's presence but also that it was Nolting's jeep that struck the boy and that it killed him.

On August 5, just two weeks before Nolting's departure, came the event that we all had feared: a second suicide by burning. It happened in the coastal town of Phan Thiet and seemed to touch off a contagion. During the next eleven days there were three more, two at Hue, one at the coastal town of Ninh Hoa. Each suicide sent a new shudder through the country. Saigon was seething with rumors of an imminent coup d'état. An AP dispatch reported that South Vietnam was caught in "the flames of general rebellion."

Nolting made one last effort, urging Diem repeatedly over a period of several days to issue a public statement appealing for reconciliation with the Buddhists. Diem reluctantly agreed, but as usual it came out as a compromise with the Nhus. In an interview with Marguerite Higgins of the New York *Herald Tribune,* Diem insisted that conciliation had been his policy all along, but he added that this policy was "irreversible." Nolting regarded this as a significant commitment. The text of Diem's remarks to Miss Higgins was given the full worldwide treatment by USIS.

On August 15 Nolting departed. At the airport he insisted stoutly that the Vietnamese Government was conducting a "winning program." Then he shook hands sadly with members of his staff and disappeared with a wave into the cavernous door of a Pan American jet, ending one of the most tumultuous tours of duty that any American foreign service officer ever experienced anywhere.

Less than six days later, just after midnight on August 21, I was awakened by an urgent call from the Embassy: "Hurry down here. The police are attacking the pagodas." It was a carefully coordinated military operation. In Hue and Saigon heavily armed Special Forces troops and police assaulted the barricaded Buddhists. Midst screams, gunfire, grenade explosions, and the eerie banging of gongs, they rounded up hundreds of bonzes and hauled them away in trucks. Dozens of Buddhists were wounded and reportedly (the facts were never clarified) several were killed. The pagodas were occupied by troops. It was ruthless, comprehensive suppression of the Buddhist movement, accompanied by a proclamation of martial law and curfew throughout the country, obviously timed for the interim between Nolting and Lodge.

Thus the Diem regime's final gesture to Fritz Nolting: flagrant abrogation of its solemn last word to this fine man who had staked his career on the regime's defense.

(5)

In declaring war against the Buddhists the Diem regime not only defied the United States and scrapped its promises to Nolting, but also failed to make any effort at all to save American face. In Asia this was perhaps the greater insult. We were confronted with a situation that must have been unprecedented in the history of United States foreign operations.

To prevent American intervention to protect the Buddhists the regime had devoted at least as much planning to immobilization of the U. S. Mission as it had to the operation itself, and most successfully.

Within an hour after the attacks the regime cut off the home telephones of all the senior American officials in Saigon, as well as our office circuits. The only exception—in deference perhaps to the fact that there was still a war on with the Viet Cong—was Harkins' headquarters, including a tie line to the Embassy. For the next forty-eight hours this was the Embassy's sole means of telephone communication with the rest of Saigon. (To avoid a repetition of this we later installed a walkie-talkie radio net among senior American homes and offices. The practice was to leave the receiver turned on at all times, especially at night, and its soft background crackling like green logs burning in a fireplace became part of our lives.)

On the excuse of "security" the barriers around Xa Loi Pagoda were expanded to include the USOM building next door. The bizarre result was that the Americans engaged in giving away more than one million dollars a day to the Vietnamese Government were unable to go to work. The USOM director, Joseph Brent, spent the next two days sitting around the Embassy fuming with frustration.

We discovered that the regime had drawn up elaborate cover plans in advance of the operation to allay American questions about the movement of several thousand Special Forces troops into the Saigon area. It was supposed to be a raid on Viet Cong forces threatening the suburbs. Harkins' headquarters was as neatly bamboozled as the rest of the Mission.

Not so the newsmen. Several of them had acquired a high frequency radio receiver with which a Vietnamese assistant monitored the Saigon police net. Unusual radio activity just before the raids stirred their suspicions enough so they were present at Xa Loi Pagoda in time to witness part of the action. UPI's Sheehan had also done a study of the American military telephone system as a potential means for getting out the story in the event of a major development such as this when commercial facilities would be shut down. On the morning of the crackdown his enterprise paid off handsomely. Using an authoritative, official-sounding voice, he asked a sleepy American GI operator for Clark Field in the Philippines. The operator replied that Clark was unreachable, but "how about Bangkok?"

It was a fine, old-fashioned news beat. Some hours later two of Sheehan's competitors complained to me that he had somehow cheated and perhaps also been helped secretly by the U. S. Mission, which was a huge joke in view of the way the Mission felt about Sheehan.

The city was under the command of a military governor, General Ton That Dinh, who announced on the Saigon radio that the government had been forced to act because the Buddhists were "political speculators (engaged in) illegal actions." The regime also claimed to have found hidden weapons in the pagodas and charged the Buddhists with plotting a coup d'état. Besides a 9 P.M. curfew and rigid military censorship on outgoing press cables, Dinh blocked off huge segments of the city with police and Special Forces troops, creating traffic jams that made our earlier troubles seem trivial.

Dinh himself was a boisterous, eccentric, whisky-drinking paratrooper whom most Americans liked but few would have chosen for such a critical job. For all his tough public posture he behaved privately as though he expected to be struck by lightning momentarily—for offending the Americans perhaps. On the morning after the raids he received an American visitor, an old friend, in his office, mixed drinks and delivered a four-hour desk-hammering harangue about his intention to destroy any further Buddhist plots. Throughout the four hours no fewer than four paratroopers stood around the American at a six-foot range pointing submachine guns at his head, tensing ominously if he so much as reached for a cigarette.

The lightning did strike eventually, but for the moment the U. S. Mission found itself at a dead end. Our only instructions from Washington were to await the arrival of Ambassador Lodge.

In the meantime we found ourselves in the hotel business. At the height of the raids two bonzes had managed to scramble over the Xa Loi Pagoda wall into the USOM compound, where they begged sanctuary. It was an awkward dilemma. If we permitted them to stay, the regime no doubt would say this proved U.S. complicity with the Buddhists. If we turned them over to the police the United States would seem to be acquiescing in the crackdown on the Buddhists. The decision was a compromise: they could stay unless Diem would guarantee safe conduct. The regime indignantly refused. The bonzes stayed for weeks, with free board and lodgings from the United States Government.

A day or two later three more bonzes were walking casually along the sidewalk in front of the U. S. Embassy. Suddenly they broke out and dashed for the entrance. A Vietnamese policeman on duty there tried to stop them but they made it inside. This was more serious than the USOM case. One of the three was Thich Tri Quang, one of the top leaders of the Buddhist movement, who had somehow escaped the roundup and was badly wanted by the regime. The Mission nevertheless applied the same policy: safe conduct or they stayed. They stayed until the coup d'état, living in a newly completed, air-conditioned conference room. The Embassy became known as "the Buddhist Hilton."*

Two other bonzes sought refuge during the August 21 attack at the apartment of a resident American correspondent. He tried to persuade them to leave, explaining that he had no way to protect them. They replied to his dismay that if they were turned out they would burn themselves to death in his front hall. They finally departed, unnoticed by the police, two or three days later.

It was my fate too to be confronted with a refugee problem. Around 4 A.M. on the night of the raids Sheehan of UPI and Halberstam of the New York *Times* sought me out at the Embassy. They said they were afraid of arrest or worse by Diem's police and asked if they could move into my house, which was U. S. Government property and therefore relatively secure. This was before it was clear what kind of madness the regime was up to, and there certainly was no doubt that the palace regarded the newsmen as enemies. With Trueheart's permission I said yes, of course. They stayed for three weeks. Several other resident correspondents, who were similarly fearful, moved into hotels for a few days.

---

* Tri Quang later emerged as one of the leaders of the neutralist tendency in the Buddhist movement, and an apparent United States adversary.

Sheehan and Halberstam had legitimate cause to fear for their personal safety. A foreign correspondent's lot in a hostile city can be extraordinarily uncomfortable, especially if he is racially different from the population and therefore easily spotted in crowds. One of Sheehan's predecessors, Gene Symonds of United Press, who was a friend of mine, was beaten to death by an Asian mob in Singapore in 1955 simply because he was white and carrying a camera. A correspondent's duty requires him to be present at the most dangerous times and places, yet he has none of the diplomatic protection of a U.S. official, except as the local American Mission chooses to provide. In Saigon in 1963 the newsmen were regarded as enemies not only by the local authorities but also by the American Mission, which must have been a lonely feeling indeed.

On the other hand there was a hint of a dare in the way Sheehan and Halberstam put their request, as much a demand for a debatable right as an invocation of friendship, a challenge to me to choose sides or be forever damned. They were the two most controversial newsmen in town, whose hostile but competent reporting had harassed both the regime and the Mission to distraction. They must have known that it would hurt my own relations with almost everyone to take them in.

It did indeed. Within a few days reports began coming back to me of unfriendly remarks by other officials of the Mission. Months later in Washington I learned that no lesser men than Secretary of State Dean Rusk and CIA Director John McCone had both complained to USIA that since Sheehan and Halberstam were living at my house I must be leaking secrets to them. This was silly. As any good cloak and dagger man should know, the last way an official gives away secrets is to invite the spy into his house. It was an alarming glimpse of the degree to which the U. S. Government had been poisoned at the very highest level by its feud with the American news media over Vietnam.

The damage done to my reputation at such a level also severely compromised my future with the government. In retrospect, however, I can think of no acceptable alternative to what I did.

Altogether the Diem regime's August 21 raids on the pagodas were a decisive turning point. There probably will be debate for years on the wisdom of U.S. support for Diem, but the debate should be limited to what happened before August 21. The pagoda raids made it categorically impossible for the United States to try to go on with the regime thereafter.

The raids were an act of political bankruptcy, confession of a catastrophic failure of leadership. The regime had permitted a minor blunder at Hue—which literally could have been repaired overnight—to build up to mass revulsion. Its actions had turned its own people into a chimera—where there had previously been only the Viet Cong, a large amount of apathy, but also a large amount of support. Its handling of the Buddhist issue conclusively discredited the regime's claim to the political savvy that would be essential in the long run to defeat the Viet Cong. It was true that the regime was confronted with such general rebellion that it had no choice but to resort to force, but this was like slugging an opponent in a debate who refuses to accept that the world is flat.

It may be argued that the U. S. Mission tried to push the regime too much, or in the wrong direction, or in the wrong tone of voice. In fact, in my opinion, nothing the Mission might have done would have made much difference.

In any case the American role developed into a critical element in the equation and the Diem regime chose to treat us with open contempt. The raids also were an unmistakable signal that Diem had abdicated a large portion of his power to Nhu and the furies who possessed Nhu's wife. We had lost such face that if we had tried to go on, no Asian regime could have regarded us with anything but scorn.

Right or wrong we had arrived at one of those breakdowns in human relations that neither side may have wanted but now was beyond repair.

CHAPTER SIX

Playing God

(1)

Ambassador Lodge was already en route to Saigon, on an orientation circuit through Tokyo, Hong Kong and Manila, at the moment of the crackdown on the pagodas. On orders from Washington he changed his plans and flew nonstop from Tokyo aboard a special U. S. Air Force transport, arriving at 9:30 P.M., a half hour after the curfew, on August 22, 1963.

It was a somberly dramatic spectacle as the big plane lumbered up to the VIP terminal at Saigon's Tan Son Nhut Airport on that oppressively hot night. It was drizzling rain and there were puddles on the hardstand that glistened in the television floodlights. The airport observation balconies were dark and empty. Straw hat in hand, wearing a dark suit, Lodge appeared alone at the cabin door. There were no cheers, only the whirr of cameras and popping of flashbulbs as he descended the gangway to be greeted by a small group of American officials, a protocol officer from the Foreign Ministry and about forty newsmen who had come out in special buses escorted by armed police jeeps through the curfew.

Lodge had radioed from the plane that he did not want to talk to the press upon arrival. When he saw the waiting newsmen, however, he instantly recognized that this would be a bad start. Accordingly he stepped up to a microphone, regretted that he could not discuss substance, nor answer questions, and then talked for five minutes about the vital role of the press in American democracy and how much he welcomed any opportunity to help the newsmen do their job. This was the nicest thing anyone except the Buddhists had said to them in a long while and the newsmen were pleased. The effect was capped by the discovery that Lodge had allowed four more American newsmen to hitch a ride on his plane from Tokyo.

This was a first glimpse of Lodge's masterful way with newsmen. As far as the U. S. Embassy was concerned, the so-called press problems ended then and there.

Lodge and his wife, Emily, drove into the city with an armed police escort through streets gleaming starkly in the rain, empty except for shadowy helmeted troops guarding the route. There had of course been widespread speculation on Lodge's intentions when he left Washington, including Mme. Nhu's helpful remark that he would be "on probation" for a while. It had been generally assumed that he would be tougher than Nolting in dealing with the regime. The pagoda raids had made this all academic. The state of American policy in Vietnam was now as bleakly empty as the streets of Saigon on that rainy night—except for the fact that unlike Nolting, Lodge would be spared the ordeal of trying to live and work with the Diem regime. That option was gone.

There was a grim element of truth in the lame witticism circulating among Americans in Saigon (relating to the aristocratic backgrounds of both Lodge and Diem) that U.S. policy had been reduced to the Americans telling the Vietnamese: "Our old mandarin can lick your old mandarin."

Lodge had a suitably hectic first day on the job. He began it by ostentatiously visiting the two Buddhists who had taken refuge at USOM, a deliberate affront to the regime. Then came the news from Washington that Mme. Nhu's father, Tran Van Chuong, Ambassador to the United States, had resigned in protest against the pagoda raids (he was still Buddhist, unlike his daughter), asserting that there was "not one chance in a hundred for victory" over the Viet Cong under Diem. His wife, the Vietnamese observer at the United Nations, also resigned. Simultaneously in Saigon, Diem's foreign minister, Vu Van Mau, resigned, shaved his head like a bonze and applied to Diem for permission to make a pilgrimage to India. (The reply a few days later was arrest.) The regime was clearly in deep trouble internally.

And just before lunch the Embassy received a flash intelligence report that the Ambassador's residence was about to be attacked by a pro-Diem mob. Lodge hurried home, along with such help as could quickly be assembled, literally to see to the protection of his wife. The report turned out to be a false alarm, the first of many that Nhu apparently planted to try to scare us.

Lodge's second day, Saturday, began with a riot. Police using clubs and tear gas broke up an anti-Diem demonstration by students at the University of Saigon. It was the first outbreak since the pagoda raids three days earlier. More significantly it was the first time in memory that Vietnamese students, traditionally apathetic in contrast to students elsewhere in Asia, had been stirred to political action, and thus an ominous development for the regime.

During the course of the rioting, three newsmen (Larry Burrows and Milton Orshefsky of *Life* and Burt Glinn of the *Saturday Evening Post*) were arrested, apparently because they were taking photographs. They were held for three hours and then offered release if they agreed to turn over their pictures. Unbeknown to the police, they had managed to switch their film around. So they politely took the spools out of their cameras, unrolled and exposed the film before the eyes of the startled police. Released, they then shipped off to New York the film they had salvaged with pictures of the riot.

All this happened without Lodge's knowledge. As soon as he heard about it, without even waiting for the details, he went immediately to the Foreign Ministry and protested to the highest ranking official he could find. And there was no foolishness this time about withholding news of his action from the correspondents.

On Sunday there was still another Buddhist demonstration, including a large number of students. During the melee with police a teen-age girl was killed. Despite the curfew and presence of heavily armed police and Special Forces troops everywhere, Saigon was seething—and at least part of the stimulation was popular anticipation that Lodge had come to put things right, meaning to apply American power to destroy the Diem regime. A good many Americans in Saigon, perhaps a sizable majority, felt the same way.

It may be a decade, or longer, when the pertinent telegrams are declassified, before we will know the exact American role in the events of the next two or three days in Saigon. Cable traffic between Lodge and Washington was top secret. Lodge was so wary of leaks that only two or three other officials of the Mission saw any of his dispatches. I doubt that anyone except Lodge himself saw all of them.

As of Sunday evening, August 25, almost five days after the pagoda raids, there had been only one formal public reaction in Washington. This was a State Department statement on the day of the raids asserting that they were "a direct violation by the Vietnamese Government of assurances that it was pursuing a policy of reconciliation with the Buddhists. The United States deplores repressive actions of this nature." This was the long-threatened "dissociation," and a significant step, but it seemed trivial in the earth-moving context of the moment.

At eleven o'clock Monday morning, August 26 (Saigon

time, which was twelve hours ahead of Eastern Daylight Time), Lodge was scheduled to present his credentials to President Diem at Gia Long Palace. I was one of a dozen officers of the U. S. Mission assigned to go with him.

At breakfast that morning I tuned in the 8 A.M. Voice of America newscast in English. Instantly I noticed an odd tone in the announcer's voice, a kind of tension, signaling something unusual. Then came the first item:

"High American officials blame police, headed by President Diem's brother Ngo Dinh Nhu, for anti-Buddhist actions in the Vietnam Republic. The officials say Vietnam military leaders are not, repeat not, responsible for last week's attacks against pagodas and the mass arrest of monks and students.

"Washington officials say Vietnam secret police carried out the raids and arrests, and that some of them were disguised as army troops or members of the youth corps.

"They say the military leaders agreed to martial law in the hope it would lead to a peaceful settlement. But, they say, the military men were not advised of secret police plans to attack Buddhists.

"*The officials indicate the U. S. may sharply reduce its aid to Vietnam unless President Diem gets rid of secret police officials responsible for the attacks.* (Italics mine)

"The new U. S. Ambassador in Vietnam—Henry Cabot Lodge—is said to be under instructions to make it clear to President Diem that the U. S. considers those measures a violation of President Diem's assurances that he would seek a peaceful settlement of Buddhist complaints against the government. . . ."

(The same text was also beamed to Vietnam in the Vietnamese language at approximately the same time.)

This, unmistakably, spectacularly, was it. There could be only one interpretation of the broadcast's meaning: fire Nhu or else.

I leaped for the telephone. Paul Garvey, our press attaché, who was staying at my house and also heard the broadcast, had picked up his extension phone at the same instant. "Did you hear *that?*" he cried. I asked Garvey to call the office and arrange for a transcript (we regularly transcribed the 8 A.M. news on tape) to be sent immediately to the Ambassador. Then I hurried to Lodge's residence, arriving at the same time as General Harkins and two or three other officials who had heard the same broadcast—all of us resplendent in white suits and uniforms for the credentials ceremony. The VOA transcript arrived a few minutes later.

We sat around a coffee table, Lodge on the end of a sofa with his back to a picture window and a view of the residence grounds. It was obvious immediately that Lodge had had no advance notice of the broadcast. He studied the transcript carefully. Then he tossed it on the table. He was angry, first because the broadcast had been timed at such an embarrassing moment for him, and second because he had not been consulted about it. "Jack Kennedy would never approve of doing things this way," he said. "This certainly isn't his way of running a government."*

The broadcast was such a slap in the face to the regime that it was at least possible that the credentials ceremony would be called off. Lodge apparently thought something even worse could happen. When the time came to go to the palace he turned to Harkins and said: "Paul, perhaps you better not come. If they try any funny business, it might be better if one of us were on the outside." Harkins went back

---

* The U. S. Information Agency later accepted the blame. It said the broadcast was a VOA "goof" and did not represent U.S. policy. In fact, it was U.S. policy but ineptly timed. The State Department blundered by leaving clearance of the text to a junior officer on Sunday duty and by failing to discuss it with other Washington agencies.

to his office. The rest of us climbed into our cars and headed for Gia Long.

There was no funny business. It was a standard Vietnamese ceremony, bowing and scraping, tea and small talk. But it was surely one of the few occasions in history—if not the only one—when an American Ambassador was concerned about his personal security in presenting credentials to a friendly government. None of us at the time thought the concern was unreasonable.

It was widely reported by Washington newsmen that Lodge was sent a cable from the State Department during that memorable weekend instructing him to advise the Vietnamese generals secretly that the United States would no longer oppose a military coup d'état. Press accounts said the cable was sent without consulting Defense Secretary McNamara, and that he was enraged since he would have opposed it.

Whether or not these reports were accurate—or Lodge initiated something on his own—they fitted the known events of the period. Dissatisfaction with the Diem regime had long been chronic inside the Vietnamese officer corps. After the outbreak of the Buddhist upheaval in May of 1963, there had been multiplying undercover approaches to officials at every level of the U. S. Mission (as well as American newsmen) from Vietnamese officers asking if the United States would countenance Diem's overthrow. These approaches by late August were coming from officers in such powerful positions that it was not unreasonable to assume that Diem could be toppled simply by flashing an American green light to the Vietnamese officer corps.

Within days after the pagoda raids the United States was publicly flashing lights like a Christmas tree. Apart from what Lodge may have been telling the Vietnamese generals secretly, if anything, there was the State Department statement "deploring" the raids. Then came the VOA broadcast, which clearly seemed to be designed to "sanitize" the Vietnamese Army, to separate it from the regime and to prepare world opinion for an Army takeover. And the American press was full of authoritative dispatches from Washington—many of which were relayed on VOA—to the effect that the Kennedy Administration had run out of patience with Diem.

In less than a week after his arrival Ambassador Lodge thus found himself presiding over an evident American effort "to play God" in Vietnam by encouraging destruction of the Diem regime and the establishment of a new government which would be more to U.S. liking, and hopefully perhaps could even defeat the Viet Cong.

(2)

In the depths of its retreat from reality the Diem regime's reasoning in cracking down on the pagodas probably went something like this:

The Buddhist upheaval is a shallow political conspiracy, perhaps inspired by the Viet Cong, and therefore can be suppressed like any other plot, by force. It will soon thereafter be forgotten, just as other attempts against the government have been forgotten. The Americans have stupidly misjudged the situation, and it is therefore necessary to do the job quickly, blocking their intervention until they can be confronted with a *fait accompli*. The interregnum between Nolting and Lodge is an ideal moment to act because the Americans will be leaderless. Once the job is done and stability restored, the Americans will recognize their error and continue their support, since they will have no alternative. The exercise thus should put a decisive end to U.S. meddling in Vietnamese domestic affairs, and the Americans forever after will accept the regime's superior wisdom in such matters.

As a military operation, the job was expertly done, with an efficiency that all too often had been lacking in clashes with the Viet Cong—perhaps because the Viet Cong shot back. With one or two exceptions, particularly Tri Quang, the known Buddhist leaders were arrested, along with hundreds of their supporters. The regime began reopening the pagodas only a day or two after the raids, installing "tame" pro-Diem bonzes (reportedly including disguised police agents). It was able to "persuade" some of the previous leaders to make public recantations and then permitted them to return to the pagodas. The population was assaulted with a massive propaganda campaign on the theme that the whole Buddhist affair had been a foul Communist plot.

The regime's façade of total control of the rebellion was, however, short-lived. The first cracks were the student demonstrations immediately after the pagoda raids. The regime promptly closed the country's two universities (Saigon and Hue). A fortnight later there was a series of demonstrations against the regime by secondary school students and then, to the regime's despair, by grade school children. The regime closed most of the schools in Saigon and arrested more than a thousand students on a single morning, hauling them away in trucks.

One of my most poignant memories of that period was the spectacle of hundreds of bicycles abandoned in neat array outside a shut-down school near my house where the boys and girls had stacked them that morning. They were there for several days, repeatedly drenched and rusting in rainy season downpours.

The regime gradually released the children in the custody of their parents, who were required to come for them. The parents were a cross section of the most respectable and influential citizens of Saigon, including numerous armed forces officers who went to the police stations in uniform to free their sons and daughters. It was dramatic, visible evidence of the degree to which the regime had isolated itself from the population.

It soon developed that even a Buddhist leadership had survived. Within a few days after the raids an underground organization began distributing leaflets in the streets.

But once again it was the foreign newsmen who played a critical role in thwarting the regime. There were at least sixty of them in Saigon by the end of August.

The government's attempt to control them by military censorship, which was maintained during the three weeks of martial law after the raids, was a comedy. It was done by young army officers whose only qualification was that they knew some English, and it was absurdly excessive. Almost all descriptions of the pagoda raids were cut out and the word "raids" was changed to "searches," for example. In a dispatch referring to "Roman Catholic President Diem," the word Catholic was cut, so the sentence read "Roman President Diem." One newsman was forbidden to call the raids a "dramatic" turn of events. Another was forbidden to say that Lodge had arrived "in this troubled country." Mme. Nhu granted an interview to a newsman on condition that she be permitted personally to censor his copy. Throughout the dispatch she inserted adjectives like "despicable" and "miserable" in front of every reference to the Buddhists.

The censors quickly lost their customers. The newsmen resorted to "pigeons" who carried their dispatches, film and tape to neighboring countries, mainly Hong Kong, Singapore, Bangkok and Manila, where colleagues relayed them to the United States.

The pigeons were airline passengers, pilots, stewardesses, rotating GIs, anyone who was flying out of Vietnam. For particularly hot stories, one of the newsmen himself would fly out with his pockets stuffed with press material. There was one occasion when a correspondent arrived at the airport just as a plane had begun to taxi away from the terminal. He recklessly ran out in front of it, waving his arms at the pilot like a runaway windmill. The pilot realized what he wanted, cut the engines on one side, caught a bundle tossed up to him by the reporter, started the engines again, waved and took off. The only effect of the regime's censorship was to delay dispatches by a few hours.

The uncensored reports of what the regime had done to the Buddhists aroused public opinion not only in the United States but around the world. The Cambodians, for example, broke off diplomatic relations with Saigon on August 27. The violence of the reaction in the Buddhist world generally led eventually to a United Nations investigation. News of the world's indignant reaction, particularly the mounting bitterness of official American comment, was relayed back to the Vietnamese people by VOA and other foreign radios. The green lights flashing from Washington were no less visible to the Vietnamese people than they were to the generals. This was unquestionably a major factor in keeping the Buddhist rebellion alive. The newsmen, in effect, provided the element of hope which is always essential to sustained resistance to an authoritarian regime anywhere.

The Diem regime's behavior as its position crumbled reminded me of a newspaper comic strip called "Peanuts." One of the strip's characters was a little boy called Linus who felt secure only when sucking his thumb and clutching a baby blanket. Loss of the blanket reduced Linus to shock, disbelief, panic. Now the Diem regime had lost its blanket: nearly a decade of blank-check, unquestioning U.S. support. The events that followed turned Saigon into a psychiatric wonderland.

The truth about who was thinking and doing what inside Gia Long Palace was lost forever when Diem and Nhu were killed on November 2, if indeed they could even have explained it themselves. The regime's actions suggested, however, that it could not bring itself to believe that the United

States had really abandoned it, i.e. that the blanket was not really gone at all. To rationalize this it created a fantasy in which the U. S. Government had come apart. It was only an evil group of traitorous officials who were doing and saying such dreadful things, the regime seemed to be thinking, and they would of course be disciplined as soon as the real powers in Washington found out about it. The palace apparently decided that the main sinners were the Saigon offices of CIA and USIS.

I think the regime hit on CIA because there had recently been such an uproar in the United States about that agency's alleged role in the Bay of Pigs episode, including widespread charges that it had recklessly operated as a "government within a government." The regime seemed to be thinking that whatever was happening now was a CIA operation and, like the Bay of Pigs, would be disowned by the American people as an unauthorized CIA adventure.

Why the regime turned on USIS made even less sense, since we were by far the smallest (twenty-four Americans) and least influential of all the American agencies operating in Vietnam. Part of the explanation probably was the regime's obsession with the idea that the U. S. Government really did control the American newsmen in Vietnam, despite our innumerable efforts to explain how wrong this was, and that USIS was the malevolent secret hand behind their hostile reports. More immediately, however, it was USIS, especially the Voice of America, that was transmitting all the bad news from Washington. I think the regime, in its frustration and anger, turned against us like a man heaving a brick into a television screen because he dislikes the program.

The first brick came on August 31 via my Australian friend Denis Warner, who often used one of the guest rooms at my house.

From a Vietnamese tipster Warner learned that General

Dinh, the excitable military governor of Saigon, had decided that Warner was an American spy, working for CIA in cahoots with Mecklin, also described as a CIA operative, to help the Buddhists upset the government. The tipster said that as "proof" Dinh had produced a photostat of a typewritten document headed "Diem's Decline, from Denis Warner." Dinh said that the police had found it in Xa Loi Pagoda. It began: "The Ngo Dinh Diem regime appears to be moving slowly but surely to its end . . . doomed if they do not crush South Vietnam's Buddhist leadership and no less doomed if they do."

The tipster said that Dinh then announced that Warner, Mecklin and a number of other newsmen and American officials would shortly be assassinated.

Warner recognized the document as a copy of the first page of an article he had written for *The Reporter* magazine during his previous visit to Saigon three weeks earlier. Reconstructing how he had handled the manuscript at the time, we decided that it must have been stolen from the guest room in my house, photostated and then returned—an unnerving discovery indeed. We never found out who did it.

Next day another Vietnamese source told Warner essentially the same story, asking him to warn me of danger. This source specified that names on the assassination list included CIA Chief John Richardson, an unidentified USOM official, another CIA official, my two house guests Halberstam and Sheehan, and one or two other newsmen, besides Warner and me.

Then came the September 2 issue of the *Times of Vietnam* with an eight-column headline on page one reading: CIA FINANCING PLANNED COUP D'ÉTAT. The story ran for four solid, chaotic columns of type. Its gist was that CIA, in cooperation with the Viet Cong (sic!) and the military attachés of three unnamed embassies, had spent $24 million in bribes to organize a coup d'état which had been planned for August 28 but had failed because the government got wind of it. The story said "the whole diplomatic corps was aware of the plan," that Lodge was now expected to fire the responsible "adventurers," and that "some observers on the scene are wondering whether the whole fiasco is a desperate effort of those who helped lose Cuba for the Free World to try to recoup their loss of face by taking control of Vietnam in time to proclaim her victory as their own."

The story also said that "the CIA group, *which is reported to have complete control of USIS* (italics mine), is said to have gone underground and to be clandestinely calling on the armed forces of the Republic to demonstrate and provoke the several times postponed coup d'état."

The daily *Times of Vietnam* was an English-language newspaper published in Saigon by an American couple, Gene Gregory, who first came to Vietnam briefly as a USIS officer in the early fifties, and his wife, Ann. Gregory was a competent journalist but he became involved in a number of complicated business ventures. He was out of the country during the last months of the Diem regime. Mrs. Gregory ran the paper—which had a circulation of only three to four thousand and little advertising—allowing herself increasingly to become a propagandist for the regime, and especially for Mme. Nhu. The *Times of Vietnam* was regarded with mixed anger and amusement in the American community. The U. S. Mission assumed that anything printed in it closely reflected government policy.

On September 2 President Kennedy personally contributed to the chorus of indignation with the Diem regime that was coming from Washington. In a television interview he said the Diem regime's "repressions" had been "very unwise," that the government had "gotten out of touch with the people," and, most significantly, that its chances of winning the war were "not very good" unless there were "changes in policy and perhaps personnel." He unmistakably meant dismissal of the Nhus, but the regime still missed the point. The *Times of Vietnam* charged that USIS had quickly distributed the text of Kennedy's remarks "because it follows the CIA line." The President evidently was now working for CIA too.

Next the *Times* printed the photostat of Warner's story (omitting his name), saying it was an example of "the role of a large section of the foreign press in preparing world opinion for a coup." In successive articles, it went on that VOA personnel and, by implication, myself were all "foreign adventurers." It accused us of trying to plant stories discrediting General Harkins (known to be pro-Diem) with the hope of having him removed, and of printing and distributing clandestine leaflets to stir up the students against the regime.

In a press conference on September 11 Nhu announced that VOA "is not the voice of the government of America at all but the voice of a group of capitalists who control it." He said VOA "wants the fall of the Vietnamese Government to set up some other government which may bring back the Bao Dai era." Thus from Nhu himself, a brick at the TV screen.

This was followed on September 19 by another haymaker in the *Times of Vietnam* under an eight-column banner reading PARDON, CIA, YOUR SPLIT IS SHOWING. The story reported that "CIA in Vietnam has split wide open into pro-coup and no-coup factions. . . . Most of the pro-coup elements (are) agents in USIS. . . . The agents there (USIS) are now feverishly trying to convince Washington to help overthrow the government."

Meantime the regime tried to work on my nerves (as well as the other "victims") through multiplying new rumors that I was about to be assassinated. Nhu told an official American visitor that I was plotting a coup. General Dinh gave another visitor a list of names for assassination, including mine. Additional reports surfaced almost daily through intelligence channels. The murders were to be done variously by the secret police disguised as Viet Cong agents, the Army Special Forces, or a special "assassination squad" headed by Tran Van Khiem, an eccentric brother of Mme. Nhu, whom I had known fairly well when he was Diem's press officer in 1955.

Lodge called me in one day and said: "Your name has been at the top of almost every list. Would you like to be transferred?" I said no thanks, that I thought this was exactly what Nhu was trying to achieve, and that I did not take the threats seriously. He said he agreed, but added helpfully: "But of course you never know."

It was true that I was not seriously worried by the threats. One reason was my feeling that the signal had been flashed and therefore the Diem regime would be undone at any moment by a coup d'état. In any case it simply did not figure that even the Nhus would commit an act so utterly destructive to their last hopes of recovering U.S. support—though there was always the possibility that it could be made to look convincingly like a Viet Cong outrage, or that they really were insane. As far as I know, the other people on the "lists" felt the same way. I took a few precautionary measures, like reminding the guards on the gate at my house that they were not to permit anyone inside the compound without my permission. One day I even tried carrying a small pistol in an inside pocket of my jacket, but it was so heavy and the sagging bulge seemed so conspicuous that I gave up that idea; any kind of professional attack would certainly be so sudden and swift in any case that a pistol would be useless.

It was the funny farm atmosphere that really worked on me. I recall a bad dream one night in which I went to a play. It was about an American diplomatic mission that gradually discovered it had been dealing for years with a government of madmen, where words were meaningless, where nothing that was supposed to have happened had really happened, yet there was no escape from continuing to try to deal with the madmen forever. I woke up without learning how it all came out.

Or perhaps I had not been dreaming at all?

Which certainly seemed to be confirmed a day or two later when I received a telephone call at the office from Tran Van Khiem. "John," he said, "have you heard that story about how I'm supposed to be head of an assassination squad?" I said yes. "And how I'm going to assassinate you?" I said yes, I had heard that, too. "John," said Khiem, "please don't believe stories like that. You and I are old friends. I would never assassinate you." I said I was glad to know that, and thanks for calling. "Let's have a drink sometime," said Khiem. I said fine, we must do that.

(3)

Some years ago I saw a delightful film—by Walt Disney, I think—to the music of a scherzo called "The Sorcerer's Apprentice" by Paul Dukas (from a poem by Goethe). As I recall it, the young apprentice experimented with magic chemicals and suddenly found himself being chased by hundreds of fearsome, animated broomsticks. He ran and he ran but the broomsticks, multiplying like demons, were gaining on him, in time with the frenetic crescendo of the music. That was the way it was in Saigon after the green lights were flashed from Washington. Our chemistry produced a phantasmagoria of assassins and other demons, but there was no coup d'état, and there was no way we could retreat.

Events were to prove that there was no lack of interest in a coup among the generals, but we had overlooked the fact that the Diem regime had been possessed for years by fear of this situation and had prepared its defenses well. There were some seven or eight thousand heavily armed, highly trained, loyal troops—mostly the palace guard and Special Forces units—in Saigon or the outskirts, under Diem's direct command. Additionally Saigon was contained in the Army's III Corps, commanded by General Ton That Dinh, besides his temporary assignment as the city's military governor. Dinh was an eccentric but he was intensely loyal to Diem. There could not be a coup, in short, without a dingdong battle.

One day during this period I asked Ambassador Lodge why the generals had failed to move. "Perhaps they're afraid to die, like anyone else," he said. It was as simple as that. The United States had miscalculated. There was still a war to be fought against the Viet Cong, and there was still the Diem regime. We were forced to reconsider the whole U.S. position.

In Washington on Friday, September 6, 1963, President Kennedy decided to send a special two-man mission to Vietnam immediately for a fresh look at the situation, with particular emphasis on (1) the state of the war and (2) the state of popular support for the Diem regime. The mission drew little public attention. It was composed of a general from the Pentagon and a senior FSO (foreign service officer) from the State Department who were both relatively unknown, though experienced Vietnam hands. They were given an Air Force C-135—the military version of the Boeing 707 jet—and ordered to report back on Tuesday the tenth. It was a remarkable assignment, to travel twenty-four thousand miles and assess a situation as complex as Vietnam and return in just four days. It was a symptom of the state the U. S. Government was in.

In Saigon that Saturday morning, to my consternation I received a cable instructing me to fly back to Washington with the general and the FSO, and to be prepared to discuss the situation. The AP reported that I was called back for "urgent consultations . . . carrying detailed reports on the current political, military and economic situation." In fact I had no idea why I was called, or who wanted to talk to me, or what kind of presentation I was expected to make. Neither did the general nor the FSO. I took some paper and a typewriter on the plane and tried to write something with an authoritative sound.

The flight itself was an unlikely experience. We took off from Saigon Monday afternoon and flew nonstop to Anchorage, Alaska, in an even twelve hours, and then nonstop across Canada to Washington in six hours. The C-135 had been called a "flying submarine" because it had no windows for the passengers except for a pair of after portholes about the size of a copy of the *Reader's Digest*. Its huge hydraulic door closed on tropical Saigon and opened twelve hours later to let in a spectacular, windswept view of Nissen huts and distant mountains in Alaska. Life in between was like a decompression chamber, no night, no day, only the roar of the engines and the glare of electric lights overhead. Except for meals and sleep (the plane was fitted with bunks), the three of us worked at separate tables, trying to make sense on paper of a situation that already seemed to me like a half-forgotten nightmare.

The *non sequitur* tone of the whole trip was capped by the fact that the general and the FSO not only appeared to dislike each other, but also disagreed on what should be done about Vietnam. On the whole flight they spoke to each other only when it was unavoidable.

The plane reached Washington around 5 A.M. on Tuesday the tenth. Five hours later I found myself attending a meeting of the National Security Council midst the most impressive gathering of VIPs I had ever seen in one place: the President, Attorney General Robert Kennedy, Secretaries

Rusk and McNamara, CIA Director McCone, General Taylor, AID Director David Bell, USIA Director Edward R. Murrow. The President nodded to the general, who read the report he had written on the plane. Then he nodded to the FSO, who read his report. The general argued impressively that the situation was, let's say, orange. The FSO argued earnestly that it was purple. When they had finished President Kennedy asked wryly:

"Were you two gentlemen in the same country?"*

For the next four days I was permitted to sit in on some of the multitude of emergency meetings that were going on all over the city to talk about Vietnam. Just about every meeting produced a blizzard of new position papers, most of them top secret, few containing new ideas. I was struck by the impression that there was almost no relaxed, reflective thought given to the problem. What counted seemed to be the paper itself, not what it said. It was usually a race between Officer A and Officer B to produce a paper first, and often they would both be outdone by Officer C working in another task force in another corner of the building—or the whole project would be dropped, after everyone had missed lunch, because somebody at a higher echelon had decided to try a different approach. And we would all find out what was really happening only by reading James Reston's column in the New York *Times* the next morning, if indeed anything was happening at all.

One reason for the empty-air flailing was the fact that this was an unusual exercise. The Pentagon, unpersuaded that the war had been affected by the Buddhist upheaval, continued to agitate for no real action at all, and for a re-

---

* Regrettably, security regulations prohibit me from reporting anything further about that meeting. I have withheld the identities of the general and the FSO, as well as what they had to say, in order to be able to record this remark by the President. It was a good example of the Kennedy style, and a rare bit of humor such as the problem of Vietnam very badly needed.

turn to normal relations with the Diem regime. CIA was more or less of the same opinion. Just about everyone else seemed to think that it had become essential to apply some kind of pressure to force the regime to reform if not to topple it.* As far as I could make out, President Kennedy was wholly undecided but profoundly uncomfortable about the suggestion that the U. S. should apply sanctions against a non-Communist, sovereign regime, much less try to unseat it.

This kind of thing had always been repugnant to Americans because of our own history as a onetime colony. To be sure, there had been numerous cases of U.S. meddling in foreign countries since World War II and the principle of nonintervention was eroding midst the pressures of big power responsibility. But this would be the first time that we had attempted such a thing with a government engaged in a shooting war against a Communist enemy. On the other hand the outcome of the war was of vital concern to the long-range security of the United States. If it had now become a certainty that the Diem regime would be defeated, was it not an obligation—both to the American people and to the rest of the Free World—to take whatever action was necessary to prevent disaster?

As usually happens in such a dilemma the debate during the few days I was in Washington was tending toward a compromise. There was increasing interest in the idea that somehow the U. S. could separate the Nhus from the government and that then we could work with Diem. The idea had been tried repeatedly in previous years—even Ambassador Nolting had suggested in one of his final meetings with Diem that Nhu might usefully take a "vacation"—and

* On September 12 a group of twenty-two senators headed by Frank Church, Democrat of Idaho, introduced (with Kennedy's blessing) a resolution demanding that aid to the Diem regime be shut off unless it stopped its "cruel repressions."

never worked. The scheme now was to reinforce our approach to Diem by direct sanctions, which had not been tried before.

My own feeling was that this was unrealistic. To anyone who would listen I argued the "Siamese-twin" theory, that Diem was psychologically a captive of his dependence on Nhu and that he could not go on without him. I said we must think in terms of unseating the whole regime, or of doing nothing at all—the regime itself being beyond persuasion. I also argued that too much accent had been placed on Nhu's undesirable influence. Even at that late date, I said, Diem still controlled the real power in Saigon, e.g. the armed forces, and whatever was wrong in Vietnam was basically Diem's responsibility.

My line therefore was:

1. The regime's actions against the Buddhists had decisively alienated such a large portion of the population that it could no longer hope to win a war in which popular support was vital. The rot was so widespread that it would eventually weaken the military effort disastrously, even if the Pentagon was right that this was not yet evident in the field.
2. The time had come for the U. S. to apply direct pressure to bring about a change of government, however distasteful. Maneuvers such as suspension of critical types of nonmilitary assistance would almost certainly stir the Vietnamese military to act on their own initiative, and it would not be necessary for the U. S. to involve itself in the plotting. The fact that the generals had not responded to the "green light" in August was irrelevant because on that occasion there had been no accompanying U.S. sanctions to make action of some sort mandatory.
3. This would unavoidably be dangerous. There was no way to be sure how events would develop. It was possible, for example, that the Vietnamese forces might frag-

ment into warring factions, or that the new government would be so incompetent and/or unstable that the effort against the Viet Cong would collapse. The U. S. should therefore resolve now to introduce American combat forces if necessary to prevent a Communist triumph midst the debris of the Diem regime.

(All of the foregoing was my personal opinion, not necessarily reflecting the views of anyone else.)

The first part of this was essentially what happened. The last argument, that we might be forced to use American forces against the Viet Cong, riled almost everyone I tried it on. "You have forgotten," snorted one senior official, "that politics is the art of the possible." Events in the months that followed reinforced my belief that we should be ready to use American forces as a last resort to save South Vietnam from the Communists. In the context of American domestic politics in 1963, however, such a suggestion apparently was unthinkable, like a Sunday school pupil asking the teacher to talk about sex.

It was a short-lived taste of high policy. Minutes after I arrived back in Saigon on September 16 the padded-cell world remorselessly closed in. Incredulously I listened to an account of the newest crisis from David Sheppard, the Deputy Public Affairs Officer, who had been in charge at USIS during my absence.

He reported that a USIS Vietnamese employee had heard a suspicious noise coming from the servants' quarters at my house while I was gone, a sort of clanking sound like a machine, he said. Sheppard went to the house with another officer, searched the servants' quarters and found nothing. Then, on a hunch, he decided to search the rest of the property. In a bedroom, hidden under some bed clothing in a packing case, he discovered a mimeograph machine. A stencil was still attached to it. A translation quickly established that it was a Buddhist propaganda leaflet savagely attacking the Diem government. Under interrogation, a servant whom I had hired temporarily, confessed that he had been given the machine by the Buddhist underground and had been operating it in his quarters. He said the Buddhists had explained that this would be a "safe" place to work since I was out of the country, and that he had agreed because he hated Diem.

Verging on an emotional breakdown the servant said that if he had done anything wrong he would burn himself to death.

This was as serious as it was grotesque. In a sense the wild charges against me and USIS in the *Times of Vietnam* had been true. However unwittingly I was involved in underground agitation against the regime. If the regime found out about this I would certainly be declared *persona non grata* immediately, and the United States would be embarrassed at an extraordinarily critical moment. We assumed that if the police learned of the affair through their own tipsters, and we had tried to conceal it, it would be futile to try to explain what really happened.

In my anger at the servant for putting me in such a spot, my first impulse was to turn him in to the police, make a clean breast of everything, and hope that the regime would believe us. We decided against this, partly because the regime was in such a psychotic state that it quite possibly would not accept our story even if we volunteered it, and partly because of the human considerations. The servant had worked for years for a succession of American families. One could never be sure of course, but our interrogation indicated that he was a low-level accomplice of the Buddhist underground and quite possibly unaware of the gravity of what he had done. If we turned him over to the police, his treatment would certainly be very unpleasant indeed. There was also the broad political consideration that if we turned him over and the affair was publicized, we would appear to be collaborating with the regime in its excessive campaign to suppress its own people.

Accordingly we impounded the mimeograph machine, lectured the servant in the strongest possible language, threatening him with a horrible fate if such a thing ever happened again, and dropped the matter there. It was a risky procedure. We had no idea, for example, of how many people knew about the affair among the Buddhists. There was always the possibility that the police would penetrate their organization, or find out from a panicky prisoner arrested for other reasons. For the next six weeks until the coup, mere mention of the word "mimeograph" gave me the heebie-jeebies. It still did a year later.

(4)

In Washington the blizzard of top secret paper apparently convinced President Kennedy that the most sensible thing to do was to throw it all away and start over. For the umpteenth time the U. S. Mission in Saigon was obliged to drop everything and prepare for a top level visitation to investigate what was really going on. The principals were Defense Secretary McNamara and General Taylor, along with a battalion of solemn lesser officials loaded with briefcases and evasive answers to newsmen.

Since a primary objective was to assess the state of the war, it was fitting perhaps that a Viet Cong sniper knocked out an engine of a Pan American 707 jet coming in to land at Saigon on the same day—September 24—that McNamara's special plane arrived (the same incident that sabotaged the farewell party reported earlier). The sniper may even have been shooting at what he thought was the Secretary's plane.

In a series of hours-long briefings in Saigon, McNamara and Taylor were at least able to establish quickly that the division in Washington of most civilian agencies versus the military and CIA extended all the way to Vietnam. Broadly Lodge and most civilian officials (including myself) felt that Diem had lost so much popular support that he could not win the war. Harkins, most military officers and John Richardson of CIA felt the war was still going well enough to keep trying with Diem. Unlike his previous visits, McNamara waded boldly into the argument, harassing each briefing officer with pointed questions, challenging undocumented assertions, and otherwise making life miserable for supposed experts who had not done their homework.

Then, while Taylor pursued details in Saigon, the remarkable McNamara set out to see how things were going in the field. Wearing an open-necked, short-sleeved shirt and GI boots, he traveled for the better part of a week all over the country, by jeep and limousine, helicopter and flivver plane, interrogating scores of Vietnamese and American officials at every level. McNamara was rightly famous for a steel-comb mind that specialized in weeding out fluff, and he was probably as good, or better, than anyone else in the Pentagon at that kind of on-the-spot inquiry.

The exercise nevertheless was largely superfluous. For one thing, the general with whom I traveled to Washington had done almost exactly the same circuit only a fortnight earlier, talking to more or less the same people and no doubt hearing essentially the same stories. However commendable the public image, it was debatable whether a man in McNamara's position should have exposed himself to the hazards of that kind of travel. And it was contrary to human nature to expect that the young captains and majors to whom McNamara spoke in the field would express their minds freely to that kind of visiting brass—especially when they knew what Harkins believed and Harkins was often present.

Moreover, the issue before us was not only the state of

the military effort but also of popular support for the Diem regime. There were, of course, many American military advisors who were intensely sensitive to the political question, but this was not their mission. The American civilians to whom McNamara talked in the field—mostly USOM men concerned with economic help to the hamlets—were less inhibited on political judgments, but they too were not primarily working on this—and again the presence of the American and Vietnamese brass who accompanied McNamara would have discouraged much free-wheeling talk. Altogether what McNamara tried to do was beyond the skill of any man in such circumstances.

The embarrassing reality was that the U. S. Mission at that time had not been keeping tabs on Vietnamese public opinion. (This was not as inexcusable as it may sound. Such an effort would have been impossible to conceal from the Diem regime, which would have regarded it as an intolerable invasion of its internal affairs.) Such knowledge as we had was based on a crash exercise following the pagoda raids to put together a meaningful judgment on the basis of responsible but haphazard comment from American military and civilian officials working in the field on other primary assignments.

The U.S. civilian-side judgment proved later to be right, that the people had run out of patience with the Diem regime, but we could not conclusively prove it at the time. On the other hand, Harkins' people had impressive, correlated evidence, e.g. government vs. Viet Cong losses, which seemed to prove that the military situation had not yet seriously deteriorated.

This was the nub of the dissension inside the U. S. Mission. In a sense, neither side was wrong. What to do hinged on an assessment of future probabilities, particularly whether or not the Vietnamese forces would keep fighting. What McNamara and Taylor recommended to the President was not revealed, but their report for the most part could only have accentuated his dilemma.

Kennedy thus was confronted with one of those lonely moments of decision that are characteristic of the presidency. It was one of the last big decisions before his death, and surely one of the toughest, with his principal advisors at loggerheads. The decision was lastingly controversial, since it led to the coup d'état. It was also one of President Kennedy's wisest decisions, in my opinion. From Saigon at the time, however, his first public action looked like a supine compromise.

Its gist, as announced by the White House on October 2, shortly after McNamara and Taylor had returned to Washington:

> We will adhere to our policy of working with the people *and government* (italics mine) of South Vietnam to deny this country to Communism. . . .
>
> The military program in South Vietnam has made progress and is sound in principle, though improvements are being energetically sought. . . .
>
> Secretary McNamara and General Taylor reported their judgment that the major part of the United States military task can be completed by the end of 1965. . . . They reported that by the end of this year (1963) the U.S. program for training Vietnamese should have progressed to the point that one thousand U.S. military personnel assigned to South Vietnam can be withdrawn.
>
> The political situation in South Vietnam remains deeply serious. The United States has made clear its continuing opposition to any repressive actions in South Vietnam. While such actions have not yet significantly affected the military effort, they can do so in the future. . . .

To many of us in Saigon, this was sickening news. It paid lip service to U.S. disapproval of the regime's actions against the Buddhists, but it seemed unmistakably to imply that this was now to be forgotten and we were expected to try to resume normal relations as though nothing had happened—that we were, in short, about to sink with Ngo Dinh Diem. The statement noted the civilian contention that popular discontent with Diem might eventually hurt the war effort, but this was made meaningless by the business about withdrawing one thousand Americans in 1963 (a long-standing plan designed for its propaganda value) and the reckless implication that the war would be won by the end of 1965.

Kennedy seemed to have chosen this moment of blackest crisis to permit the Pentagon once again to indulge its obsession with excessive optimism, which so long had dogged our efforts to establish a degree of credibility for the U. S. Mission.

Not long thereafter, however, we began to realize in Saigon that the White House statement was only part of a plan that was brilliantly realistic and imaginative, yet also offered a compromise between the two U.S. factions that both sides could honorably live with. It appeared to be Kennedy the politician at his best in an indescribably difficult situation.

On the basis of the limited information available in Saigon, the White House statement apparently was designed to appease the CIA and the Pentagon by publicly accepting their judgment on the state of the war. At the same time the statement neatly offered the Diem regime a face-saving opportunity to repair its relations with the United States, since we appeared to have swallowed our pride and abandoned further public pressuring. In effect the statement offered all parties a chance for one last try with a minimum of public embarrassment.

The other part of the plan was set in motion with no announcement at all. This was the quiet suspension of several segments of U.S. aid to Vietnam. They were selected so that the least possible damage would be done to the military effort against the Viet Cong, but also to generate the maximum possible internal political pressure on the regime.

By far the most important suspension was the Commercial Import Program, commonly known as CIP, which represented an annual American expenditure of almost $100 million. CIP was a complicated financial operation designed to convert American dollars into Vietnamese piasters to pay for war-supporting needs, such as Vietnamese troop pay, without inflation of the Vietnamese economy. In effect it was a device for providing piasters that the regime should have been able to collect through taxes which it was unable and/or unwilling to impose. This was accomplished by using dollars provided by USOM to pay for imports from abroad, with the importer making his remittance in piasters which were then turned over to the Vietnamese Government. The government's legitimate needs for piasters were so great that USOM would authorize CIP dollars for virtually any kind of import requested, whether it was Scotch whisky, Mercedes limousines, Japanese textiles or baby food—altogether an oddly unaustere but necessary program for this embattled country.

The beauty of suspending CIP was the fact that dollar allocations were normally made four or five months before the goods were delivered to Vietnam, and the piaster payments were made mostly on delivery. Deliveries already authorized were not affected. Thus there was no immediate damage to the economy, nor to the regime's piaster income. At the same time, however, the psychological impact was enormous. The suspension would eventually hit hundreds of private businessmen in the pocketbook, with resulting heavy pressure on the palace to do something about it. The CIP maneuver was experimental, probably unprecedented in American foreign aid programs, and highly successful. As such it was a valuable study in how to use an aid program to achieve a political objective which should be useful if and as the United States finds it necessary to play that kind of game again somewhere else.

Another suspended program was the several hundred thousand dollars we had been spending to support the Vietnamese Special Forces. This was done to express U.S. displeasure with the fact that Special Forces units had been used for the crackdown on the pagodas. Also a large portion of the Special Forces was now being held in the Saigon area to protect the palace and not being used for the purpose for which we had been putting up the money: to fight the Viet Cong.

A third was the $4 million worth of condensed milk that the U. S. had annually been sending to Saigon. This item was selected for suspension because Mme. Nhu had been quoted as saying that the Vietnamese people did not like condensed milk and therefore had been feeding it to pigs.

Thus behind the camouflage of the White House statement the United States signaled the Diem regime loud and clear that it meant business. It did so in such a way, moreover, that the regime could still bend to our will relatively gracefully if it acted before news of the aid suspensions began to come out.

In approaching the problem this way the United States had not turned off the "green light" to the Vietnamese generals. It did modify its position, however, in the sense that it now was indicating that we did not necessarily want a change of government, as long as the existing regime would change some of its policies and personnel. Specifically this meant real and lasting reconciliation with the Buddhists and dismissal of the Nhus. If the regime refused, it was a reasonable probability that the mounting pressures created by the aid cuts would eventually provoke its destruction.

Since it was highly unlikely that the regime would give in, it is hairsplitting perhaps to argue that the United States did not deliberately "dump" Diem. This nevertheless was the fact. All that was ever asked of Diem was a government and politics that would meet what the United States believed to be the urgent needs of the situation to prevent disaster—or to put it another way, that he honor the reform promises he made to General Taylor in the fall of 1961 in return for a massive increase in U.S. help.

For years there had been a campaign among supersensitive foreign leaders, especially in newly independent countries, to establish a principle that aid should be given without "strings." There had been previous cases of aid manipulation for political reasons, such as Secretary Dulles' withdrawal in 1956 of U.S. financing for Egypt's Aswan Dam, but U.S. policy on "strings" had never before been tested in such decisive fashion in such a critical situation.

President Kennedy's decision thus had implications reaching beyond Vietnam. It was conclusive rejection of the idea that the United States may not attach "strings" to its aid. Ambassador Lodge went so far as to say at the time that, on the contrary, it was our "right" to expect specific actions in return for our assistance. The argument no doubt will arise again in other circumstances elsewhere. In the case of Vietnam in 1963 the alternative to assertion of this right would have been tantamount to asking the American advisors in the field to risk their lives in support of policies that were doomed to failure.

For application of the new policy, which was likely to be an unpleasant operation, President Kennedy had found exactly the right man. Ambassador Lodge proved to be an able executioner.

CHAPTER SEVEN

Heat Lightning

(1)

Like so much else about the U.S. position in Vietnam, the role of Henry Cabot Lodge was unique, controversial, and hard to live with.

Even the question of why he came to Vietnam could start an argument.

The pro-Lodge version was that he was bored with inactivity after his defeat in the 1960 election, that he wanted to serve his country again, and that he asked President Kennedy for a job, stipulating only that it be a "tough" one. This version went that Kennedy had come to know Lodge well as a political opponent, had a high regard for him and therefore welcomed the opportunity to use his services in an assignment of such importance to the U.S. interest.

Lodge himself liked to say that he took the job because "I'm too old to play touch football, but too young to retire." He was sixty-two at the time.

The anti-Lodge (and anti-Kennedy) version went that Kennedy sent him to Saigon as a cynical political maneuver, hoping to cancel out the explosive issue of Vietnam in the 1964 election by filling the post with a prominent Republican. A New Frontier leader was supposed to have quipped: "If we have to lose Vietnam, we might as well let a Republican take the blame."

This version held that Lodge was aware of all this, but

that he figured he could outsmart the Democrats by (1) resigning indignantly if things went badly, blaming everything on stupid leadership in Washington, or (2) bringing off a miracle by putting things right in Vietnam, in which case he could only be hailed as a national hero, or (3) somehow exploiting the glamour of his front-line post to promote a draft to the presidential nomination from the Republican Convention.

Lodge's critics read personal political motivation into many of his actions in Saigon. They charged him with posturing for photographers to keep his image alive back home. Political meaning was read into the fact that Lodge and his wife brought few personal effects, such as books and paintings, to Saigon, suggesting that they did not plan to stay long, and wanted to be able to leave quickly—as they did, ten months later.

A large segment of the American community in Saigon disapproved of Ambassador Nolting's policy, but he was regarded personally with real affection. In contrast, most of the community favored Lodge's policy, but they were alienated by his patrician ways.

One of his first moves set the tone. He ordered removal of a brass plate reading "Ambassador" from the door of his office and had it replaced with a plate reading "Mr. Lodge." Most of the other paraphernalia of a standard American overseas mission went the way of the title, including the country team—until Washington specifically ordered him to revive it.

Lodge insisted that the Mission become a one-man operation, conducted in total secrecy and insulated from the staff he had inherited from Nolting by a pair of special assistants he had brought from Washington.

"Lodge has never been betrayed," one of them once told me. "He seldom confides in enough people to be betrayed."

Circulation of cable traffic to and from Washington was

cut so drastically that even General Harkins, with responsibility for sixteen thousand American military personnel, was left in the dark on Lodge's activities and policies—until the State Department, probably at the Pentagon's request, began using the slug "Please pass to General Harkins" at the head of each message. There were occasions when senior officials received direct Washington instructions pertaining to projects they had never heard of.

Lodge also claimed for himself a monopoly on direct contact with top officials of the Vietnamese Government, to the point where he ordered several senior Americans to cease working with Vietnamese whom they had known for years. This sometimes had the effect of delaying, or permanently canceling, projects because Lodge was too busy with other matters, or not interested. Lodge's attitude profoundly hurt a good many officers who had been working sixteen- and eighteen-hour days, and now were told, in effect, to become bench-warmers.

Lodge regarded the newsmen in the same category with cable traffic: as his private domain. "The leak," he said, "is the prerogative of the ambassador. It is one of my weapons for doing this job." Leak prevention was one of the main reasons for his blackout on information to his staff. He was uncomfortable if other U.S. officials even had social contacts with reporters. In his relationship with the newsmen, Lodge not only repaired the dismal situation inherited from Nolting. He also converted the newsmen into disciples. "The correspondents," said a bitter official who had shared Nolting's ordeal with the press, "were patsys for Lodge."

Lodge had not been particularly successful in his previous press relations. Some of the newsmen who covered him as U. S. Ambassador to the United Nations disliked him. Lodge himself once remarked to a friend that the personal animosity of a handful of the reporters assigned to the 1960 campaign might even have made the difference in the narrow defeat of the Nixon-Lodge ticket. He was determined not to make that mistake in Saigon.

Lodge sent instructions to the Mission before he arrived to invite the three hard-core regular correspondents—Halberstam of the New York *Times,* Sheehan of UPI and Browne of AP—to successive private lunches at his residence. We were told to explain that the Ambassador wanted their "advice." This was the pattern that Lodge was to follow with almost every other reporter of any consequence who came to town. Except for his arrival and departure ten months later, Lodge gave no press conferences, no off-the-record briefings. Instead he met frequently but always alone with individual American newsmen, thus at once flattering them and minimizing the risk of broken confidences.

He was not an exceptionally good news source, but he knew how to talk to newsmen so they went away happy. Unlike Nolting and Harkins, he did not try to debate with them. Instead he invited their ideas, confided enough information to make a story, and treated them as equals—tried and true devices that should have been used much sooner in Saigon.

Lodge enjoyed a special advantage in the coincidence that he agreed with the newsmen's view that Diem had to go. They were therefore relatively forgiving when things went badly after the coup. Lodge, in short, came at a golden moment. He was smart enough, however, to keep it going for the whole ten months of his tour in Saigon. He survived without a single serious attack upon him personally, or his policy, by the newsmen who regularly covered Saigon. In this respect he was a successful ambassador.

Lodge's arrival did not, however, shut off the unauthorized news dispatches that so long had harassed us. Shortly after his arrival there was a series of stories from Saigon savagely attacking members of Lodge's own staff. Their source was never established. The primary targets were the two senior officials who had led the minority element of the U. S. Mission that favored trying to keep going with Ngo Dinh Diem: the CIA chief, John Richardson, and General Harkins.

The stories came in three waves.

The first was on the theme that the U. S. Mission was "a five-headed monstrosity," as UPI columnist Lyle C. Wilson called it (September 18, 1963), because of bickering among its component agencies: CIA, USIS, State (i.e. the Embassy), AID and Defense. Halberstam reported in the New York *Times* of September 15 that Lodge and Harkins disagreed on the state of the war, and that there was "tension" inside the Mission. The effect of such stories was to accent the idea that strong leadership was needed and Lodge was the man to provide it.

The second wave of stories was directed at Richardson personally. The main one was a dispatch from Scripps-Howard correspondent Richard Starnes published in the Washington *Daily News* (October 2, 1963) under a headline reading: "ARROGANT" CIA DISOBEYS ORDERS IN VIETNAM. The dispatch said that Richardson refused twice to carry out Lodge's orders and asserted that CIA's role in Vietnam had been a "dismal chronicle of bureaucratic arrogance, obstinate disregard of orders and unrestrained thirst for power." It continued: "One very high American official here, a man who has spent much of his life in the service of democracy, likened the CIA's growth to a malignancy, and added he was not sure even the White House could control it any longer."

Some of Richardson's men strongly disapproved of his dogged support for Diem, but the CIA station in Saigon was nevertheless outraged by this kind of public humiliation. It was, of course, possible that Richardson had been insubordinate, but nobody else in the Mission had heard of any such thing. What little we knew of CIA activities indicated exactly the contrary, that Richardson had loyally bowed to Lodge's attitude. I was a witness on one occasion when Lodge gave Richardson an order that I knew he strongly disapproved. His response was "Yes, sir."

Apart from the merits of the charges, CIA was obliged to remove Richardson because his identity had been revealed. CIA chiefs of station the world over are usually known to newsmen and other outsiders, since they seldom work under so-called "deep cover," but their identity is technically classified. Traditionally newsmen have honored this elsewhere. In this case there was the added consideration that it was CIA practice not to try to defend itself against public criticism (on the theory that this only tends to reveal more of its operations), making Richardson's position untenable. He left quietly on October 5. There was widespread satisfaction in Saigon shortly afterward when President Kennedy publicly praised him and his work by name.

The third wave of stories came after the coup d'état, aimed this time at Harkins. A dispatch from Halberstam to the New York *Times* (November 13, 1963) reported that the positions of Lodge had been "strengthened" and of Harkins "weakened" by the coup. It said the coup leaders advised "the Americans" of their plans in advance, but not the U.S. military for fear the latter would betray them to Diem. The dispatch asserted that the Embassy and CIA sent a joint message to Washington on the morning of the coup saying that a coup was coming, but that Harkins' headquarters dissented. It said that after the shooting began, the military asked that its dissent be stricken from the message. By implication the point of the dispatch was that Harkins was not trusted by the new regime, and that he had been woefully out of touch with what was happening.

The Pentagon was incensed and so, I heard later, was President Kennedy. On November 15 Kennedy told a news conference: "I have great confidence in General Harkins.

There may be some who would like to see General Harkins go, since the coup, but I plan to keep him there." Kennedy's pique led to an extension of Harkins' tour in Saigon by several months.

In overall performance Cabot Lodge managed to separate himself from a significant part of the American community in Saigon. He disrupted the morale of some of us to a degree that even Mme. Nhu had failed to achieve. Failure of the newsmen to report this fact further deepened the bitterness of Mission officials who had watched them dismember Ambassador Nolting.

The community's emotional reaction to Lodge was, however, only a part of his impact. Much of the resentment was mixed with reluctant admiration. In the spring of 1964, when Lodge was briefly a leading contender for the Republican nomination, some of the same officials whom he had outraged incredulously found themselves tempted to vote for this enigmatic man if he became a candidate for President of the United States.

Lodge himself was indifferent to what his immediate associates thought of him. He operated on the assumption that he was surrounded by adversaries, with the predictable result that would-be friends were soon converted into adversaries.

I was often struck by the contrast between his bearing in small, give-and-take gatherings, where he appeared bored and uncomfortable, and the way he behaved on a public platform. When the floor was his, even without prepared remarks, he was one of the most articulate men I had known. He could deliver his thoughts—and they were almost always penetrating thoughts—in succinct, often colorful language, with the polished manner of a professional orator. It verged on charism. His cables to Washington, the few I saw, were written with exceptional literary persuasiveness.

In the barracuda world of government service, Lodge's protective shell was an invaluable asset, enabling him to operate as he thought best with serene ruthlessness—which is exactly what it often requires to get anything done in the government. Right or wrong, he knew what he wanted. He crushed the spirits of many of us, but he also disengaged the operations of the U. S. Mission from the endless, agonized soul-searching that prevailed before his arrival. He was a commander by instinct, in a situation where resolute commanders had been hard to come by.

Lodge expected to be judged on performance, not on the affection of his staff.

(2)

Lodge's application of the new U.S. policy of sanctions against the Diem regime was superbly done. His personality exactly fitted the requirements of the job. It was this performance that stirred many of his sourest critics among Americans in Saigon to grudging admiration.

During his first weeks in Saigon, Lodge called on Diem, Nhu and two or three other top officials to register precisely what the United States wanted from the regime. Press dispatches reported on September 10, for example, that he had bluntly asked Diem to remove Nhu from the government. He encountered the same amorphous, tangential monologues that had frustrated his predecessors. Lodge, however, did not attempt to negotiate. Instead, he stopped making calls. Soon thereafter Washington quietly began suspending the aid program.

"They have not done anything I asked," Lodge said. "They know what I want. Why should I keep asking? Let them come to ask me for something."

Instructions were circulated throughout the U. S. Mission that if anyone asked about the suspended aid the answer was to be simply that it was "under review." If a Vietnamese official requested U.S. assistance of any significance, the reply was to be that perhaps President Diem would care to take it up with Ambassador Lodge. The result was that our relations with the Vietnamese Government began to dry up at all levels, except for military operations. It became a standoff, a test of wills, with the odds heavily favoring Lodge.

Lodge's strategy suggested a shrewd understanding of human nature. He knew that any approach to him from the palace, especially in face-conscious Asia, could only be tantamount to surrender. The technique not only preserved but exploited American dignity, in effect turning an Asian characteristic against Asians, yet it never closed the door to reconciliation—on American terms.

There was a yeasty irony in the fact that Lodge did not tell his newfound friends among the newsmen about any of this, allowing them to be scooped on the first really important news story since his arrival. *Newsweek* (September 30) even reported that the U. S. had "capitulated" to the Diem regime. It remained for the much scorned *Times of Vietnam* —no doubt on the regime's orders—to break the story on October 7.

USOM FREEZES ECONOMIC AID PROGRAM, said an eight-column headline. The article erroneously said that all economic assistance had been suspended, but it correctly placed main emphasis on the cutoff of the Commercial Import Program. Next day in Washington a State Department spokesman commented: "Our aid program to South Vietnam is under close and continuing review. In line with the President's statement at his last (September 13) press conference, what helps win the war we support and what interferes with the war we oppose. In the close and continuing review, I include the Commercial Import Program."

Curiously, in view of the intense interest that Vietnam

continued to command in the United States, news of the suspension of aid to the Special Forces did not come out until October 21, in a UPI dispatch from Washington. The *Times of Vietnam* reported on October 31, the day before the coup, that the regime had suspended domestic sale of milk products because of hoarding resulting from the U.S. cutoff. The stop orders on one or two other projects never were reported. The carefully calculated, surgical nature of the suspensions—as well as their unique political implications—were lost in the rush of other events.

News of the CIP suspension was enough, however, to shock the Diem regime out of its euphoric idea that somehow it was villains like CIA and USIS that were making the trouble, not the U. S. Government itself. This realization was reinforced on October 9, when President Kennedy told a press conference that CIA had "done a good job" in Vietnam. At the same time Kennedy was asked if there had been any change in the situation since his September 2 remark about the desirability of new "policies and perhaps personnel." The President replied that "we are still dealing with the same problems we were dealing with a month ago." The *Times of Vietnam* glumly, and correctly, interpreted this as presidential "blessing" of what it called the Saigon "intrigues" against the regime.

News of the CIP suspension also alerted the American public to the fact that a major policy decision had been reached. Judging by what we could observe from Saigon, its full import apparently was fuzzed by official evasiveness, and the fact that Republican critics were inhibited by the presence of a Republican as Ambassador in Saigon. Nevertheless a domestic U.S. political uproar now was superimposed on the backlash maneuvers of the Diem regime itself against the U. S. Mission in Saigon, aggravating our trials.

From Washington insiders some months later I heard that

pro-Diem pressures on President Kennedy were building up so rapidly that he possibly would have been forced to capitulate to Diem within a few weeks if the issue had not been settled by the November 1 coup d'état. It was a curiously uncomfortable experience to be personally involved in implementation of a policy that was stirring varying degrees of opposition from some of the most influential voices in the United States: the Hearst newspapers, a number of prominent Roman Catholic leaders, Senator Goldwater and several other prominent politicians, columnists like Alsop, Marguerite Higgins and Walter Lippmann, the Scripps-Howard newspapers, and *Time-Life,* plus CIA and the Pentagon.

Many of the forces that now were coming to Diem's support had been relatively noncommittal during the preceding, critical months of decision. On the other hand, some of the up-and-at-'em liberals who had been so hostile to Diem were now running for cover, rather than be associated with the unpleasantness of unseating him and thus of unliberal meddling in another country's affairs.

There was concern among some Americans in Saigon that we might be risking future political difficulties such as those experienced by the foreign service officers who had opposed American support for Chiang Kai-shek in China in the forties. Some of the pro-Diem forces were already making the comparison. There was a distinct parallel. Chiang and Diem were both Christians. They were both leading a national struggle against a Communist enemy. They were both Asians who had tried to cooperate with the West. And the issue before us in Saigon in 1963, when it was not conclusively established that Diem would lose, was roughly similar to the earlier dilemma when the U. S. was trying to assess Chiang's chances of defeating the Communists.

There was one critical difference. Many of the anti-Chiang forces thought in terms of some kind of compromise with the

Communists. There was no such thought in Saigon in 1963. The anti-Diem forces sought a military regime that not only would continue the struggle against the Viet Cong, but also would be more effective than the Diem regime. Hopefully there was also the difference that there would not be another McCarthy era in the United States wherein foreign service men who had sincerely supported controversial policies would be accused of disloyalty.

A whiff of this sort of thing resulted from a Saigon visit during that period by a group of junketing congressmen. I became involved with them because they asked for a private meeting with a group of American newsmen, which I arranged one evening at my home. The proceedings lasted until 2 A.M. and it was a healthy, slam-bang bull session. There was a noisy dispute about U.S. support for Diem, but some of the newsmen and some of the congressmen were on each side.

A fortnight later, after the congressmen had returned to Washington, columnists Robert S. Allen and Paul Scott quoted members of the group as reporting that William Trueheart, the deputy chief of mission, and I had slyly "spent their time channeling the legislators to briefings by U.S. civilian officials strongly biased against President Diem." The column continued: "According to South Vietnamese sources, Trueheart and Mecklin were the ringleaders behind the abortive attempt by a small group of USIA and State Department officials to oust the Diem regime two months ago. The legislators, who will issue a report strongly supporting Diem this week . . . were able to document that these two officials were the source of a number of anti-Diem stories leaked to U.S. reporters in Saigon."

The story was absurd, if only because of its failure to note that the leading anti-Diem civilian official in Saigon was Ambassador Lodge himself. It was an uncritical acceptance of the *Times of Vietnam* fantasy about plots. I wondered if the source could have been the congressman who fell asleep in a chair during the session at my house, snoring blissfully through the evening, and perhaps wanted to get even for his embarrassment. The significance of the story, however, was its tone, its implication that to oppose Diem was somehow sinful, or un-American.

Of all the noise reaching Saigon from the United States about the showdown with Diem, nothing came near to the performance of Mme. Nhu. When she left Saigon on September 9, her announced mission was to represent Vietnam at a meeting of the Inter-Parliamentary Union at Belgrade. It was only after she arrived in Belgrade that she revealed her intention to visit the United States. She already had a valid visa, but there was a debate inside the U. S. Government on whether she should be permitted to come. For all the vaunted political savvy of the New Frontier, the Administration was divided. Would the American people be charmed, or disgusted?

The decision was to have faith in the people and take a chance.* The result was certainly one of the most bizarre political phenomena of modern times. Mme. Nhu was the personality who probably had done more to turn the United States Government against the Diem regime than any other single person, especially if her claim was true that she personally persuaded Diem to attack the pagodas. She was the most articulate spokesman of the regime, and certainly its prettiest. By chance she arrived in the United States (October 7) at a moment when the nation was just beginning to realize the gravity of our new pressures on the Diem regime, and was torn by doubt. At that moment things were so touch-and-go that she conceivably could have saved both the regime and the lives of her husband and brother-in-law

---

* Unlike the Johnson Administration which refused her a visa in June 1964.

if she could have moved American public opinion only a few percentage points in their favor.

There was irony in the attitude of the American press and radio-TV networks which she had attacked so savagely as Communist dupes. The motivation perhaps was less fair play than audience interest, but Mme. Nhu nevertheless was given a hearing such as seldom had been granted to a foreign visitor with a political message (except perhaps Khrushchev), projecting her person and what she had to say almost daily for three weeks into millions of American homes. She failed spectacularly. Public opinion polls indicated that the American people disapproved of her as much as by thirteen to one. In Saigon at the time, however, we had no inkling of this, and we followed her press notices with bug-eyed fixation.

Mme. Nhu's prepared speeches were relatively reasonable appeals for sympathy for a nation engaged in bitter struggle against Communist insurrection. When she submitted to questions from newsmen, however, she repeatedly came up with remarks reflecting the same irrationality that had so harassed us in Saigon.

In Rome on September 25, for example, she said: "The junior officers of the U.S. military mission are acting like little soldiers of fortune." This drew an angry riposte from Ambassador Lodge: "It is incomprehensible to me how anyone can speak so cruelly. These men should be thanked and not insulted. These junior officers are risking their lives every day. Some of them have been killed side by side with their Vietnamese comrades." It was Lodge's first public statement as Ambassador, and was published all over the world. It nettled Mme. Nhu, who spent the next week or two in complicated explanations about how she did not really mean what she had said.

In Paris, October 3: The Buddhist burnings were "barbarous sacrifices . . . a Communist-inspired plot."

In New York, October 9, her first public statement in the U. S.: The United States Information Service, the New York *Times*, United Press International, the Associated Press and the Voice of America were "working feverishly" to overthrow the Diem regime.

In New York, October 12, in a national TV show ("Meet the Press"): "Your government is following the new fashion of liberalism, which is much closer to Communism than we are." Again she accused USIS, "which in my opinion speaks too freely," and the Saigon newsmen of plotting against the regime.

Her tour must have been a remarkable spectacle. There were demonstrations, e.g. placards reading MME. NHU, PENTAGON PUPPET. Columnist Alsop beseeched the U. S. Government not to behave like a "bee-stung adolescent" in reacting to her "egomaniacal maunderings." At the same time, often in the same cities, her father, the resigned ambassador Tran Van Chuong, was making speeches bitterly assailing the Diem regime. He asserted that any one of "hundreds of men" could do a better job than Diem, that "there is no possibility at all of victory over the Communists under the present regime . . . which has become the greatest asset of the Communists and the greatest obstacle to victory."

The comedy reached some kind of peak on October 18, when Mme. Nhu told the National Press Club in Washington that the economic aid suspensions were "treason" and "a childish gesture," and that "I have the impression that American policy is *led* (italics mine) by USIS, which we find strange."

This particular brick in the TV screen caught the attention of my fourteen-year-old son in the U. S. He commented in a letter that "you must be very busy if you are trying to upset the government." I replied that this was like saying that the New York Mets would win the World Series, but I did not really think it was funny. On the contrary it was a scary business, like a nightmare about being accused falsely of a crime by an insane judge.

In Saigon during those last weeks, the regime's public utterances were only moderately less hysterical than Mme. Nhu's outbursts abroad. There was less accent, however, on such bugaboos as CIA and USIS and more recognition of the reality that the enemy was the whole U. S. Government. In their desperate efforts somehow to turn the tide of events, Diem and Nhu struck out against the American press and radio/TV networks, on the theme that it was they who had poisoned the American public and government. As often as possible they vented their bitterness to visiting non-American journalists, presumably in hope of more sympathetic treatment.

On September 22, for example, Diem told a German TV correspondent that the American press had presented news of the Buddhist affairs "in an utterly wrong light. . . . Thereunder lies a campaign of intoxication relayed by the international Communist agitation-propaganda apparatus, which has greatly prejudiced relations between the two countries."

In the *Times of Vietnam* a page-one headline cried UPI LIES, LIES, LIES.

Diem complained to an Indian journalist that the "televised murder" of Thich Quang Duc, the first suicide by burning, was part of a plot to topple the government through "a systematic and well-orchestrated international distortion campaign by means of the press."

Nhu suggested to a Canadian correspondent that Communist agents had infiltrated the Buddhist movement and were deliberately trying to exploit the movement to disrupt Vietnamese-American cooperation and thus to avoid certain defeat. Nhu added that one of these agents, meaning Thich

Tri Quang, "is now hiding in the American Embassy in Saigon."

On September 27 the regime went through the motions of a general election for the National Assembly. It announced that in their respective constituencies Nhu won 99.99 percent of the votes and Mme. Nhu 99.8 percent—her constituency was in Long An Province, where at least half of the people were controlled by the V.C.

In a speech to the new assembly on October 7 Diem claimed that the Communists had already been defeated, asserted that they therefore had turned to other means, and cried: "The Communist atheists and slave-traders have in a certain measure succeeded—thanks to the demagogic and criminal complicity of a certain number of traitors and foreign adventurers, and thanks also to a huge Western press which serves them gratuitously as a soundbox—in intoxicating a not negligible portion of national and international opinion with the so-called Buddhist affair."

For one of his last interviews, with CBS on October 17, Diem was in a different mood, perhaps because he now realized both the futility of further outbursts and the extreme danger of his position. "With or without American aid," he said, "I will keep up the fight, and I will always fully maintain my friendship towards the American people." This was a tone that he might usefully have adopted earlier.

In a press conference two days later, Nhu appeared to be similarly shaken. He made the familiar charge that "CIA agents plus some other employees of American civilian government agencies" had tried to provoke a coup d'état through the Buddhists. His main theme, however, struck a note that was almost plaintive: "People here are wondering what the United States is doing. There is an atmosphere of distrust. People have lost confidence in the United States. . . . I do not see what U.S. policy is at this state." This was

Nhu's last public appearance before his death thirteen days later.

Behind the scenes Nhu reacted like a cornered animal. He was increasingly possessed by scornful hatred of the United States, and spent his last weeks exploring every conceivable avenue of escape from his country's dependence on the Americans, or at least to salvage some kind of continuing power for the regime.

Attempting to dig in for a prolonged test of wills with the Americans, Nhu ordered top officials of the regime to conserve funds and supplies with the objective of surviving for a year or even longer without American aid. This was not as silly as it sounded. U.S. aid had been shoveled so generously into Vietnam that the regime had built up enormous stockpiles of foreign exchange (about $150 million) and war materiel. If conditions had been otherwise stable, it could have kept going for months before the aid cuts would hurt badly—long enough probably for pro-Diem pressures on Kennedy at home to force him to capitulate.

There were multiplying indications that Nhu also thought seriously about trying to establish contact with the Viet Cong to discuss a negotiated settlement. His idea presumably would have been to use the threat of such a settlement as a weapon against the Americans, or perhaps to bring about a "neutralist" government in which he could hope to retain a degree of power for himself and Diem. There were reports that Nhu actually did make contact with Hanoi, via the French. Such a move would have played neatly into the hands of President de Gaulle, who had broached his ideas about neutralizing Southeast Asia only a few weeks earlier, on August 30.

There was a glimpse of the depth of Nhu's despair, and bitterness, in his remarks to a foreign, non-American visitor in mid-October. He said he wanted all American advisors to go home forthwith, including the helicopter crews, though material aid should continue. Said Nhu: "Without the Americans we could win the war in two or three years. With the Americans, who knows? Perhaps never. The United States does not understand this kind of war." The visitor asked what he thought of Lodge. "Mr. Dulles applied moral principles in his diplomacy, though he often made mistakes," Nhu replied. "There is no morality in present American diplomacy."

(3)

Saigon during those last grim weeks became an eerie, *non sequitur* world. In the presence of the isolated fortress that its brooding, pathological occupants had made of Gia Long Palace, almost nothing made sense, and the rumors multiplied. The sorcerer's broomsticks were everywhere, lurking in the shadows of our half-knowledge of what was happening, or about to happen. There were signs that they were also invading the minds of the Vietnamese, eroding their Asian placidity, working on ancient superstitions.

Thousands of people flocked to a lake near Hue where there was supposed to be a magical fish that occasionally surfaced to utter oracular comments on the state of the world. Thousands more were said to have climbed a mountain in the central highlands where a Buddhist nun was performing miraculous cures. In Saigon a rumor swept through the city that a Buddha in one of the pagodas had been seen to weep real tears. (Not so, said the Saigon press; there had been a heavy rain and the roof leaked.) Another rumor raced through the streets that the sun had been seen swinging back and forth in the sky, encircled by a great ring of fire.

One day a clipping from a proof sheet of the *Times of Vietnam* found its way to my desk. This is what it said:

"Eleven monkeys with shaven heads and sporting tags bearing the name of the President (Diem) were released by mysterious 'agents' at the Central Market square yesterday afternoon. The monkeys, presumably shooed out from a moving car, scampered about amidst shrieks and screams by market vendors and fishwives. They melted away underneath market stalls.

"There was wild speculation among the hundreds of eyewitnesses to the monkey business that the animals were of foreign breed. Said one woman: 'Certainly they must have been imported monkeys since they were decidedly bigger than the local breed.' It was the second time monkeys demonstrated against the government. Last week five monkeys staged a similar demonstration at the same place.

"Investigations are underway to trace the sponsors of the monkeys and determine their foreign origin."

The item was never published, presumably pulled out of the paper on orders from the censors. We never found out whether the story was true, or where it came from, or what it was all about.

Even a foreigner could sense something of how the people felt. Except for what they heard via the Voice of America, or rumor, they knew few of the details, but they were unmistakably aware that the United States had moved against the regime. This was what a majority of politically conscious Vietnamese had wanted, but there was nevertheless a feeling of awesome expectation in the air, of recognition that a mighty world power was calling the tune. Some Vietnamese no doubt related this to memories of the French colonial era. Others regarded it in the same way as the sun swinging in the sky, as an act of forces beyond their comprehension. But everywhere there was suppressed excitement.

One night in a Tu Do bar I was talking to a Vietnamese hostess. Softly, without warning, after a furtive look around the room, she began singing "Dixie" under her breath, in beautifully accented English. There was something about the tone, or the look in her eye, that reminded me instantly of a moment nearly twenty years earlier. It was in France, when I was a prisoner of the Germans, being marched through a village. On a street corner a Frenchman looking blandly down at the gutter began whistling "Tipperary." In both cases the sense was: Courage, we are with you. Then she giggled with embarrassment and demanded another three-dollar glass of fake vermouth.

Among the Indian merchants around the Caravelle Hotel, there was a more cynical recognition that something was up. The Indians for some reason seemed to have a near monopoly on black market money transactions in Southeast Asia. The rate for one dollar (officially 73 piasters, normally around 90 on the black market) began climbing steadily, to 110, then 130, then 150. During the days just before the coup there were reports of frantic Vietnamese and Chinese businessmen offering as much as two hundred to a dollar in desperate efforts to convert the wealth that close association with the regime had produced.

Saigon was like a deathly still summer night with heat lightning flickering on the horizon. Then on Saturday, October 5, there began the last episode of this insane period.

In an article for the New York *Times* house organ, correspondent Halberstam described how it looked to him: "I was sitting in the office last Saturday . . . when there was a brief anonymous phone call suggesting that I be in the Central Market at high noon. . . . I went there, found most of my colleagues already assembled and waited. Thirty minutes passed and we had just about decided to bug out when a man burst into flames. I shall not describe that scene in any detail. Watching a human being burn himself to death gives a man a helpless feeling and a reporter a rare confusion of personal emotion. . . . Well, we covered it. . . ."

The burning—a Buddhist bonze—was the first since the

pagoda raids six weeks earlier. It was spectacular defiance of the regime's harsh campaign to pacify the Buddhists. Secret police on the scene, apparently alerted by the suspicious assembly of newsmen, reacted in fury, concentrating on photographers. They managed to catch up with one, Grant Wolfkill of NBC, and attempted to seize or smash his camera. John Sharkey, also of NBC, and Halberstam (who had also starred in the July 7 clash) went to his defense. In a slam-bang free-for-all, they managed to beat off the police and escape. All three sustained bruises, Sharkey seriously enough to be briefly hospitalized for a head wound.* Ambassador Lodge immediately registered a strong protest with the palace.

Photographs of the burning—including a color shot this time—were flashed around the world to give the lie undeniably to the regime's claim to have settled the Buddhist dispute. The regime was incensed.

Its first impulse was direct reprisals against the newsmen. The *Times of Vietnam* suggested that the newsmen had "instigated" the burning. It reported that the government was considering their arrest as accessories to a crime since they had known about it in advance and failed to notify the police. There was also a rumor that no fewer than eight reporters were about to be expelled summarily. The regime eventually decided against that kind of action, perhaps because it was shaken by news of the U.S. aid suspensions which came out two days after the burning.

Instead it flailed out in a renewed war of nerves against its own people, the correspondents, and the U. S. Mission. Nhu was the force behind this. He may have thought he could scare us into a change of policy. More likely he was

---

* NBC promptly flew Sharkey back to New York where he appeared, head still bandaged, on a TV panel of newsmen with Mme. Nhu. She was quoted as saying she hoped he would soon recover.

simply venting his anger. (There was speculation that Diem may not even have known about it.)

Police all over the country were ordered to tighten surveillance and general harassment of persons friendly to the Americans and of Vietnamese employees of American agencies. We learned after the coup, for example, that a teen-age girl student at the University of Hue was arrested and brutally tortured—electrodes attached to her nipples—on suspicion of being an "agent" for USIS, apparently because she had been a regular visitor to the USIS library.

Not one of our Vietnamese employees resigned, or otherwise wavered in loyalty to USIS, but many of them were frightened, and increasingly resisted assignments outside of Saigon for fear of police reprisals. I tried to damp down some of this by delivering a speech to the Vietnamese staff explaining the absurdity of the regime's charges against us and strongly reminding them of our long-standing policy not to engage in any sort of political activity. I then arranged for a copy of the speech to reach Nhu through his own clandestine channels. There was no evidence that it did any good.

Much of the regime's ugly repression of its own people went on without our knowledge, but we heard enough to realize that it was whimsical and usually inept. In the ultimate clutch the regime's own secret apparatuses were coming apart, its agents resorting variously to panicky torture, or quietly pocketing such funds as were easily available and disappearing, or defecting to the Americans and/or the Viet Cong. The Diem regime, in short, was not even a good police state. The result among its people was a feeling of contemptuous terror.

Many Americans had close Vietnamese friends who were now being persecuted uselessly, often because they merely had been friendly to Americans.

One such case was a Vietnamese widow who had long

been an intimate friend of several American families. One day she appeared at an American home and begged for refuge, sobbing convulsively that she knew she was about to be arrested. On instructions from the Embassy, the answer was no. She went to a second American home and received the same treatment. She tried a third home, this time belonging to a senior Embassy officer whose wife begged him tearfully—and uselessly—for hours to forget his protocol and be a human being. The widow finally went back to her own home. She never was arrested, saved perhaps by the coup a few days later.

Nhu tried secretly to poison the minds of the Vietnamese armed forces against the United States. We acquired one directive asserting that:

1. There was no difference between the Buddhist crisis in Vietnam and the Negro crisis in the United States.
2. President Kennedy ordered his brother Robert to force the South to accept integration, just as President Diem ordered his brother Nhu to discipline the Buddhists.
3. The Vietnamese Government in fact had been less extreme in its actions because it had not used dogs and cattle prods against the Buddhists.
4. The U. S. Government controlled the American press, just as the Vietnamese Government controlled the Vietnamese press.
5. Therefore press reports that the U. S. had stopped aid to Vietnam were merely a lie designed to dominate Vietnam. The U. S. was too deeply committed in Vietnam to risk withdrawing its support.

To harass Americans directly, Nhu planted a new crop of assassination rumors, but the main accent this time was on a flood of reports deliberately fed into American intelligence channels that various U.S. installations were to be attacked by "spontaneous" mobs protesting U.S. policy. The scares continued, almost daily, for two or three weeks until the coup. The main supposed targets were the Embassy, USIS, and the AP and UPI offices, never any of our military installations. The regime at least was rational enough not to interfere with U.S. military aid.

We realized of course that most if not all the tips were palace plants—which was easy to do because of the intimate relationship that existed between the U.S. and Vietnamese intelligence and security organizations. But it would have been risky to ignore them. For one thing it was possible that Nhu's mind was cracking and that he was capable of any kind of madness. In my case there was also the gnawing memory of the day in 1955 when I had witnessed a precedent, the "spontaneous" pro-Diem mob attack on Saigon's Majestic Hotel to protest the policies of the International Control Commission which had its headquarters there. The mob was so spontaneous that it came equipped with crowbars and sledgehammers (useful for breaking up toilets). It made a shambles of the hotel but carefully avoided damage to rooms occupied by Americans, who were then in good standing.

There were persistent reports that the mission of a mob attack on USIS would be to "discover" proof that we had plotted a coup, supported the Buddhists and otherwise maneuvered nefariously against the regime. The ironic truth was that a search of our files would have proved conclusively that the regime's ideas about us were crazy. By that time, in fact, Lodge had so completely cut off everyone from his operations that a thorough analysis of our files would also have proved that USIS knew little more about U.S. activities than Nhu himself, perhaps less.

As the rumors multiplied we took such precautions as we could. There were steel anti-mob gates on the stairways of our building for closing off the upper floors, so we made plans about who would be responsible for closing them. We dusted off the metal barrels and special chemicals that many American government offices maintain overseas for burning classified papers in an emergency, and listened to instructions on how to do it. We also made a study of possible escape routes in case a mob broke through the steel gates. They all involved some formidable gymnastics, like climbing over balconies to an adjoining building.

Apart from what we could do ourselves, the hundred and fifty Vietnamese and twenty-odd Americans working in the USIS building were largely dependent for help, in case of an attack, on the small, overextended U. S. Marine Corps guard attached to the Saigon Embassy. They were the unsung heroes of that whole traumatic period. Repeatedly they were on duty as much as thirty-six hours in a stretch without rest, and never complained. Their commander, Gunnery Sergeant Leroy W. Westrom, was a relaxed, soft-spoken combat veteran, six feet six inches of solid muscle, who looked as though he could handle any ordinary mob single-handedly. By comparison the rest of us felt like panicky kids in a thunderstorm.

Westrom and his men stored tear gas grenades, gas masks, pistols and eventually a submachine gun, plus ammunition, at various points around the building. It was all out of sight, but I began to feel as though I were working in a pillbox. The system was that two or three Marines would show up to defend the place every time there was a report of an imminent attack. My third-floor office, on a corner with a view of the main approaches to the building, would then become a sort of command post. Besides the Marines, alerts regularly attracted reporters and cameramen who would clutter the place with their paraphernalia like a Hollywood studio. It was part of the exercise each time to lock up classified papers. Our staff of three American secretaries got so much practice that they could do it in one minute forty seconds flat.

The high point of this wild period came on Tuesday, October 22. Early that morning there was a routine report that we would be attacked. Then came a series of reports that a mob of four thousand men, supposedly secret police and Special Forces troops disguised in civilian clothes, was gathering on the edge of the city. Its targets reportedly would be the offices of UPI, AP and USIS in that order, and perhaps also the Embassy. At about 11:30 A.M. there came a still more strident report that an attack on one of these targets was "imminent." Westrom and his men began removing tear gas grenades from their boxes and lining them up on my desk. At exactly 12:10 P.M. the Embassy security people called to warn excitedly that an attack was to come "now."

This was the worst scare yet, and it sounded authentic. Should we evacuate the building? Many of the people milling around my office said it was essential to do so, immediately.

But the square outside looked normal, with traffic dying down for the midday siesta. In twenty minutes, at twelve-thirty, our staff was scheduled to go home for lunch. An order to evacuate would seriously damage the morale of our people. If this was another false alarm, a panicky reaction was just what Nhu wanted. Yet if an attack came, and members of our staff were trapped in the building and injured, or worse, it would be my fault for ignoring an urgent warning. The square was still quiet, and now it was twelve-fifteen, just fifteen minutes to go. I thought dammit a mob simply cannot materialize out of nothing in an instant, that we surely would have a few minutes notice after the first demonstrators appeared. But suppose they arrived in trucks? Would Nhu dare be so blatant?

Partly on hunch, partly in anger at the whole grotesque mess I was in, I announced "the hell with it, let's take our chances." It was a long, long fifteen minutes, but nothing happened. At twelve-thirty the staff went home normally.

Next day I went to the Embassy to ask Ambassador Lodge if anything could be done to put an end to this kind of harassment. He was displeased. "At least you have a modern building," he snapped. "This place is a firetrap. Look at these wooden floors."

Via the grapevine we heard, however, that Lodge had not been inactive. One story circulated widely, though it possibly was apocryphal, that he had said something like this to a top Vietnamese official: "You surely do not intend any harm to Americans in Vietnam. If you do, of course we will bring in the Marines. The Japanese tried to fight the Marines. On a lot of those islands in the Pacific there were not enough Japanese left to bury their own dead after the battle. You wouldn't like that, would you?" There were rumors, which we all hoped to be true, that the U. S. 7th Fleet was cruising just over the horizon in the South China Sea while Nhu played out his vicious little game.

There was not much more of it. On October 26 the regime staged its annual national day parade. The diplomatic corps appeared solemnly in white suits and sat in the blazing sun for four hours. (With Lodge's permission I stayed away, in unnoticed protest of the indignities that the regime had been heaping upon USIS and myself.) Diem reviewed the troops and tanks and armored cars—many of which were shooting at the palace only six days later—from an open limousine. His speech was moderate, even conciliatory, deploring that unnamed enemies "have sought to sow discord among ourselves, and between us and friendly nations, in order to undermine our fighting strength, but thanks to our wisdom and self-control we have successfully withstood all trials. . . ."

Next day another bonze burned himself to death, this time in front of the Saigon cathedral just as the faithful were emerging from Sunday Mass.

On the same afternoon there was a last-minute invitation

for Lodge to accompany Diem to the inauguration of an atomic energy research laboratory, financed by American aid, at Dalat north of Saigon. During the course of the trip Diem also escorted Lodge to visit a nearby strategic hamlet. This was the first contact between the two men since the McNamara-Taylor visit a month earlier. It was also a first hint of response to Lodge's deliberate silence to force the regime to "come to me."

Months later, in an interview with the New York *Times* on June 29, 1964, Lodge remarked that "we wanted reform and a change for the better and, as a matter of fact, we came awfully close to doing it. I think Mr. Nhu, for instance, came very close to leaving, and if he had, he'd be alive today." It was a reasonable guess that this was one of the subjects that Diem and Lodge discussed on that occasion just three days before Diem was killed.

Thus the stage was prepared. There was a glimpse of its setting in the last issue of the *Times of Vietnam* which appeared just an hour or two before the coup began on November 1.

On page one, a photograph of Diem, pudgy, intent, confident, chatting with two visiting officials of an American oil company . . . A photograph of Admiral Felt arriving for an overnight visit, warmly shaking hands with General Tran Van Don, then acting chief of staff of the Vietnamese armed forces, who would emerge next day as one of the leaders of the coup . . . A story quoting a senior American officer as saying that Vietnamese soldiers were "just like American soldiers, loyal to their government" . . . A dispatch from Los Angeles quoting Mme. Nhu as saying that Henry Cabot Lodge "has become more mysterious than an Asian." On page two, a report on an interview with General Harkins paraphrasing him as saying that "'victory, in the sense it would apply to this kind of war,' is just months away."

By chance that last issue also carried an interminable article entitled "The Truth About the Buddhist Question in Vietnam," running for six columns of invective against the American press and government. Its final thought:

"Why does the American government show more animosity towards strong anti-Communists like Presidents Park (of Korea) and Diem than toward Communists like Castro? . . . That is another story. A long, dark, and sad story that some day must be unfolded. But the crushing fact is there. In Vietnam, once again, the West has fired in the back of its friend for the sole benefit of its enemies."

CHAPTER EIGHT

"A Change of Personnel"

(1)

On that Friday morning, All Saints Day, November 1, 1963, Ambassador Lodge played out a last parody on seven years of American support for Ngo Dinh Diem. He knew that the Vietnamese armed forces were poised to destroy the regime, but he nevertheless went through the motions of a courtesy call on Diem with Admiral Felt at ten o'clock at Gia Long Palace. The small talk included a remark by Diem that the Americans should not be alarmed by a new rash of "rumors" about an imminent coup d'état. Everyone chuckled.

Immediately after the visit, Felt went to the airport and took off for his headquarters at Honolulu. Whether he knew about the conspiracy was never clarified. There were press reports at the time, however, that the coup leaders had asked Lodge not to inform the American military of their plans for fear the latter would tip off Diem. Felt's visit to the palace was normal protocol and Lodge would have had to go along anyway to prevent palace suspicions, which would be particularly pertinent if the upcoming coup were a failure. It was at least possible, however, that Lodge also went through the exercise to avoid awkward questions from the U.S. commander-in-chief for the Pacific. Felt had known and worked intimately with Diem for years.

The plotters not only had shrewdly chosen a Roman Catholic holiday for the coup, but they had fixed H-Hour for 1:30

P.M., at the height of the midday siesta when most of Saigon's population would be asleep, and the streets conveniently clear for military movements. For those of us who were not in the know, the surprise was complete, as it apparently was also for the regime, despite months of innumerable rumors that a coup d'état was coming at any moment.

At one forty-five, at lunch with a friend from the Embassy, I had just served myself a lamb chop when the telephone rang. It was the Embassy reporting that a detachment of Vietnamese Marines had seized the central post office and suggesting that perhaps we should get back to work. The lamb chop was abandoned.

We took a taxi, one of the hundreds of blue bug-sized Renaults that abound in Saigon, and asked the driver to go to USIS and the American Embassy. The driver knew some French and immediately volunteered that there had been some *coups de feu* (shooting) near the airport. He looked at us quizzically, as though we might know about it—perhaps because of the address we had given. We asked who was shooting. "Who knows?" he replied, with an eloquent shrug. Our route took us past the post office. Indeed there were some troops in full battle dress, lounging around the entrance, plus one or two armored cars with guns covering the adjoining square. Otherwise, however, the city was normal, somnolent in the scorching midday sun. Back at my office I telephoned the Embassy and was told that I would be advised if and as there were special instructions such as closing up shop for the day. Then I tuned in the Armed Forces Radio Station (AFRS). It was broadcasting "White Christmas."

At this moment, just before 2 P.M., troops were swiftly carrying out the rebel plan. It was simple: seize the city's two main radio stations, occupy police stations, deploy in blocking positions to prevent loyal reinforcements (there were none) from entering the city, seize the central post office (which also contained commercial facilities for cable and telephone communications with the outside world), seize the airport, prepare to attack the barracks of the presidential guard, and finally prepare to assault the palace itself. As it turned out, the whole operation required only eighteen hours. But little of this was evident at the time.

On the contrary, the dominating characteristic of a battle, or street rioting, or a breakdown of law and order of any sort is always the unsettling, often frightening vacuum of information on what is going on. A man caught in such chaos must reasonably assume that there may be danger, perhaps desperate danger, but he cannot tell what the danger is, nor where it may come from. Worst of all, there is always the gnawing thought that perhaps he should be taking actions now that may be the only hope of averting disaster a few minutes later. But what actions?

In those lonely ten or fifteen minutes one of my first thoughts was the possibility that whatever was happening had been instigated by the regime itself. There had been repeated rumors that Nhu was planning a false coup as a means to expose his enemies, who would then be exterminated. If this was now happening, there was the uncomfortable possibility that Nhu would use the disorder to send his much-rumored "spontaneous" mobs against American installations, including USIS. I picked up a telephone. Still working. This was temporarily reassuring since it probably could be assumed that if Nhu was still pulling the strings, he would cut off our telephones as he had for the pagoda raids in August. I was to find myself testing the telephone perhaps a dozen times in the next hour or two. The dial tone became a frail symbol of security in the midst of the pandemonium that followed.

It was an incongruous moment. Still nothing on AFRS but a disc jockey program. Still no word from the Embassy. Still no unusual sound or movement in the streets outside. I sat at my desk and contemplated the fact that the U. S. Information Service in Saigon was fresh out of information, except that perhaps the host government was coming apart, and perhaps the U. S. Government wanted it to come apart. Or perhaps it was all a false alarm.

It was a brief interlude. First came the welcome sight of two or three of Sergeant Westrom's Marines, who swiftly began preparing their familiar defenses again, posting a man downstairs to close the steel gate if we were attacked. Then the telephone and the voice of one of our American secretaries, Ann Horne, wonderfully calm and matter of fact: "Mr. Mecklin, there are some people shooting at each other out in the street. Shall I come to work?" I could hear gunfire in the background as she spoke. The USIS building was steel-reinforced concrete, defended and provisioned with emergency food and water supplies. In the event of widespread street fighting, it would probably be more secure than a private home or apartment building. Since Miss Horne had no dependents to worry about, I told her to come to the office if she could make it without taking risks. She waited for a pause in the shooting, hailed a taxi and arrived safely, and unperturbed.

Soon most of the rest of our staff had showed up, several after similar experiences. Around two forty-five AFRS began intermittent broadcasts of an official announcement that all Americans should stay off the streets and at home except on urgent official business. It said there was a "civil disturbance." Between bulletins, more popular music. At about this time, the rebels gained control of the main Saigon radio and began a series of proclamations, mixed with martial music. They were a strident mixture of invective against the Diem regime and orders to the population, e.g. a 7 P.M. curfew.

Suddenly a burst of heavy machine-gun fire rocked the

air, then another, and another. One of the Marines, craning his head out a window, shouted: "It's a plane. Attacking the palace. Salvo of rockets." The firing had been antiaircraft guns in the palace area. One of the rockets struck the U. S. Marines' barracks a couple of blocks beyond the palace. Fortunately the Marines all had been called out on duty around the city, but one man's bunk and personal effects were destroyed. The attack reminded us effectively that USIS was only about two hundred yards from the palace, by far the closest of any American installation except a BOQ (bachelor officers' quarters) next door called the Rex. If it were a true coup—which remained to be established—this meant that heavy fighting easily might develop all around us, which was just what happened.

By now, about 3 P.M., there were twenty or thirty people milling around my office—newsmen, Marines, USIS personnel, and a number of others I had never seen before.

Two armored cars lumbered into the square outside our building. We had no idea whether they were rebels or loyal to Diem, though the latter seemed more likely. They took up positions, side by side, commanding Le Loi, a broad, tree-lined boulevard leading to the Central Market a half mile away, and on for several miles beyond to Cholon, the Chinese section of the city. By now there was almost no traffic in the streets, but the sidewalks were teeming with people who watched apprehensively.

Without warning, both cars began firing their cannon down Le Loi, barrels depressed almost to horizontal. This was the heart of Saigon. It was comparable with stationing a tank in New York's Times Square and firing down Broadway. The people flung themselves on the pavement, jamming into doorways and shops, scuttling around corners, cringing in fear of the unknown.

The crack of a heavy gun is an awesome thing in the open. In the closed-in passages of a city, where the noise ricochets from walls and pavements, it becomes obscene. The muzzle blast hammers at casements and windows like a rude, arrogant giant. The noise is so severe that it can rupture an eardrum. It becomes unthinkable, wild, barbaric desecration of orderly, civilized living. The impact of the noise, the blast, and the stench of gunpowder is overwhelming and terrifying.

We could not make out what the two armored cars were shooting at. (We found out later that it probably was the rebel troops who had occupied the police station about a mile down Le Loi. The cars were trying to prevent them from advancing farther toward the palace.) There was obviously an imminent possibility, however, that somebody would begin shooting back. In this case the targets would be about twenty-five feet from our front door. It now seemed clear that whatever was happening was happening for keeps. We ordered immediate evacuation of the USIS building, with the understanding that if anyone preferred to remain he could do so. With the building rocking every few seconds from cannon blasts, almost all our Vietnamese employees and most of the American staff with families went home.

The firing continued for a half hour or more. By now we had a two-way radio tied in with an emergency American net. Against the background of the guns in the street a voice was asking repeatedly: "This is Buster. Where is Horatio? Repeat, where is Horatio?" Horatio was the code name (i.e. my substitute for the true one) for Ambassador Lodge. It turned out later to be a communications mix-up. Lodge was safely at his residence where he remained throughout the upheaval, leaving his deputy, William Trueheart, in charge at the Embassy. But until I could get through to the Embassy by telephone, the chaos was compounded by the thought that something might have happened to the Ambassador.

Midst the confusion a woman correspondent for a European newspaper, who had arrived in Saigon only the day before, nervously pressed a note in my hand. "It's my mother's address," she said. "You will write, please? If anything goes wrong."

I made a tour of the building. In the library on the ground floor, protected only by plate glass windows, I found thirty or forty Vietnamese who had come in from the street to seek shelter, most of them lying on the floor in panic, the blast of the guns outside slapping the windows at ten- or fifteen-second intervals. One of the American Marines was there. "What am I supposed to do about this?" he asked. We decided to try to move the people to an inside office where they would be less exposed to flying glass. I pointed to the office door, shouting *"Di, di"* (go, go), but they refused to budge, apparently thinking I was trying to throw them out in the street. Finally a little boy got the point and persuaded everyone to move.

By 4:30 or 5 P.M. the armored cars mercifully stopped shooting and disappeared. In the distance, however, there was continued sporadic firing. It seemed fairly certain that a genuine effort was under way to destroy the Diem regime —which hopefully meant there would be no direct attack on USIS—but the vacuum of information on what was happening was more uncomfortable than ever. Among other things, we had no idea who was winning, except that the rebels controlled the Saigon radio. Apart from the Marines, most of our visitors had departed. Our building, like the streets outside, was virtually deserted, our telephones silent. It was like the waiting room in a hospital maternity ward.

David Sheppard, our Deputy Public Affairs Officer, suggested that whatever good I could do would be at the Embassy, which had become a command post for the American community. He volunteered to stay on at USIS "to answer the phone" (translation: to help the Marines protect the building). In the circumstances I guess this was the right move, but I was glad he suggested it.

(2)

Except that its heavy iron grill gates were closed, I found no unusual activity around the Embassy. It looked the same as it had for more than a decade—a disgrace to the United States.

The building was located on a shabby street corner in a congested commercial district with no grounds, no parking space except the street, and little dignity. A onetime office building, it had six floors but they were so narrow that there was space for only six or eight closet-size offices on each floor. The washroom on each floor could be reached only by an open walkway. The building was flanked by a rundown apartment house so close that the American Ambassador could look through a window over the shoulder of his receptionist into a back terrace cluttered with refuse and the burned-out joss sticks of an unkempt Buddhist family shrine.

Every Ambassador who had ever served in Saigon had appealed to Washington for something to be done. A State Department request for funds to build a new Embassy had been before Congress for several years, but regularly passed over. World capitals were blossoming with new American Embassies—in politically comfortable places like Stockholm, Mexico City and London. But in Vietnam where we were spending more money in one day ($1.5 million) than it would cost for a new building, where a show of lasting American respect and confidence in the country's future would have been psychologically valuable, Congress was content to permit the American flag to be displayed on a building that would risk condemnation as a firetrap in many American cities.

That kind of building does, however, tend to encourage a special kind of camaraderie among the people who must work there. On that memorable Friday night this was accentuated by the shared uncertainties and the absence of Ambassador Lodge, who had remained at home since lunch. The top floor, normally dominated by Lodge's presence, became a gathering place. A few adventurers even risked watching the battle from Lodge's air-conditioned office, where the view was not quite as good as the roof but there was better protection against stray bullets.

The Saigon Embassy had been through so many eruptions of this sort over the years that it was well equipped to keep track of what was happening and had swung into action like a well-drilled fire company when the coup began. Two or three "language officers" (a bureaucratic euphemism for foreign service officers who know the local language) were monitoring radio broadcasts. Other officers with walkie-talkie radios were moving around the city in automobiles trying to observe events and reporting in to a control center in the Embassy. By late afternoon an American had even talked himself into the headquarters of the Vietnamese Joint General Staff (JGS) which had now become the rebel command post; he was able to report by telephone on what he could pick up, though it was far from comprehensive or even consistent. (It would have been physically difficult, if not impossible, for anyone to reach the palace to establish himself similarly there, even if Diem and Nhu would permit it, which was doubtful.) Embassy political officers were firing off "flash" cables (absolute priority, usually used only for material to be seen immediately by the Secretary of State or even the President) on such information as could be obtained. By morning the cable file was as thick as a Dagwood sandwich, and almost as interesting.

In contrast to the vacuum of information at USIS the Embassy was flooded with rumors, conflicting reports, and speculation. By 5 P.M. we had several persuasive reports that the reason for the apparent lull in the shooting was an effort by the coup leaders to convince Diem by telephone that he should surrender. We also had reports that the rebels had given him an ultimatum, to surrender by 6 P.M. or the palace would be obliterated by the Air Force.

As the deadline approached we watched from the Embassy roof. Saigon from that angle was a city of towering trees, spreading greenery everywhere with occasional buildings reaching up among them. We could see only parts of the red slate roof of the palace, just to the left of a block of office buildings. The palace was about six blocks from the Embassy.

Sure enough, there was a plane. It looked like a T-28 fighter, coming in low, apparently heading directly for the palace. On, and on it came. We braced for the crash of a bomb. Then at the last moment it turned away. A second plane performed the same maneuver. Then both of them orbited for fifteen or twenty minutes over the distant outskirts of the city. We never found out what they were doing. A third plane, meantime, whooshed directly over the Embassy, also apparently headed for the palace, but we could see immediately that it was a C-47 (the military version of the ancient DC-3). Were they planning to drop a bomb out the door? Then it too veered away and wheeled at low level around the city—dropping rebel leaflets, we learned later.

The deadline came and went. Soon thereafter nightfall. No air attack. They were still negotiating, we heard. We never did find out if that was the real reason, though there was no question that the Air Force was solidly with the rebels. Through most of the night we could see the navigation lights of one or two planes maneuvering over the city. A U. S. Air Force officer among the rooftop spectators assured us repeatedly that the Vietnamese Air Force lacked training in night attacks and that an air strike before dawn was therefore impossible. But we never knew for sure.

There were multitudinous reports of troop movements around the city and outskirts, but the observing officers were never sure where they were going or whose side they were on. Several ten-ton army trucks went by the Embassy, loaded to capacity with troops, who waved to the U. S. Marines on guard downstairs. Politically the situation was so confused that this did not prove whether they were rebels or loyal Diemists.

Around 6 P.M. the rebels began a heavy bombardment of the presidential guard barracks with mortars and perhaps artillery. During the next hour they pumped at least a hundred rounds into the barracks area—mostly old, sprawling two-story wooden buildings, located about a half mile from the palace. From the Embassy roof we could hear the crack of each round being fired, then a few seconds later the brutal crrrr-ump as it crashed into the target area. Black smoke from fires appeared over the trees. We visualized carnage and devastation among the flimsy barracks and marveled at the courage of the guardsmen to hold out so long. We failed to notice the absence of small arms fire which would have meant a real fight. It turned out later that the barracks were deserted at the time of the bombardment, the guardsmen having long since deployed around the palace.

Then came another lull, broken only by occasional distant bursts of small arms fire. It lasted about eight hours. In our ignorance of what was happening, it seemed like an infinity.

By now there was a misty drizzle adding to the discomfort of the heat and extreme humidity. The tar and gravel roof radiated the smell of musty dust and soot. But nobody left. Perhaps thirty or forty people were there, rotating between the roof and downstairs offices, throughout the night, some on duty, others trapped at the Embassy by the curfew, some (like myself) on hand in case they could be useful, some just plain afraid to go home. Mostly Americans but also a few Vietnamese employees of the Embassy.

Continued reports of troop movements. Another convoy of trucks jammed with troops, helmets gleaming in the street lights, went by the Embassy and turned down a street toward the palace. In the distance we could see the lights of a convoy crossing a bridge over the Saigon River. "I hope they're friendly," said a voice in the darkness of our rooftop. "Who do you mean by 'friendly'?" said another voice. "Three guesses," came the answer. Scattered, anonymous laughs in the darkness. A poll of the people there would have shown a heavy majority who hoped the coup would be successful.

A smothered curse as somebody walked into one of the radio antennae strung across the roof. The voice of a girl: "I was supposed to go on leave tonight. Nothing ever goes right in this cotton-pickin' dump." A language officer carrying a transistor radio joined the gathering. The radio played semiclassical music in the background, adding to the unreal atmosphere. Then he turned up the volume as the music was interrupted by a torrent of strident Vietnamese. The language officer began scribbling notes under a flashlight. "It's the generals," he explained. "Each one of them is coming on to say in his own voice that he's supporting the coup."

With one or two unimportant exceptions, they included every general in the Vietnamese Army. There was always the possibility that they were speaking under duress, e.g. a pistol in the belly, but for me this was the moment of persuasion, that the Diem regime at long last was truly finished. This had to come, but it was not a proud moment. In a way it was our own failure, as well as Diem's—a tragic verdict on seven years of American support.

Around 9:30 P.M. the telephone rang in Trueheart's office. His part of the conversation went like this:

"Yes, Mr. Ambassador."

"No, I can't think of anything. No change."

"No, I see no reason why not."

"Yes, of course we'll call if necessary."

"Good night, sir."

The Ambassador was about to go to bed, as he always did at nine-thirty unless there was an unavoidable obligation to stay up later. (When an Embassy officer telephoned to tell Lodge about the second coup in January 1964, the Ambassador rebuked him for calling in the middle of the night.) Lodge apparently reasoned that the coup, which he had expected, seemed to be going well, that there was nothing he could do to help it go better, and that morning would probably confront him with dozens of difficult problems, such as how to recognize the new regime as quickly as possible and still be dignified. A fresh, well-rested Ambassador in the morning would be more in the U.S. interest than an exhausted, fretful man who had been up all night worrying.

As the night wore on, the Embassy's control center for the radio reporting network became a gathering place. It was clear that resistance to the rebels, which had been negligible anyway, had ceased inside the city except for the defenders of the palace. The rebels now were deploying their forces for the decisive assault. The big unknown was whether or not units outside the city would come to Diem's defense, as they had at the last moment in the attempted military coup of November 1960. We had received no reports of anything like this, but we also had poor communications with many parts of the country. All we could do was wait.

The radio net by now was so inactive that the Embassy operator occasionally would check each location to make sure there had been no technical breakdowns. From the lonely men spotted around the city came responses like "Roger, I read you loud and clear, but we don't have any cigarettes and I hope you're having a happy night too."

Somebody produced a case of U. S. Army C rations from the Embassy's emergency stores. It was stamped 1948, tasted accordingly, but was ravenously consumed, littering file cabinets, desks and coffee tables with empty cans, dehydrated lemonade, crumbs (the crackers were so old that a bite made them explode) and other unlikely refuse. A bottle of Kentucky bourbon materialized. We drank it from paper cups expropriated from a drinking fountain in the hall. They soon ran out and after the original cups became so soggy that they leaked, we passed around the bottle.

We made bets. Among them: the Communists would get control of South Vietnam within eighteen months; American combat troops would be brought in within a year to fight the Viet Cong; the generals would never be able to agree and there would be another coup d'état within six months (which was wrong, it was only three months).

A CIA man remarked: "If the coup is successful, they'll say back home that it sure was a good thing the CIA stayed out of this one so it wasn't mucked up. If it fails, they'll say the CIA was behind it and we ought to keep our goddam fingers out of other countries' affairs. Pass the goddam bourbon."

There was also some byplay relating to Mme. Nhu's charges that USIS was behind the conspiracy against the regime. Very funny remarks like: "John, now that we're all here together and there aren't any reporters, how did you do it?" Or: "Hey, Mecklin, can I be minister of women's welfare?"

In the midst of all this, around ten-thirty, there was a telephone call. An officer answered and motioned for silence. It was Nguyen Dinh Thuan, assistant minister of defense, secretary to the presidency, and by far the most helpful top official in Saigon. He said he was calling from a private home, not his own, and that he had heard on the radio (as we had) that the generals had offered clemency to all members of Diem's government who would surrender before 11 P.M. The radio had said that those who did not do this would be regarded as enemies. Thuan wanted to know if we thought the generals could be trusted, and asked our advice on what to do.

By chance the officer who answered the phone knew Thuan well, as did several others in the room. Yet his call implied that he believed the United States was somehow involved in the coup and had special access to the generals, if not indeed control over their actions. There was still the possibility that the coup would fail, and whatever we said now to a man in Thuan's influential position could be held against the United States. We probably had better information on the general situation than Thuan, particularly the apparent hopelessness of Diem's position, but we knew no more than he did about the clemency ultimatum to Diem's ministers.

The American said: "Mr. Minister, we know only what we have heard on the radio." Thuan evidently pressed, with emotion, for more guidance than that. Gripping the telephone with fingers that were sticky from cold C ration pork and beans, the American repeated: "We know only what we have heard on the radio." Thuan persisted. The American repeated the same sentence several times more, increasingly embarrassed. After perhaps five or six minutes of this, he said: "Good night, Mr. Minister." Then he put down the phone, looked around the room noncommittally, and reached for a soggy cup of bourbon. Nobody spoke. (We heard later that Thuan did surrender before the deadline, by telephone to JGS. He was placed under house arrest but eventually managed to leave the country for Paris.)

Not long after this an Embassy officer came into the room

to report that a convoy of trucks had been organized, with American GI drivers, to evacuate Americans living within five blocks of the palace. He said he had the addresses of about sixty Americans who lived within that area. Should we try it while there still might be time before the assault on the palace, which presumably was imminent? They could be evacuated temporarily to U.S. military installations.

It was an immensely difficult decision. (Six or eight USIS people were among the sixty persons involved.) We had no idea how the forthcoming battle would develop. It was possible, for example, that rebel troops might use some of the buildings housing Americans—one of the main ones was just across the street from the palace—for gun positions, which would attract return fire. If Diem succeeded in calling in reinforcements from outside Saigon, street fighting could break out all through the center of the city. Or a prolonged siege could develop, cutting off the Americans in no-man's-land.

On the other hand, few of the sixty Americans had telephones and trying to alert them by messengers would take too much time. The evacuation trucks thus would probably have to remain in the danger area for an hour or more while everyone was rounded up. Fighting could break out in the midst of the operation, with much greater danger to the evacuees exposed in the streets than if they remained in their homes. Even if the operation went smoothly, there would be a risk of panic. Morale problems would probably develop among families in areas of marginal danger who were not evacuated. And in any case it might be impossible to make foolproof arrangements with both sides to permit safe passage of the trucks through the curfew. It was a reasonable assumption that the palace defenders particularly were scared and trigger happy because of the increasing hopelessness of their position.

We decided, at least for the time being, not to risk it. We

turned out to be right. Not a single American was injured in the whole fracas.* But it was an uncomfortable gamble, and a good example of life in a "hardship post."

Back on the roof around 12:30 or 1 A.M. the soft misty rain continued. The city around us lay silent and enigmatic, its lights burning but its streets deserted except for the troops and armored vehicles we knew to be gathering around the palace. The tinsel sound of dance music from a transistor radio. The occasional conversation of boredom. Mostly the watchers leaning on the chest-high parapets to gaze out over the city, trying to imagine perhaps, as I was, what it was like inside the palace. Presidential guardsmen desperately strengthening their defenses? Diem and Nhu still appealing for help on the palace radio? Or philosophically waiting for whatever the night would bring? My guess was the latter, at least in the case of Diem.

It was none of this. Diem and Nhu had both secretly fled the palace around 8 or 9 P.M. But nobody knew that until midmorning, neither the Embassy, nor the coup leaders, nor the rebel troops—nor the palace defenders preparing to risk death to protect a President who had abandoned them.

Suddenly the night was rent by a crescendoing rustling sound that could only be an incoming shell. I dived to my hands and knees behind the parapet, as did many of the other rooftop watchers who had heard that fearful sound before. There was a flash high above us, followed a second or two later by an explosion, and then the spectacular sight of a magnesium flare dangling from a parachute. It seemed to be about midway between the Embassy and the palace, drifting toward us. It drenched the neighborhood in white

---

* Four American and two Australian secretaries spent the night in an apartment only a block from the palace, watching tracers flash by the windows. After the battle they found a small shell fragment—still too hot to touch—lying on the doormat. One of the girls had it framed.

light almost as bright as day, sharply etching even the distant trees around the palace. After a minute or two it fell into the street so close to the Embassy that we could see the shower of sparks when it banged against a building on the way down.

The shell evidently had come from a rebel gun across the river. For a moment we wondered uneasily if the intention had been to light up the Embassy—there was nothing else in the neighborhood of any possible significance—and if so, why. It apparently was the error of a gunner who misjudged the wind. A few minutes later another shell whistled out of the night, placing its flare this time directly over the palace. There were several more during the next hour or two. We guessed that the idea was to try to see what dispositions the palace defenders had made of their forces, perhaps in coordination with an observer in one of the planes still droning around the city.

At 4 A.M. the rebels attacked. First the staccato guttural of a 50-caliber machine gun, then the rocking shock wave of a 75-mm tank gun, soon a wild confusion of noise that was to continue unabated for an hypnotic two and three-quarters hours. The rebels had positioned tanks, armored cars and armored personnel carriers in every street and alley offering a field of fire into the palace area. They proceeded to let go with countless thousands of rounds of ammunition, gradually tightening the ring as the defenders' answering fire diminished. Contained as it was among concrete buildings five or six stories high, the noise compared with the hottest engagements I had experienced in World War II, and perhaps was even greater. On our rooftop six blocks away, we could communicate with each other only by shouting, and even that was sometimes useless.

The flat angle of our view was such that we could see the tops of the buildings around the fighting, as well as the tops of the trees clumped around the palace, but not what was happening in the streets. The effect was like watching a restless volcano spewing deadly flickers of fire and smoke through ancient fissures in the floor of its crater.

Always against the background of savage, unrelenting pandemonium, brilliant red tracers lined through the night, gracefully arching over the city in floating blobs of light, or striking a building or pavement and ricocheting like colliding electrons in a vapor chamber in crazy patterns of angles. There were occasional monstrous explosions, sporadic and usually unrelated sudden tongues of fire that would quiver upward for an instant, creating ghastly silhouettes of the buildings around it, and then collapse. At frequent intervals there were more parachute flares, dripping fire as they drifted into the caldron, illuminating billowing towers of smoke that flattened and drifted far across the city to our right.*

A vehicle was hit—a personnel carrier we discovered later—and exploded in a balloon of dancing orange flame. Intermittently through the night thereafter its ammunition stores went off, shooting a new mass of flame into the air for an instant. Its smoldering wreckage, exuding oily black smoke, became a sullen constant in a kaleidoscope of nightmarish movement.

From the Embassy roof we watched in awe and fascination. Occasionally a ricochet came our way, its disrupted aerodynamics creating an eerie wailing sound in the night, and we would duck behind the parapets. The shooting was so wholly constricted by buildings, however, that there was no real danger. The dance music, interrupted now by news bulletins, continued on the radio.

As the frightful spectacle wore on, and indeed became a

* The shooting was so intense and continual that a French television crew was able to make a spectacular close-in film of the battle by relying exclusively on light from gun flashes.

sort of tortured normalcy, the trance waned among the watchers. "I wish we could get them to fight that way against the Viet Cong," said a voice in the darkness during a moment of relative quiet. "You know who's paying for all that ammo, don't you?" said another. "It's the good old American taxpayer." A third voice, evidently a military man, remarked: "This must be the first time all those tanks have ever been worth anything. They sure aren't any damn good against guerrillas." Said a fourth: "Do we have a course for teaching them how to shoot up a palace?" There was no response. Mostly the faces illuminated in the fitful glare from the battle were fixed and expressionless.

By 6:30 A.M. the shooting had diminished to occasional, isolated cracks of a tank gun, or a burst of machine-gun fire echoing through the streets. In the first light of dawn the city emerged a steely gray, empty, still and desolate, a pall of smoke stretching away to the horizon, motionless against a slatelike sky, as though it had been painted by an inept artist. At six forty-five the radio announced that the palace had been overrun.

At seven I drove back to USIS. The streets were still empty, just as the curfew was ending. The building was intact, indeed no evidence of damage anywhere around it. Upstairs I found Sheppard, bright-eyed and spirited, despite telltale mountains of cigarette butts. A longtime motion picture officer, he had just come back from making some film of the palace. For an hour or two during the battle he had shot what he could from the roof of the Rex BOQ next door, looking down into the palace grounds. I remarked that it must have been a rough night, judging by the way things looked and sounded at the Embassy.

"Noisy as hell," he said, "but no sweat." That was about all I could get out of him. A wartime Air Force flier, Sheppard was as cool in a pinch as he was sensible all the time, a fine officer.

We made a brief tour of the city. Rebel troops had cordoned off the palace area but there appeared to be surprisingly little damage, a few shell holes in the walls, hundreds of scars from bullets and shell fragments, but nothing like the pile of rubble I had expected. The same was true of the buildings around it. The new regime completely repaired the palace in less than a month.

By now the streets were a turmoil of people and vehicles. Most of the Saigon police force had demobilized itself for fear of reprisals by the new government.* So there was nobody to direct traffic. But nobody cared. Asians are not a boisterous people, and the Vietnamese were particularly inhibited after interminable years of war and disorder. There was little of the wild joyousness that I had seen, for example, during the liberation of France in 1944. But there nevertheless was a refreshing change in the atmosphere, a sense of new hope, and certainly of release from the oppressive, eccentric ineptness of Diem and his family.

Later that morning, when full appreciation of the night's events had sunk in, there were instances of crowds lifting rebel soldiers on their shoulders. Mobs—probably spontaneous, though maybe not—attacked and burned out several newspaper offices, including the *Times of Vietnam* (Mrs. Gregory took refuge in the Embassy), and a bookstore owned by the Ngo Dinh family. They also tore down a statue of the Trung Sisters erected by Mme. Nhu.

Sheppard and I sensed a new friendliness toward us as Americans. Where there once had been impassive courtesy, we now encountered smiles and even a few waves and hand

* Not long after the coup began Friday afternoon, a policeman dashed into the offices of Pan American World Airways, apologized hastily to the Vietnamese girl on duty, ripped off his uniform, put on the black peasant clothes he had brought with him, thanked the astonished girl for her hospitality, and disappeared.

clapping. Rightly or wrongly this certainly indicated a belief that the U. S. had a hand in the coup. But were the smiles in gratitude? Or merely a new respect for American power? I think it was gratitude, but we will never know.

From the palace we made our way down Thong Nhut Boulevard to the barracks of the presidential guard. Here again, like the palace, there was almost none of the devastation I had expected after the bombardment of the previous evening. The streets were cluttered with branches wrenched from trees. The fragile wooden barracks had plentiful pockmarks and two or three gaping holes from direct hits, but for the most part they were intact. Again there obviously had been a vast amount of high explosive flailing, random shooting, which is often a characteristic of panicky and not very good troops. If the Viet Cong had been defending the palace it would have taken a good deal more than a month to put it back together again.

Random shooting does, however, usually hit something. As we turned down a side street from the barracks, we passed a blood-spattered Vespa scooter lying in the gutter. Next to it was a sandal, with a human foot still in it.

(3)

Incalculable quantities of printer's ink, radio/TV time and official cipher were expended in explanations of how the coup came off. It was certainly one of the most elaborate plots in recent history. What really happened may never be known. What counted was the fact that the Vietnamese armed forces turned against the Diem regime almost to a man.

All accounts agree that there were several rings of conspirators, working independently for the most part, and perhaps even competing with one another to get started first. Two of the also-ran leaders reportedly were Dr. Tran

Kim Tuyen, chief of Nhu's secret police, and Lieutenant Colonel Pham Ngoc Thao, a reformed Vietminh who had won Diem's favor as a successful province chief. The resulting complex of plots within plots, with all sides hoping for American support, explained the multitude of seemingly genuine reports reaching the U. S. Mission over a period of two or three months that a coup was imminent. Despite the regime's panicky charges, there was no evidence that the Buddhist leaders played a role of any significance, except as they kept the country stirred up and thus contributed to the necessary political climate.

The plot that prevailed was engineered at the very top of the Vietnamese military hierarchy, by General Duong Van Minh, a former chief of staff who had been relegated to a meaningless job as special advisor to Diem because of the latter's suspicions of him, and General Tran Van Don, acting chief of the joint general staff. (The normal JGS chief, who might have blocked the coup, was mortally ill.) General Minh, known as "Big Minh" among Americans to distinguish him from another General Minh, was a longtime American favorite, particularly including General Taylor, who had often played tennis with him during visits to Vietnam.

All accounts also agreed that the critical problem in plotting the coup was to persuade General Ton That Dinh, the volatile III Corps commander, to join, since he controlled the troops around the capital who would have to do the job. In an article for *The Saturday Evening Post*, correspondent Stanley Karnow reported that Dinh, whom he described as a "courageous but not very bright soldier," was swayed by flattery. The plotting generals persuaded him that he was such a remarkable man that he should ask Diem to appoint him minister of interior. Dinh fell for it, and did ask Diem for the job. Diem flatly refused. Dinh was bitterly resentful. According to Karnow the other generals then promised that *they* would let him be minister of interior if he would join the plot, and Dinh eventually agreed. (The generals kept their promise, but not for long. After the Khanh coup, Dinh was arrested, to be released some months later.)

There evidently was substance of some sort behind the repeated reports, beginning as early as August, that Nhu was intrigued with the idea of a false coup. Karnow's version went that Nhu's idea was for "rebel" troops to seize the city, proclaim an anti-American neutralist government, and invite all anti-Diem forces to rally round. Then a day or two later Diem would be "saved" by loyal troops from outside the city. The idea would be to scare the Americans into renewed support for Diem, while at the same time exposing the regime's true enemies. Karnow reported that General Dinh tricked Nhu into believing that the genuine coup was the false one and that the palace did not realize what was really happening until several hours after the operation began.

A number of local commanders around the countryside sided initially with Diem when the coup began. In most cases, however, this appeared to be opportunism, a wrong guess about the outcome, rather than conviction. There was one commander who sent a telegram to Diem pledging all-out support, followed a couple of hours later by another telegram urgently advising that the first one was an "error" and should be ignored. Except for the resistance of the presidential guard, not a weapon was raised in the regime's defense anywhere in Vietnam.

Casualties of the coup were officially placed at 55 rebel soldiers (nine dead), 48 palace guardsmen (four dead) and 166 civilians (20 dead). The only senior officer casualty was Captain Ho Tan Quyen, commander of the Vietnamese Navy, who was shot dead just before the coup began. One version of this was that he was shot for refusing to join the plot. Another version was that a personal enemy took advantage of the confusion to murder him.

The regime collapsed like an empty shell. There was a brief wave of reprisals against its supporters. In Hue, Brother Can was tried and executed. But even that stirred only limited popular interest. The regime was so remote from its people that nobody cared—except Vietnamese Catholics, and their concern often was less grief than fear of persecution under a Buddhist government.

In view of the fact that Vietnam was engaged in a bitter struggle with the Communists for the people's loyalty, the relative indifference that greeted its destruction was grim proof of its failure.

Little was known about the activities of Diem and Nhu during those last desperate hours. They evidently faced the end alone, isolated from human counsel except for flunkies, palace domestic servants and officers of the presidential guard. Diem used the palace radio repeatedly, as he had so successfully during the attempted coup of 1960, to try to communicate with commanders outside the city to come to his rescue. Nhu attempted to stir his Republican Youth to rise in the regime's defense. All was silence.

Diem telephoned Ambassador Lodge on the afternoon of the coup. The exact conversation was not made public. According to press accounts, Diem asked if the Ambassador knew what was happening. Lodge replied that he had heard shooting and offered U.S. assistance if Diem wanted to leave the country. Diem refused. If this was all that was said, Lodge's failure to express support for the regime would probably have led to his departure as *persona non grata* if the coup had failed.

There were a number of telephone conversations between Diem and the rebel leaders Friday afternoon and evening. These reportedly included several exchanges of bitter, obscene invective. Diem refused repeated demands that he surrender. Beyond this, all that was definitely known was that Diem and Nhu had disappeared when the rebel troops entered the palace at dawn on November 2 and that they turned up an hour or two later in Cholon, the Chinese section of the city, several miles from the palace.

It was generally accepted that they fled the palace secretly during the evening, probably via a tunnel, and proceeded by automobile to Cholon where they went to a prearranged hideout. This reportedly was the home of a Chinese businessman which had been rigged with an extension of the palace telephone switchboard. Diem thus was able to continue the telephone dialogue with the generals without betraying that he had abandoned the palace. Sometime during the early morning hours they went to a nearby Roman Catholic church where they were eventually arrested. One story was that they were recognized and betrayed by another worshiper. Another version went that Diem made a final telephone call to the generals and agreed to surrender in return for a promise of honorable treatment.

All versions agreed that Diem and Nhu were taken into custody at the church and placed aboard an armored vehicle which then headed for the rebel headquarters. This was around 9 or 10 A.M. Saturday. En route they were both killed. The new regime initially announced that it was "suicide." This immediately stirred a row because the Roman Catholic Church regards suicide as a sin. The regime then issued an amended version, that it was "accidental suicide" resulting from a scuffle with the escorting officer. The latter's identity was not revealed, except that it was a relatively junior man with the rank of captain or major. Stories were given unofficially to newsmen that the officer became involved in an exchange of insults with Nhu, lost his temper, and killed both Nhu and Diem as the armored car rolled through the streets.

This could be true, but it was hard to believe that a junior officer entrusted with such prisoners as these would kill them without authority, however outrageously he may have been provoked. A good many Americans in Saigon thought it was more likely that Diem and Nhu were killed on orders from someone since they could only be an embarrassment and a divisive force if they lived, not only in Vietnam but also abroad.

The new military regime further obscured all this by imposing secrecy on what happened to the bodies. It was announced that they were buried with appropriate religious ceremony, but the exact location of the graves was not revealed. The new regime also refused to publish photographs of the bodies to prove to the population that Diem and Nhu were really dead—despite widely circulating rumors, especially in Catholic communities, to the effect that they were still alive.

Photographs of the corpses that appeared in the foreign press were mysteriously acquired, never acknowledged by the regime, and of such poor quality as to leave reasonable doubt of their authenticity. All that was ever shown to American officials, including myself, was a brief motion picture film of the backs of two bodies jammed face down between the seats of what we were told was an armored car. The bodies were both dressed in neat dark suits and they were the right bulks for Diem and Nhu, but it was otherwise impossible to confirm their identity. There were spots that could have been stab wounds in the back on the smaller figure, i.e. Nhu, but no other signs of injury.

It looked as though the new regime imposed the secrecy for the same reason that it may have ordered the killings, to damp down a difficult aftermath, and suppressed photographs because they would not support the "accidental suicide" explanation.

What of the American role in the coup?

In his homecoming interview with the New York *Times*

(June 30, 1964), Ambassador Lodge said: "The United States was not involved in the overthrow of the Diem regime. The United States was trying to change—bring about a change in the behavior of the Diem regime. It was trying to bring about a change in the personnel of the Diem regime. . . . We were trying to bring about this by thoroughly legitimate political means. . . .

"The overthrow was—of the Diem regime—was a purely Vietnamese affair. We never participated in the planning. We never gave any advice. We had nothing whatever to do with it. I—*there were opportunities to participate in the planning and to give advice,* and we never did. (Italics mine) We were punctilious in drawing that line. . . ."

This was surely an admission that the coup was not a surprise to Lodge. It also implied that he knew something about who was planning it. This may have been the explanation of the fact that Lodge had scheduled a trip to Washington on October 31, the day before the coup, and postponed it at the last minute. A story circulated in Saigon after the coup that Lodge was advised of the date a full week before it happened, and so reported to President Kennedy. American participation in the plotting itself would have been contrary to Lodge's strong personal objection to "colonial" behavior. If he knew that the top men of the Vietnamese forces were behind the plot, as he evidently did, U.S. intervention would have been unnecessary anyway.

But to assert that the U. S. was "not involved" in the coup was a bit like claiming innocence for a night watchman at a bank who tells a known safecracker that he is going out for a beer.

To recapitulate, here was a country at war against a formidable enemy, and doing badly. This was a country totally dependent upon massive U.S. support. Its government was weak and in grave trouble with its own people because of the Buddhist upheaval. The Vietnamese military had already tried one coup, in 1960, and only narrowly failed. Some of the most powerful officers in the Vietnamese armed forces were now advising the U. S. secretly that they were ready to try again, and in effect asking U.S. approval. It was increasingly well known inside Vietnam, furthermore, that the government was blatantly ignoring American advice on issues that the U. S. regarded as vital.

Then, against this background: (1) the State Department publicly "deplored" the government's attacks on the pagodas; (2) the Voice of America publicly sanitized the Vietnamese armed forces and strongly implied that Nhu should be removed from the government; (3) President Kennedy publicly asked for new policies and personnel; and (4) the United States began suspending aid programs without which Vietnam could not hope to survive. There was the widespread report that Lodge had secretly passed the word to the generals in August that the U. S. no longer objected to a coup. And finally the U.S. position in Vietnam was so vitally important to the Vietnamese that if Lodge knew about the coup in advance, as he indicated to the New York *Times*, he probably could have prevented it, if he had tried.

Otherwise, we were "not involved."

CHAPTER NINE

The Guerrilla Gap

(1)

A coup d'état in such circumstances, with the nation locked in struggle with Communist insurgents, was desperate surgery. The odds against success were comparable with, say, a kidney transplant. U.S. encouragement of the coup was justified only by the judgment that the odds against trying to continue with Diem were even worse.

The operation itself came off neatly. There was virtually no interruption of command authority over the nation's armed forces and civilian administration. There was so little tension that the military junta was able to lift martial law in six days. Just a fortnight after the coup Ambassador Lodge gave an elegant black-tie dinner for the new chief of state, General Duong Van (Big) Minh, and the leading members of the junta—small talk, champagne and cigars, as though we had all been working together for years.

In the towns and cities there was a feeling everywhere of a fresh breeze in a musty room. Dozens of new newspapers sprang up in Saigon. Dancing resumed in the nightclubs and dancehalls. For the first time in nearly two years the streets around Gia Long Palace were cleared of police barricades and barb wire, easing Saigon's traffic congestion like the lancing of a boil.

Among the peasants, for whom the central government had never had much meaning anyway, news of the coup circulated slowly. In some of the more remote regions the Viet Cong appeared at the gates of fortified hamlets, announced that the government had been overthrown, and demanded that the hamlet militia turn over their weapons. In a few instances the trick worked. Generally in the rural areas the feeling was *che do nao cung vay* (all rulers are the same), but there was willingness to go along with the military junta. In a few places there were even hamlet celebrations.

The Diem regime was so universally disliked, and alien to the people, that its destruction left few significant pockets of resentment. Minh was granted a fleeting opportunity to breathe new life into his war-wracked country.

It was also a bright moment of hope for the U. S. Mission. The new warmth toward Americans among the Vietnamese people that I had observed on the morning of the coup continued for some weeks. The Minh regime indicated eagerness to work closely with us. In Honolulu on November 20, 1963, Secretaries Rusk and McNamara presided over a conference at which it was decided to give all possible support to the new regime, with no basic change in American operations, except that hopefully they might now be more effective.

Ambassador Lodge, in effect, was invited to demonstrate whether he was as good at rallying the Vietnamese to fight the Viet Cong as he had been in presiding over the undoing of Diem and Nhu.

He was not. Neither was Big Minh. In the months that followed, there was relentless deterioration everywhere, confirming in dreary succession all the black predictions of those who had opposed the coup.

The coup released an avalanche of new information on the true state of the struggle against the Viet Cong, all of it bad. It was a story of decay that had been under way for months, or years—certainly not a swift result of Diem's collapse as some of his apologists argued. The strategic hamlet program, which had been the heart of our joint effort, was revealed to be a Potemkin-style illusion. From local Vietnamese officials, now unafraid to speak out, we learned that perhaps seventy percent of the thousands of "completed" hamlets were insecure, often controlled secretly by the V.C. Corruption was everywhere, especially in the use of forced labor to build fortifications. In many areas the strategic hamlets had become a symbol of government tyranny rather than new hope against the V.C.

Minh was dangerously hesitant. Rather than assert his considerable popularity he chose to share authority with a committee of twelve officers who were torn by jealousies, contradictory motivations and personal ambitions. They could agree only that all vestiges of the Diem era must be destroyed. There was a sweeping purge of virtually every official of any importance in the country: military commanders all the way down to company level, province and district chiefs, often even hamlet chiefs. The result was to discredit not only the Diem regime among the peasants but also the concept of government of any sort. Government military operations fell off. V.C. gains mounted. On top of this there was a poor rice harvest, and then a cholera epidemic.

At USIS we were unable even to find out whether the new regime wanted to retain the term "strategic hamlet," forcing us to suspend our considerable propaganda effort in support of this key program. (Months later it became "new life hamlets.")

Lodge also hesitated. He appealed to Washington for two or three months of patience to give Minh a chance to organize a government and do things his own way. Washington reluctantly concurred.

Such glimpses as I had of Lodge's thinking indicated that the new situation surprised and puzzled him. He was an idealist in the New England liberal tradition, with a built-in aversion to anything smacking of "colonialism"—a word that he frequently used—and an uncritical faith in the righteousness of the American cause. This had been a reservoir of fortitude for ringing declarations in defiance of the Russians when he was Ambassador to the United Nations.

As I judged it, he had been able to rationalize the destruction of Diem on the grounds of an overriding American interest, especially since the job could be done in dignified, relatively sanitary fashion. His personal discomfort nevertheless may have been one reason why he stayed home throughout the coup itself. But he was not prepared, or so it seemed to me, for the complex and shabby realities of the ways in which American power now needed to be applied.

There was nothing orientally inscrutable about the multitude of things that needed to be done—like pressuring Big Minh to decide what to call the strategic hamlets, to cite a minor example—but Lodge seemed to shy away from that kind of meddling. He seemed to have built his policy on the hope (like our previous attitude toward Diem) that Minh would be a natural leader, who merely needed our material support. When it turned out that Minh instead was stalling his country into the ground, to the benefit of the Viet Cong, Lodge was fresh out of a policy.

Lodge, I think, recognized this, but he resisted plunging into the problem. This perhaps was partly because he was distracted by the multiplying reports from home that he had a real chance for the Republican nomination. It may also have been related to the fact that except for a brief visit in the twenties, Lodge had no experience with Asia. He seemed to be reluctant to tangle with its monumentally complex problems—just as many another American had been reluctant, including myself.

He had been in Vietnam for four months before he took

time to be briefed on USIS activities, for example, and he allowed us only one hour.

He was similarly reluctant to be educated in the principles and techniques of guerrilla warfare. At a meeting one day, five months after his arrival, he asked why government military reinforcements had failed to drive the Viet Cong out of a province near Saigon. He was told that the people there still supported the V.C. because of government indifference to the peasants' needs. He brightened and remarked: "You mean we need precinct workers?" Which was correct, except that we already had thousands of them—civic action teams, psychological warfare teams, local government officials—who were doing almost nothing except squeezing the villagers for money.

Lodge's apparent inhibitions about being informed combined with his insistence on a personal monopoly of negotiations with the Vietnamese Government. There was one occasion when he went alone to a meeting with Minh and several other members of the junta. The session lasted an hour or more, covering a multitude of subjects—many of them complex, some of them new to the Ambassador. Lodge's report was so sketchy on what was said that there was genuine doubt inside the U. S. Mission on whether it would be safe to proceed with the actions he ordered—for fear that Lodge's understanding of what was agreed might be embarrassingly different from Minh's.

Lodge did have time, however, to proceed with reorganization of his own staff. Among the departures were the Army, Air Force and Navy attachés, whose jobs were abolished, Lodge's deputy William Trueheart, and myself. I was ordered to return to Washington in late January 1964. The New York *Times* magazine (May 10, 1964) reported: "Mecklin was sent home, not so much for differences of policy as, apparently, for taking too much responsibility for dealing with the press, particularly the American press, a preserve Lodge wanted to keep for himself."

Meantime, the Minh government collapsed, signaling the start of the musical chairs regimes we all had feared. The new coup was executed bloodlessly in the early hours of January 30, 1964, by General Nguyen Khanh, a thirty-six-year-old, French-trained officer whom the junta had distrusted and banished to a distant corps command. Khanh promptly began firing people again all over the country. The Viet Cong accelerated its gains again in the resulting confusion. The U. S. shifted its affections again.

McNamara and Taylor flew out to Vietnam and embraced Khanh with such back-to-the-wall fervor as to make our previous "sink or swim" support for Diem seem standoffish. McNamara toured the countryside with Khanh and had himself photographed, taped and televised repeatedly holding Khanh's arm aloft and shouting *Vietnam muon nam* (long live Vietnam) to the cheers of puzzled peasants who had been rounded up for the occasion. Then Rusk flew out a few weeks later and announced to newsmen that things were showing "steady improvement."

Two days later (April 22) the New York *Times* headlined REDS INFLICT HEAVIEST TOLL ON SOUTH VIETNAM ARMY. It reported the bloodiest week of the war with a thousand Vietnamese Government and twenty-three American casualties. It said the Viet Cong now were often making attacks with as many as three battalions (450 men each) at once—which they had seldom been able to do before Diem's collapse.

From Saigon, columnist Joseph Alsop reported that seven million peasants (half the total population) had slipped under V.C. control since Diem's fall. He warned that "a great national disaster is creeping up on the United States. . . . The disaster is a final Communist triumph in South

Vietnam." There were multiplying street clashes between Catholic and Buddhist mobs in Saigon.

The U. S. Government began to panic. For the first time in the long years of U.S. involvement in Vietnam, there were indications that responsible policy-makers were tempted to "escalate" the struggle by attacking North Vietnam. In May, McNamara and Taylor hurried back to Saigon. "Excellent progress," reported McNamara. It was so excellent that President Johnson asked Congress for an additional $125 million for Vietnam, an increase of twenty-five percent over existing programs. In June, in Honolulu, still another crisis conference. Rusk asked newsmen to report that the U.S. commitment to Vietnam was unlimited, comparable with West Berlin. In a speech Johnson warned the Communist world: "If a nation is to keep its freedom, it must be prepared to risk war. When necessary, we will take that risk."

It was at this point that Lodge announced that duty called him to leave beleaguered Saigon immediately to join in a futile, last-minute effort to deny the Republican nomination to Barry Goldwater. In a homecoming, televised speech to the National Press Club in Washington on July 1, 1964, Lodge reported:

"There is vivid recognition (by the Vietnamese Government) that the Viet Cong campaign is, above all, a political affair; that we must organize for the political conflict as carefully as we have organized for military success; and that there must be a true civil-political organization to go hand in hand with the military. . . . If the people were to deny the Viet Cong, they would thus have no base; they would be through." He appealed to Americans to match Communist "patience and persistence." He suggested, however, that he was tempted to despair of winning the struggle in South Vietnam alone. "The forces working against us are strong and subtle," he said, "and sheer persistence may not suffice if hostile outside pressures grow too great. Thus we may be forced to do something more."

(The text of the speech was lifted word for word from an article Lodge had done for *Life* two and one-half months earlier, April 17, 1964, except for omission of a few paragraphs to make it shorter. In his report to the American people he unfortunately neglected to update the statistics. For *Life* in April he said 127 Americans had lost their lives in Vietnam. In the July speech it was still 127.)

In Washington, especially at State and the Pentagon, Lodge's departure from Saigon was not regarded as a disaster. Lodge had been a good choice to pull the switch on Diem and Nhu. His prestige was useful psychologically in demonstrating to the Vietnamese, and the world, that the United States meant business in Vietnam. But he had proved to be the wrong kind of man for the reconstruction job that was required after the November coup, and he had declined to accept help from his staff. The state of the war effort when Lodge left indicated clearly that he had accomplished even less with the post-coup regimes than Ambassador Nolting and General Harkins had achieved with Diem.

The Lodge appointment demonstrated that, in the long run, VIP status was no substitute for experience and professionalism in a situation as subtle, complex and urgently critical as Vietnam.*

President Johnson nevertheless chose to appoint another VIP to the job: General Maxwell Taylor, chairman of the joint chiefs of staff. Taylor was one of the nation's most respected soldiers, though some critics noted that he also

* Which was not a unanimous opinion. In San Francisco on October 21, 1964, the Thomas A. Dooley Foundation presented Lodge with its "Splendid American" award. The citation said he was the American who had "most effectively exemplified the ideals of America to the people of Asia."

shared with McNamara responsibility for the shortsighted American military policy in Vietnam during the previous two and one-half years. Whatever the merit of Taylor's appointment it was much to the credit of this admirable man that he was now willing to lay his career on the line to try to set things right.

In what appeared to be a hedge against the VIP gamble this time, Johnson also appointed U. Alexis Johnson, deputy undersecretary of state for political affairs and a professional foreign service officer, to the newly created job of deputy Ambassador. Coincidentally Harkins came home to retire and was succeeded by Lieutenant General William C. (Westy) Westmoreland, fifty, a paratrooper who had been serving as Harkins' deputy. Like Harkins two years earlier, Westmoreland's press notices described him as a "no nonsense" officer.

It was evident that the don't-escalate forces had prevailed in the Washington debate, at least until after the November election. It was announced in late July that an additional five thousand American military personnel (an increase of nearly one-third) and some three hundred more economic aid field workers would be sent to Vietnam. This was to be accompanied by still more material aid such as helicopter outfits, artillery and M-113 armored personnel carriers. Taylor was given what amounted to a blank check for one more heroic effort to get the Vietnamese to win their own war.*

Only a fortnight after Taylor's arrival the Viet Cong ambushed a battalion-strong government truck convoy in the Delta, inflicting nearly a hundred casualties. Then, in classic guerrilla fashion, the V.C. ambushed a government relief column rushing blindly to the scene, cutting it to pieces too. Grimly the action happened ten years, to the day, after Viet

* Said a British observer in Saigon: "Every time the Americans double their effort they thereby square the error."

Minh guerrillas, using exactly the same tactics, completed destruction of the famous French Groupement Mobile 100, so eloquently and tragically described in Bernard Fall's *Street Without Joy*.

After a decade, so pitifully little had been learned. Taylor was asked about the action in a television interview. "We just cannot get them to put out patrols to avoid ambushes," he said wearily.

In early August the world stiffened to face a sudden, dangerous broadening of the crisis. In the Gulf of Tonkin two U.S. destroyers were attacked by North Vietnamese torpedo boats. The U. S. retaliated swiftly by air attacks on the boats' ports and supply depots on the North Vietnamese coast, inflicting heavy damage on Ho Chi Minh's navy. It was the first U.S. attack upon Communist territory anywhere since the Korean War. "Escalation" was no longer an idle word. In a savage editorial directed to the United States, the official *People's Daily* in Peking warned: "The debt in blood you owe the Vietnamese people must be repaid."

In Saigon the Khanh regime was momentarily heartened by this show of American force. The action turned out, however, to be an isolated flare-up, at least for the time being. The malaise in South Vietnam deepened. The nation was desperately weary of war, its people verging on such despair that they would soon accept anything to get it over with.

In the months that followed, the news from Vietnam became increasingly incomprehensible, and ugly. Repeated outbreaks of bloody, senseless rioting in the streets of Saigon among students, Catholics and Buddhists. Mounting indications of Viet Cong influence in the mobs, especially Buddhist mobs. Coups d'état following one another like a grotesque game of musical chairs. Khanh was out, in again, out again, in again, engaged in a bitter public feud with

Ambassador Taylor, until finally he was exiled to New York to represent Vietnam at the United Nations in February 1965.

A parade of meaningless names marched across the headlines, mixed with reports of new Viet Cong gains. Nightclub comics in the United States amused their audiences with jokes about the absurdity of American policy.

Then, with the fury of a sudden tropical storm, in the early weeks of 1965, there came a new eruption. The Viet Cong mounted a series of direct attacks on U.S. installations in Vietnam, with frightening success, killing some threescore Americans and wrecking millions of dollars' worth of planes and equipment. Again the United States escalated, this time with a series of massive retaliatory air strikes against Communist staging areas and supply depots just above the 17th Parallel in North Vietnam on the infiltration routes to the South.

The world was plunged anew into seething dispute over the implacable problem of Vietnam.

(2)

By the spring of 1965, hope that the American "advisory" policy could save Vietnam was swiftly evaporating. It was conceivable that the sheer weight of the American presence could keep the struggle going for some time, or even that a true leader might still emerge and miraculously reverse the trend. A greater likelihood was irreparable collapse.

This could happen in a dozen unpredictable ways. It could be a coup d'état by neutralist forces who would then seek a negotiated settlement with the Viet Cong. Or defections of major military units to the Communists. Or gradual domination of the streets of Saigon by Communist-led mobs. Or a spectacular Viet Cong military success. The situation had become so unstable, and despair was deepening so universally among the Vietnamese people, that almost any new shock could be fatal.

Again the U. S. faced a moment of grim decision in Vietnam.

Exactly what were the stakes?

They were incalculable. There was little doubt that loss of South Vietnam would create a "domino" effect, as John Foster Dulles once called it, leading to eventual loss of all of Southeast Asia. Except for the Filipinos, recent history had proved the peoples of the region to be political chameleons. Fear of Red China had now turned many of their leaders into political jelly, with near anarchy in Laos, neutralist regimes kowtowing to Peking in Cambodia, Burma and Indonesia, shaky pro-Western regimes in Thailand and the new state of Malaysia.

Stretching over several million square miles, Southeast Asia was mostly underpopulated with an estimated 220 million people. Its strategic position athwart the world's east-west communications compared in importance with Suez and Panama. It had vast, largely untapped economic resources, including valuable food surpluses. It had been the goal of Japanese expansion a quarter century earlier. For Peking it was now the great hope for solving the staggering economic problems of China.

In a series of articles in mid-1964 columnist Joseph Alsop wrote that Communist capture of South Vietnam would be "the heaviest defeat of American world policy in a great many decades . . . a gigantic American failure." Alsop predicted that Vietnam, Laos and Cambodia would become part of the Chinese Communist empire, that Thailand would turn to neutralism and eventually go under, that Malaysia would "swiftly founder," that even Japan and the Philippines would move toward neutralism, that South Korea would be "convulsed," Taiwan "destroyed," and the

U. S. forced to give up its bases in Okinawa and the Philippines. "In sum," said Alsop, "the United States will be forced out of business as a Pacific power."

In an article for *Reader's Digest* (August 1964), the former Vice-President, Richard M. Nixon, expressed equal alarm. "On the fate of South Vietnam," he wrote, "depends the fate of Asia. For South Vietnam is the dam in the river. . . . The Communists' conquest of Southeast Asia would draw a boundary line from pole to pole. Overnight the United States would cease to be a power in the world's greatest ocean. Our ships and planes could thereafter circumnavigate the globe only with Communist permission. . . . And can anyone doubt that long before this happened the United States would have become involved in a major war, if not a world war?"

This was neither hysterical nor farfetched. No thoughtful analyst of international relationships could examine the geopolitical equation of which South Vietnam was a part and come to any other conclusion.

And this was only the immediate, predictable outlook for U.S. defeat in Vietnam. It would also generate shock waves inside the Communist world that could only be damaging to U.S. interests. Vietnam had become a critical, perhaps decisive, factor in the Sino-Soviet ideological dispute over "revolutionary wars" versus peaceful competition as the path to Communist world triumph. A Viet Cong victory would prove Peking's assertion that the U. S. was a "paper tiger," and shatter the Soviet contention that war of any sort had been made impractical by the nuclear stalemate. Inevitably this would encourage the Communists in both camps to launch new guerrilla wars elsewhere—Africa and Latin America, for example. Even more significantly it would now become difficult if not impossible for Moscow to continue the trend toward a détente with the West which had become a bright new hope for a peaceful world.

Vietnam had been the high-water mark of France's postwar effort to reestablish herself as a colonial power. What the U. S. did now could determine whether Vietnam would also be the high-water mark of American defense of the free world, the point at which we wavered and fell back.

What were the U.S. options?

Three were being seriously debated: (1) to seek a negotiated settlement with the Communists; (2) to escalate, carrying the war to North Vietnam; or (3) to introduce American combat forces to fight the Viet Cong inside South Vietnam.

Polls in mid-1964 indicated that American public opinion on the crisis was directionless—a reflection in part perhaps of the breakdown of dialogue between press and government that I have tried to report. There was a consensus only in the hope for some kind of quick, painless, yet honorable solution. The polls showed the population evenly divided on neutralization of Vietnam, two to one opposed to military action against North Vietnam, three to one in favor of resistance to the Viet Cong, two to one disapproving of U.S. policy. Then came a poll on public reaction to the August attack on the North Vietnamese PT boat bases. It showed eighty-five percent approval, only three percent disapproval—a suggestion perhaps of relief that at last we were going to slug the villain and get it over with, as well as an escape from the discomforts of being patient. All of which was capped by a survey in December 1964 showing that one fourth of the American people had not heard anything at all about the Vietnam fighting.

The nation appeared to be frustrated and humiliated by the realization that a few thousand Vietnamese peasants had been able to thumb their noses at all the brains, industrial genius and Buck Rogers weaponry of the most powerful nation on earth. We could go to the moon, but not to a Vietnamese hamlet without an armed escort.

The case for a negotiated settlement, which was certainly the most tempting solution, had been promoted by a blizzard of wishful arguments, beginning with President de Gaulle's proposal in August 1963 to "neutralize" all of Southeast Asia. This was suspect to begin with because it came only a day or so after the Diem regime's assault on the pagodas, suggesting—to me at any rate—that de Gaulle had read the assault as a signal that the U. S. would fail in Vietnam, just as the French had failed. His motivation, I think, was to seize the leadership in Western surrender, to ingratiate himself with the Communists, and thus to reestablish a shabby French political *présence* in Southeast Asia. This, of course, would include the perpetuation of French commercial interests, e.g. domination of the bulk of South Vietnam's rubber production.

De Gaulle's diplomats all over the world brilliantly pressed the offensive with the disconcertingly specious logic that had long been a Gallic trademark. One of their main arguments, for example, was built on the fact of historic Vietnamese fear and hatred of the Chinese. The French said that once the Vietnamese Communists had achieved control of the whole country they would seek to break away from Peking's domination to become Asian "Titoists," who would cooperate with the West. There were at least two fallacies in this. The first was the fact that Ho Chi Minh had already tried to be a "Titoist" by not taking sides in the Sino-Soviet split, and failed. In late 1963 he surrendered to intense Chinese pressure. This was dramatically confirmed in August 1964 when North Vietnam flatly rejected a Soviet invitation to tell its side of the Tonkin Gulf incident to the United Nations Security Council. The second fallacy was the fact of Vietnam's six hundred and thirty miles of common frontier with China and the historical reality that it took the Vietnamese more than a thousand years to break away the last time the Chinese got control of their country.

In mid-1964 de Gaulle pressed his campaign by formally proposing another Geneva conference to negotiate a settlement on Vietnam. The Communists were delighted (no division between Moscow and Peking on this one), and they were shrewd enough to be relatively silent, allowing de Gaulle to speak for them. More significantly a number of smaller Western nations liked the idea, besides the neutralist bloc, and it won the interest of several highly respected international figures, such as U.N. Secretary-General U Thant.

President Johnson eloquently rejected the proposal. "We do not believe in a conference to ratify terror," he told a news conference (July 24). But a number of major American opinion-makers nibbled at de Gaulle's euphoric bait. Among others, these included columnist Walter Lippmann, the New York *Times* and the Senate majority leader, Mike Mansfield. Their line was generally a cautious cliché, that we should at least hear what de Gaulle had to say, that we should not automatically rule out a negotiated settlement.

Which reminded me of a joke that circulated in West Germany after the Kennedy-Khrushchev confrontation in Vienna in 1961:

Khrushchev: "Give me your watch and wallet."

Kennedy: "No."

Khrushchev: "Be reasonable. Let's negotiate. Just give me your wallet."

A negotiated settlement with the Viet Cong could only be an American surrender. Agreements between enemy nations, or individuals, can be lasting only if there is good faith on both sides, or if the agreement merely formalizes a status quo which neither side has the power to change anyway, i.e. if there is a political and military standoff. Nothing approaching either condition existed in Vietnam.

In the decade of the sixties only a fool could argue seriously that Communists make agreements in good faith. They broke the Geneva Agreement of 1954, which de Gaulle was now seeking to duplicate, before the ink was dry, in refusing to evacuate the two northernmost provinces of Laos. They broke the Laos Agreement of 1962 by refusing again to evacuate Vietminh troops. It was basic Communist doctrine to tempt the opponent with "negotiation" in which he gives up some of his strength, and then to forget it as soon as convenient. This unquestionably was why Hanoi and Peking were so pleased (privately no doubt amazed) with de Gaulle's proposals.

Similarly the situation in Vietnam was certainly no standoff. The Viet Cong were winning everywhere. The country was demoralized. There was no reason at all for the Viet Cong to settle for the status quo. Any agreement they accepted could *only* be a cynical, temporary expedient to see what could be gained politically before resuming their military effort.

In an appeal for negotiation, columnist James Reston of the New York *Times* invoked a quotation from George Kennan to the effect that Americans irrationally tend to regard war "as a struggle to the death between total virtue and total evil," rather than a means to achieve limited objectives. This was a sensible argument against the drumbeaters in 1952 who wanted to drive the Communists out of all Korea. It was irrelevant in the case of Vietnam in 1964. In Korea the U. S. eventually settled honorably for reestablishment of the status quo ante, i.e. an approximate return to the original demarcation line. In Vietnam the U. S. had never sought anything more than to defend the status quo ante, i.e. an independent South Vietnam as provided by the Geneva Agreement of 1954.

To negotiate with the Viet Cong made about as much sense as a pitcher deliberately walking a batter with the bases full and the winning run on third.

A willingness to negotiate implies a commitment to compromise. The Communists presumably would seek an agreement on the basis of the 1962 deal on Laos: withdrawal of foreign (i.e. U.S.) troops, a new government pledged to neutralism, and Communist participation in such a government. The U. S. could not give in on any of the probable Communist demands without compromising South Vietnamese independence to some degree. We could not even offer, in short, to negotiate in good faith with the Viet Cong without signaling to the world that Mao Tse-tung was right, that aggression by "revolutionary wars" can be profitable. Next, the dominoes.

Another argument for negotiation—voiced by Lippmann and Senator Church, among others—was prefaced by a condition: that the U. S. should continue the struggle until the situation was "stabilized," meaning to convince the Viet Cong that they could not win either, and then go to the conference table. The fallacy here was that the situation could not be stabilized until the Vietnamese Government could halt the psychological deterioration of the country, inflict a series of important military defeats on the Viet Cong, and reestablish effective and lasting control of sizable parts of the countryside. To do this it would have to reverse the trend. There is such a large psychological ingredient in this kind of struggle that once it begins to move, it tends to keep going in the same direction. If the government somehow could reverse the trend, it probably could keep going and eventually destroy the Viet Cong totally.

Of all the arguments for negotiation, the most illusory was the idea that the West had successfully accepted neutralization of Austria and Finland and that therefore a similar arrangement could be made for Vietnam or even for all of Southeast Asia. This kind of talk showed deplorable ignorance of the nature of the struggle in Vietnam. The Finns and Austrians were modern, economically prosperous, sophisticated peoples, with intimate knowledge and understanding of Communism, which they overwhelmingly opposed. They were immune to subversion. The Communists could not hope to take over either country except by flagrant, open invasion of their frontiers by foreign armies, which was prevented by the American atomic deterrent.

Exactly the reverse was true in Southeast Asia, where the main Communist threat was subversion, and history had demonstrated that American atomic power was irrelevant. Instead of a protective shield the Vietnamese certainly would regard a neutral settlement as a reverse for both their own government and the United States, making them more vulnerable than ever to Viet Cong blandishments. No amount of chest-beating American rhetoric, or ironclad commitments to fight if the agreement were broken, could change this. The very fact of the agreement would be taken as evidence that we would not fight.

For the Vietnamese people, moreover, such a settlement would come after their own government had been saying for years that neutralism not only was bad but that it was illegal even to suggest it. (Nguyen Khanh tried to justify his coup by charging the Minh regime with neutralist tendencies.)

Now they would hear the Voice of America reporting that neutralism was good, that the U. S. and South Vietnamese Governments had stopped fighting the Viet Cong, and perhaps even that the Viet Cong were now represented in the legal government of the country. The people would personally witness the departure of the American advisors and helicopter companies, and they would look exactly like the defeated French troops leaving ten years earlier. The people would also witness that there was no change at all in clandestine V.C. political and military control of the countryside —except for the sham of some V.C. guerrillas caching their weapons and melting back into the population, ready to emerge and fight again, stronger than ever, on a moment's notice.

Viet Cong propagandists in the hamlets surely would say that all this was happening because the V.C. had triumphed, and the peasant to doubt them would be rare indeed. "Neutralization" of South Vietnam, in short, would quickly be followed by the fastening of close to total Communist control on the rural population, as well as final demoralization of city dwellers and the armed forces.

This in turn would create a situation where the Viet Cong leaders in Saigon, already members of the "neutralist" government, quite possibly could take over total control without firing a shot, and perhaps even with the public "consent" of intimidated non-Communist leaders. In such circumstances U.S. air and sea power would be even more impotent than before the settlement. A threat to attack Hanoi because of peaceful change of government in Saigon, for example, would look ridiculous. Once the U. S. was committed to neutralization, and the fighting ceased, there probably would be nothing we could do to enforce the agreement short of landing the U. S. Marines and seizing Saigon by force—conceivably against resistance by the same troops whom we ourselves had trained and armed.

The multiplying advocates of negotiation tended perilously to confirm a judgment of the American character that led Ho Chi Minh to predict in 1962 (in an interview with Bernard Fall) that Communism would eventually prevail in Vietnam because the U. S. would run out of patience and go home.

The case for attacking North Vietnam was often argued with the same muscle-flexing faith in American super power that we had heard in 1950 when it was assumed that a division of flabby occupation troops from Japan could put the North Koreans out of business in a few weeks.

In a dispatch from London (contradicting his paper's editorial line), columnist C. L. Sulzberger of the New York *Times* wrote: "So long as we permit the Communists to fight according to their own rules, to train and equip guerrillas in a northern safe haven and then send them south, we cannot crush them. . . . We should never contemplate invading North Vietnam. But it is time to announce that, if aggression is not stopped, we will pulverize its bases and communications. Counter-guerrilla action must be moved into the third dimension—an aerial riposte. The time for showdown has come. We certainly don't want holocaust any more than we wanted holocaust in Cuba eighteen months ago. But we cannot afford a self-defeating strategy."

The Air Force chief of staff, General Curtis L. LeMay, asserted: "We are swatting flies when we should be going after the manure pile." The chief of the Strategic Air Command, General Thomas S. Power, said that with conventional bombs alone "we could pulverize North Vietnam." Barry Goldwater said that if he were President he would tell his commanders to go out there and win the war, using whatever means they wanted. Governor Nelson Rockefeller proposed that South Vietnamese forces be encouraged to invade not only North Vietnam but also Cambodia and Laos in "hot pursuit" of V.C. guerrillas. Alsop urged a blockade of North Vietnam by mining its ports and bombing its road and rail line to China, followed if necessary by air attacks to "progressively destroy the entire military, industrial and economic intra-structure of North Vietnam."

These arguments too were less than knowledgeable, and dangerous.

There were two approaches to the get-tough proposition. One was the suggestion that the threat of generalized air attack on his country could force Ho Chi Minh to use his influence to call off the Viet Cong in the South. The other was the idea that the V.C. could be hurt so badly by selective bombing of their supply lines and bases in North Vietnam (and/or Cambodia and Laos) that they then could be defeated by the South Vietnamese forces.

In either case this would be an attempt to apply the deterrent principle to guerrilla warfare, which had never been tried before.

There was little doubt that Hanoi had the power to order the Viet Cong to call off the war. It was a reasonable assumption that Ho Chi Minh would do so if he were confronted with American air power in a vacuum. It was conspicuously not a vacuum. It was unlikely, to begin with, that the U. S.'s allies would go along with such an attack, just as the U. S. opposed the Anglo-French attack on Egypt in 1956 which grew out of strikingly similar angry frustration.

More decisively it was likely that the Sino-Soviet split would vanish in the face of such a blatant American threat against a Communist country—just as de Gaulle would close ranks with the U. S. if a secondary NATO power, say Greece, was threatened by flagrant Russian aggression. Moscow would probably have no choice, if it hoped to retain its prestige in the Communist world, but to threaten retaliation against the United States if we bombed Hanoi. This assumption could be wrong, but it could be ignored only at our peril in making American policy. The U. S., in short, was denied recourse to general air attack on North Vietnam by the same global atomic stalemate that had prevented us from helping the Hungarian rebels in 1956, or the Russians from taking over West Berlin in 1959, or the U. S. from invading Cuba in 1962.

The second proposal, to bomb only military targets in the North, would be almost as risky. It would be virtually mandatory, for example, for Chinese submarines to try to retaliate against units of the 7th Fleet, which in turn would raise the question of bombing their bases on the Chinese mainland. It would be extremely difficult to avoid uncontrollable escalation. The risk might nevertheless be justified perhaps if attacks on military targets would really hurt the Viet Cong decisively. The reality was, in my judgment, that they would not.*

Like everything else in Vietnam, statistics on infiltrated materiel and personnel from the North were highly debatable. There was no question that significant Chinese and North Vietnamese supplies had been smuggled: medical kits, radios, recoilless rifles and ammunition, machine guns and submachine guns. But the vast bulk of Viet Cong weapons and equipment were American, captured from the government forces. Nor was there any doubt that several thousand Viet Cong officers and other trained personnel had infiltrated from the North. But the overwhelming majority of their forces were recruited locally, with the infiltrated personnel acting mainly as cadres.

If such specialized men and supplies could be cut off by destruction of factories and training camps in the North, the Viet Cong would be weakened, but probably not much more than the efficiency of the Pentagon would be reduced if the air conditioning were shut off. The imports from the North that really counted were guerrilla know-how and political direction, which could not be blocked by a thousand bombers.

It made even less sense to talk about bombing supply routes. Everything that the Communists smuggled into South Vietnam moved into the country by foot, or perhaps part of the way by sampan from Cambodia into the Delta. Bombing roads and bridges in North Vietnam could delay deliveries, but not by much, since they also could move by

---

* The United States accepted this risk in the air attacks mounted against the North in February 1965, but the objective was as much political as it was military. It was a cliff-hanging experiment with "gradual escalation" in the hope that the threat of general warfare might persuade Peking and Hanoi to call off the Viet Cong.

foot in the North. Blockading the coast and bombing rail and road lines into China similarly could only delay the movement. As the French discovered so disastrously at Dienbienphu, air attack on coolie jungle supply routes is like trying to shoot a mouse hiding in a wheatfield from an airplane with a rifle.

The same objections applied to attack on Viet Cong infiltration routes, safe havens and command posts in Cambodia and Laos. To attack targets in Cambodia would also create massive international problems, perhaps culminating in formal United Nations censure. To attack targets in Laos, e.g. the air and road terminal at Tchepone where supplies for the V.C. were being delivered by plane and truck, would give the Communists just the excuse they needed to abrogate completely the 1962 agreement on Laos and quickly take over the rest of the country.

Altogether the idea that everything would be fine if only we could block infiltration from North Vietnam was irrelevant. The issue was the fact that the Viet Cong were gradually capturing the countryside, infiltrating the hamlets, intimidating local officials, fighting off the Vietnamese armed forces, and in most cases doing so with rifles, hand grenades and superior courage. Our side was losing where it counted, in man-to-man confrontations, and this was a weakness that could not be corrected with planes and bombs or by making faces at Ho Chi Minh. Talk of bombing Hanoi or V.C. supply lines sounded, in fact, like a palliative for failure.

What to do?

Introduction of U.S. combat forces to fight the Viet Cong inside South Vietnam was the only choice remaining. The moment had come to do this, to go to war, as quickly as possible. With every day of procrastination the danger mounted of a sudden upheaval, such as a neutralist coup d'état, which would make it more difficult.

The military requirement was simple: to get out and do the things we had been advising the Vietnamese so futilely to do. Among guerrilla warfare experts there was no serious disagreement about the merits of existing principles of strategy and tactics in Vietnam, if only they could be applied: to patrol and fight at night just as fearlessly and aggressively as the Viet Cong, to bring honest government to the hamlets, to dismiss corrupt officials and inept military commanders, to press home attacks and cease leaning on crutches like helicopters and artillery, in short to get out in the muck of the paddies and jungles and destroy the V.C. where they lived. And at the same time to make the strategic hamlet program work, bringing hope to the people where all had been despair, and economic and social benefits—like straightening the path at Binh Yen Dong—to win their support.

Americans could do these things just as well as Vietnamese, and there was no question that the people would respond to them. American Special Forces men were already doing it to a limited degree among the Montagnards. It was likely that the American example would gradually bring the face-conscious Vietnamese Government forces alive, just as it had breathed new spirit into the Korean Army.

There was no use trying to pretend that this could be done cheaply. One qualified advocate of American intervention, Professor Wesley R. Fishel of Michigan State University, who spent five years in Vietnam as an advisor to Diem, tried to estimate the cost in an article for the Washington *Post* (June 14, 1964). "We would have to look forward," he wrote, "to using as many as 100,000 American soldiers, spending as much as $2 billion a year and working doggedly at the job for as long as ten years." This may even have been optimistic. Other experts thought it would take 200,000 or 300,000 troops to do the job, making the undertaking comparable with Korea in expenditure of American blood and treasure.

This would still be cheaper than the longer-run costs of surrender, or the risk of atomic holocaust. An American war against the Viet Cong, moreover, would be certain to succeed, unlike the easy-way alternatives—if only by sheer weight of numbers, just as the British succeeded in Malaya and even the French might have prevailed in Vietnam if they had been willing to make the necessary effort. And success would not only save South Vietnam. It would also reverse the domino process throughout Southeast Asia, generating a healthy new respect for American power, and the dependability of American protection against Communist imperialism.

The mere suggestion that we might be forced at some point to commit American forces in the jungles and swamps of Vietnam provoked frowns and disdain when I tried to peddle the idea around Washington in September 1963. The thought was regarded as equally leprous a year later. There was a curious, and rather unlovely, psychological implication in this. Some of the same officials who opposed using American troops were desk-hammering around Washington in favor of bombing Hanoi, even at the risk of uncontrollable worldwide catastrophe. They seemed to be saying that the proud American tradition that American fighting men could lick anyone did not apply in Vietnam.

One of the many rationalizations of the win-without-fighting proponents was the specter of "bogging down" American forces midst the vast land masses and populations of Asia. This had long been basic U. S. Army doctrine. Ambassador Taylor was known as one of its strongest guardians. It was for this reason that American forces avoided challenging the Japanese on the mainland of China during World War II, that we had not gone to Chiang's help on the mainland in 1949, and that we had refused to attack Communist bases beyond the Yalu River in the Korean war. It was behind President Johnson's remark in September 1964 that "we don't want our American boys to be doing the fighting for Asian boys."

An immediate fallacy in this argument was the fact that the U. S. had already deployed some twenty-three thousand troops in Vietnam, placing our prestige on the line no less than committing them to combat. Communist propagandists had long since convinced most Southeast Asians that the Americans were already in combat anyway, which tended to magnify continued Viet Cong gains. It could be debated perhaps that it was a mistake to commit even "advisory" forces in Vietnam in the first place, that we had overextended even the mighty resources of the United States, but this was no longer relevant. We had created a situation where withdrawal of our forces, except in victory, could only be both disastrous and dishonorable.

The requirement now was not contrary to U. S. Army doctrine in any case. The objective was to *avoid* escalation which would bring us in direct conflict with China. Our mission would be rigidly limited to surgical intervention to enforce the Geneva Agreement of 1954 in support of the legitimate government of South Vietnam, hopefully at the invitation of this government. We would be fighting entirely inside South Vietnam against rebels whom Communist propagandists had long tried to portray as simple South Vietnamese nationalists with no outside connections. Morally, legally and politically, our position would be clean and defensible.

American intervention on this basis would neatly shift the escalation dilemma to the Communists. Ho Chi Minh would certainly step up clandestine support for the Viet Cong, infiltration of men and supplies, to the maximum. But there were distinct limits to this, especially with such a long supply route. To be really effective the movements and concentrations of men would become so big that the struggle would be changed into conventional war. At that point the enormous U.S. superiority in modern weapons and resources at last would begin to count. The same would be true if the Communists decided on overt, large-scale invasion of South Vietnam, which would then transform the war into another Korea with the clashing of classic, massed armies.

It was highly unlikely that the Communists would choose to escalate in any case. In Korea the Chinese entered the fighting only after our side had escalated by crossing the demarcation line into North Korea. In Korea the Chinese had also learned the hard way about the dangers of confronting Western industrial might on a confined battlefield where their enormous manpower advantage could not be exploited. Vietnam was still more restricted geographically. Even if the war expanded to include Laos and Cambodia the Chinese would still find themselves confined to a peninsula, just as they were in Korea, and this time with very long, exposed supply lines.

If an American attack on North Vietnam would probably bring the Russians into the struggle, it was equally probable that they would stay out if we limited our action to South Vietnam. Indeed it was likely that Moscow instead would try to restrain Hanoi and Peking from escalation, and perhaps would even be privately pleased to see the Viet Cong destroyed because of its bearing on the ideological dispute.

Another objection to U.S. intervention was the problem of arranging it politically. United Nations aegis, as in Korea, was impossible because of the Soviet veto. Similarly the French would probably veto a SEATO action. Even if the U. S. acted unilaterally, we would still have to negotiate a new command arrangement with the Vietnamese. Ideally this probably should be an American supreme commander working under some kind of joint Vietnamese-American political direction. There was no assurance that the Vietnamese Government would agree to this, or that it could stay in power against the wrath of street mobs if it did agree.

If all else failed, the U. S. would be obliged to bring in combat forces anyway, with whatever political window dressing was possible, or even with no political draperies at all. The requirement for action was exactly that mandatory.

There was the argument, of which Lodge was one advocate, that Americans could not take the extreme hardships of jungle and paddy fighting to which Asians were accustomed. This was certainly disproved repeatedly in the war against Japan. In Guadalcanal and New Guinea, for example, American troops prevailed despite the worst imaginable conditions.* British troops in Malaya similarly were able to take it and win. American advisors attached to Vietnamese combat units had already learned, in fact, that once they had accustomed themselves to the climate, their greater physical stature and better diet gave them considerably more stamina than Vietnamese troops. They could carry bigger loads, keep going longer, and do without the traditional Vietnamese siesta—a reflection itself of limited Vietnamese endurance.

Then there was what might be called the French syndrome, the idea that the French, who rank among the finest soldiers in the world, had failed against the Vietminh and that therefore the U. S. would fail against the Viet Cong. This was often linked with the myth—shrewdly perpetuated by Communist propagandists—that white men could never prevail over Asian guerrillas because the people would reject them.

There was certainly some truth in this, but its importance had been exaggerated. Most importantly, Americans would

---

* A Japanese general who opposed the Americans in one of those battles is supposed to have remarked later: "Americans don't fight in the jungle anyway. They bulldoze the jungle away and fight what's left."

not behave the way the French did. The French were fighting to reestablish colonial control, for purely selfish, materialistic motives, and the Vietnamese people knew it. They treated the Vietnamese as inferiors, with a special brand of arrogance that only the French can display. They did literally everything wrong. They antagonized the people, isolated themselves from the people, ignored the people's legitimate grievances, lavished puppet politicians and puppet military commanders. Witnessing some of this at the time, I often thought that a Vietnamese with any sense of pride and dignity would have no choice but to join the Vietminh. One of the remarkable aspects of Vietnam—and an indictment of Communism—was the fact that so many of its people still resisted the Communists despite the French.

The U.S. image in Vietnam was the exact opposite. This had been demonstrated hundreds of times already by the way Americans in the field had made friends with the peasants—especially children, whom the French ignored and Americans instinctively befriended. We were there to help, not to exploit; to defend, not to oppress; and the people knew this. One of our problems with the Diem regime was the ironic fact that rural communities, especially among the aboriginal Montagnards, often tended to develop loyalties to the American advisors in the area instead of the local government officials. Repeatedly, for example, we heard of cases where peasants with a grievance went to the American field advisors for justice because they knew that the American would help, while the local Vietnamese official would ask for a bribe and probably do nothing anyway.

It was a bitter reality that in Vietnam our central enemies, the Russians and Chinese, once again had found somebody else to fight their battles for them, and that our friends had failed. The security of South Vietnam was nevertheless vital to the security of the United States. It was now our unalterable obligation to send our own fighting men to defend our vital interests, just as we had through all our history. There was no cheap way, no easy way out.

(3)

There was one central lesson in the American experience in Vietnam. This was its exposure of what might be called a "guerrilla gap" in U.S. defense capability. It was a weakness no less dangerous than the missile gap of the fifties.

Vietnam was a position of such strategic importance that the secretary of state had compared it with West Berlin. Yet in fourteen years, through four administrations in Washington, and despite the expenditure of billions of dollars and deployment of twenty-three thousand elite troops, we had failed to secure it. We were facing defeat by a few tens of thousands of barefooted Vietnamese peasant guerrillas armed with rifles, hand grenades and sometimes only homemade knives. It was irrelevant that we had not ourselves engaged in combat. The damage to our national security was no less severe.

We were denied effective recourse to overwhelming American air and sea power. We were also denied recourse to negotiation, except in shameful surrender. Our last hope to salvage the situation, and American prestige, was to commit ground forces in numbers that would eat significantly into the U.S. global strategic reserve, an undertaking that seemed ridiculously big for the size of the problem—like calling out the National Guard to round up a gang of teen-age hoodlums.

This nevertheless was urgently necessary. The guerrilla techniques developed by Mao Tse-tung and Vo Nguyen Giap were comparable in some ways with the atomic bomb. They had short-circuited the industrial and technical power of the free world, and outflanked the bomb itself. They were rapidly acquiring an aura of invincibility that would stimulate more such wars in other underdeveloped parts of the world. We were confronted with a threat of our whole system of global security so serious that it could not be tolerated.

There was irony in the accident that General Taylor now found himself presiding over our comeuppance. He had split with the Eisenhower Administration because he felt there was too much dependence on the defeat-or-holocaust atomic deterrent. It could be said that his failure to correct this weakness during his two years as chairman of the joint chiefs under Kennedy and Johnson had now come back to haunt him. This, however, would be unfair. One of the main reasons for the dilemma that now confronted the nation had been the false assumption that guerrillas were primarily a military problem.

The guerrilla gap was rather a national failure to respond to the changing character of the Communist challenge.

The nation had long recognized that a complex of historical accidents had shifted the cold war arena to the undeveloped areas: the atomic stalemate which blocked Communist expansion in modernized countries, the emergence of dozens of newly independent countries after World War II which had spread the seeds of nationalism, the explosive growth of mass communications which opened political access to hundreds of millions of people who had previously lived in isolation. We were aware that the Communists were working in these areas, confronting the nation with what President Kennedy, in his inaugural address, called "a long twilight struggle" in the years ahead.

But we gravely underestimated the skill and imagination with which the Communists were developing a doctrine to exploit the fermenting political mash of such countries as Vietnam. In effect the Communists created a new *tactical* weapon: the direct application of political, economic and psychological action, backed up by military operations, to destroy an enemy government by stealing its people. In Vietnam this new weapon surprised and confounded us—just as it had the French—in much the same way that Hitler's *blitzkrieg* technique had conquered Europe at the beginning of World War II. This was the guerrilla gap.

Could it now be closed?

Probably not entirely. There was a parallel with the problem that our defenses against sneak air attack could never deny an enemy the advantage of the first strike. This was the nature of our conflict with the Communist world. The thief in the night always had an edge over the policeman on the beat. There would always be soft, troubled countries like Vietnam that were vulnerable to subversion. We would again be obliged to try to defend such countries through local governments as bad or even worse than the Diem regime. We could never escape the possibility that conditions once again would leave us no choice but to send our own troops to defend such distant frontiers—just as other great powers had done throughout history.

The problem of formulating counter-guerrilla doctrine was like the science of antibiotics, with each advance confounded by changing forms of disease. In many ways Vietnam was a special case, with conditions that might never be duplicated elsewhere—hopefully including Mme. Nhu. The odds against Diem were exceptionally heavy: his country prostrate after a decade of war, demoralized by French colonialism and Communist subversion, stripped of its elite. But in Vietnam we had also encountered many of the constants in this ugly kind of struggle against opponents who play dirty, camouflaging themselves with the aspirations of the people.

There was much to be learned from the experience.

Our own bureaucratic organization was deplorably inefficient. At least a half dozen U.S. agencies were deeply involved, with no single command in Washington. Most of them were maneuvering for control of the whole show for themselves. Decisions had to go through a morass of ad hoc committees and "task forces." There was no central responsibility for collecting intelligence or even keeping a historical record of what we were doing and learning, no central source of policy, little effort to recruit personnel with experience in guerrilla warfare, or even in Southeast Asia.

Presidential action was urgently needed to create a permanent counter-insurgency organization headed by an officer with cabinet rank, authority to cut across inter-agency lines, and direct command of missions primarily concerned with insurgency in the field.

On the maddening problem of Vietnamese refusal to heed American advice, our experience indicated three major principles:

1. The U. S. should abandon the idea, inherited from Marshall Plan days, that economic and military assistance was a strategic government-to-government operation, especially in a struggle against guerrillas. Aid should be given only on the specific understanding that American advice on its use must be heeded all the way down to the point where the last cartload of fertilizer was delivered to the peasant. We should insist that almost all of it reach that level to give us a tactical weapon to counter the Communists' political, economic and psychological action at the rice roots.
2. U.S. intelligence networks in contested countries such as Vietnam should be vastly beefed up, with or without the consent of the host government, to give us accurate, fast and detailed information on exactly what is going on among the people, on the end use of American aid, and on specific hamlet-to-hamlet activities of both the enemy and local authorities. U.S. advice to the host government should be based exclusively on our own intelligence. U.S. agents should also follow up closely on resulting actions.

3. Advice should be given sparingly, and as often as possible at a low level where less "face" is lost by compliance, but the U. S. should never permit it to be ignored, just as a good teacher never permits a student to make the same mistake twice. We should cease exacting broad, high-level promises for sweeping reforms—Diem managed to ignore perhaps a half dozen such commitments over the years—and concentrate instead on removing specific complaints—one by one if necessary—that the Communists could exploit among the people. If there must be a showdown on this issue—which was deferred in Vietnam until disaster was upon us in 1963—it is far better to have it at the outset.

None of this would have been easy to achieve in Vietnam, but all of it was attainable to some degree—vastly more, in any case, than we did achieve. There was nothing pretentious about this kind of approach, moreover. An American sergeant working through an interpreter could find out about a corrupt local official who was charging the people for U.S. barb wire that should be given away, for example, just as easily in a Vietnamese hamlet as he could in Nebraska—perhaps more easily. The evils exploited by the Viet Cong were universal human evils, no more mysterious in Asia than in any other corner of the world. Americans knew a great deal about what went wrong in Vietnam but seldom could correct it. This was an important clue to our failure.

There was an equally important corollary lesson. Just as the U. S. should insist on effective action against a guerrilla enemy, we should rigidly limit our interference to this objective. We should accept almost any extreme of public embarrassment, even at the expense of our "dignity," to permit the host government to enjoy the trappings of independence. In the case of Vietnam this should have specifically included toleration of Mme. Nhu.

This was an important part of the problem with newsmen.

The official effort to deceive the press was deplorable, but the greater mistake was our failure to create a sharp frame of reference for our actions in Vietnam. The true issue in the unseating of Diem, for example, was not whether this was wise. The true issue was our failure for years to decide exactly what we were trying to do with Diem. The official attitude created an open season for judgments of what was "right" and what was "wrong." The most articulate or noisiest man in an argument, or in pounding a typewriter, tended to prevail. There was no accepted consensus. Newsmen and officials alike fed on their own ideas and their own emotions, and the product was Babel.

If we had done all this, could we have prevailed with Diem? Not, I think, against such staggering odds. Fate very likely had preordained that we would be forced eventually to resort to U.S. troops in Vietnam, no matter what medicine we tried on Diem.

If he had been a popular leader with a charismatic appeal to his people, like a Magsaysay or a Nasser or even a Soekarno, Diem probably could have swayed the nation against the Viet Cong sufficiently to turn the tide. It was that close. If he had been an effective administrator, willing to delegate authority, to punish inefficiency and corruption, and to reward ability instead of political loyalty, he possibly could have organized his resources sufficiently to prevail. The fact that he was neither a popular figure nor a good administrator was his undoing, suggesting as a rule of thumb for the U. S. that it should be wary of giving its support unconditionally to that kind of man elsewhere in comparable circumstances.

Paradoxically it could be argued that even an eccentric playboy like Soekarno or Cambodia's Sihanouk might be preferable to a Diem in a chips-down guerrilla war where failure would lead to immediate Communist takeover. Soekarno and Sihanouk were notoriously bad administrators.

They were both leading their countries into a will-o'-the-wisp land of happy coexistence with Communist China, pretending ignorance of the fact that there was no more dangerously predatory power in the world. Unlike Diem, however, they were both loved by their people with the result that Communist subversion had never made important penetrations of either country, despite repeated efforts in both cases. Grotesquely, both countries were thus more secure than South Vietnam. Both retained a degree of free choice. If they chose to stand up to China, they could be captured militarily only by open invasion—and this the U. S. did have the means to stop with sea and air power.

This was certainly not to suggest that the U. S. should seek out eccentrics of this sort to support. Indonesia and Cambodia faced chaos if either leader suddenly died. But it did suggest that the U. S. should be more sophisticated in its attitude toward the leaders available in fragile, emergency situations like Vietnam.

The absolute measure of our interest should be the local government's control of the people, just as this was the consuming interest of the Communists. If this could be furthered by public criticism of the United States, or American newsmen, we should be silent—on the one condition that such a government was successfully resisting Communist subversion. There was even a persuasive argument for tolerating long-range neutralist inclinations of such a government if this would help consolidate its popular support—again on the one condition that its intention was first to rid itself of internal Communist penetration.

The struggle for such countries as Vietnam was in the paddies and hamlets—the exact opposite of such chancery conspiracies as the Communist capture of Czechoslovakia in 1948. It was in the paddies and hamlets that the U. S. must learn to concentrate its interest and its influence. If the struggle was moving our way in the paddies, all else was relative froth. In Vietnam we were wrong on both counts. We were distracted by the froth, and we failed to find out what was happening in the hamlets—like the crooked path at Binh Yen Dong.